National Interests
and Presidential Leadership

Other Titles in This Series

Presidents, Secretaries of State, and Crises in U.S. Foreign Relations: A Model and Predictive Analysis, Lawrence Falkowski

U.S. Policy in International Institutions: Defining Reasonable Options in an Unreasonable World, edited by Seymour M. Finger and Joseph R. Harbert

Congress and Arms Control, edited by Alan Platt and Lawrence D. Weiler

U.S.-Japan Relations and the Security of East Asia: The Next Decade, edited by Franklin B. Weinstein

Communist Indochina and U.S. Foreign Policy: Forging New Relations, Joseph J. Zasloff and MacAlister Brown

Crisis Resolution: Presidential Decision Making in the Mayaguez and Korean Confrontations, Richard G. Head, Frisco W. Short, and Robert C. McFarlane

Westview Special Studies in International Relations

National Interests and Presidential Leadership: The Setting of Priorities
Donald E. Nuechterlein

Many scholars have ignored the concept of "national interest" simply because no logical, systematic means of dealing with this key aspect of international politics has been available. A new approach to defining national interest forms the basis for this study of presidential decisions on U.S. involvement in foreign wars. Professor Nuechterlein looks at various crisis situations to determine what defense, economic, world order, and ideological interests are at stake; he identifies sixteen cost/risk and value factors that affect the U.S. view of which interest is most vital in a given situation. In any dispute, it is the interest that is considered vital—too important to compromise—that is the key element in crisis decisions.

Professor Nuechterlein uses his analytical framework to examine the ways Presidents Wilson, Roosevelt, Truman, Johnson, and Nixon perceived the national interest when making their decisions to begin or extend U.S. war involvement. He assesses the value of National Security Council participation in the decision-making process and presents case-study analyses of three imminent U.S. foreign policy concerns—Quebec's possible separation from Canada, the Panama Canal Treaty, and the potential for race war in South Africa—with an epilogue on the challenges facing Carter. The author suggests that the most important U.S. national interest in the future will be economic, with energy conservation a top priority.

Donald E. Nuechterlein is professor of international affairs at the Federal Executive Institute in Charlottesville, Virginia. He has held posts at George Washington University and the University of Virginia, and was a Fulbright lecturer at the University College of Wales. Professor Nuechterlein is the author of numerous books and articles on international relations and U.S. foreign policy, the most recent of which, *Inside the Bureaucracy: The View from the Assistant Secretary's Desk*, he coauthored with Thomas P. Murphy and Ronald J. Stupak.

National Interests and Presidential Leadership: The Setting of Priorities

Donald E. Nuechterlein

Westview Press / Boulder, Colorado

Westview Special Studies in International Relations

Published in 1978 in the United States of America by
Westview Press, Inc.
5500 Central Avenue
Boulder, Colorado 80301
Frederick A. Praeger, Publisher

Library of Congress Cataloging in Publication Data
Nuechterlein, Donald Edwin, 1925-
National interests and presidential leadership.
(Westview special studies in international relations)
Includes index.
1. Presidents—United States. 2. United States—Foreign relations. I. Title.
JK570.N83   353.03'2   78-2764
ISBN 0-89158-169-3
ISBN 0-89158-170-7 pbk.

Printed and bound in the United States of America

Contents

Illustrations

Charts

xi

Table

Figure

Preface

The idea of "national interest" has fascinated me for much of the last decade; the more I read and think about it, the more I become convinced that scholars ought to deal with it logically and systematically instead of sweeping it under the rug, as many have done since the early postwar period. The reasons for the current neglect of national interest as a key concept in the study of international politics are threefold: (1) many scholars believe that the nation-state should not be the primary focus of the study of international relations and, hence, that the interests of states should be subordinated to the study of international organization and international integration; (2) scholars who earlier rejected the "realist" school of international politics because of its efforts to tie national interest to military power have found no other suitable basis for discussing the goals of states; and (3) some have decided that the term *national interest* is methodologically so vague and loosely defined by diplomats and military planners that it is impossible to formulate generally acceptable operational guidelines; it is useless to try to resuscitate the patient, they say, and better to let him die. In my view, such attitudes represent a "cop-out" on the part of political scientists. Rather than passing off a concept that has been in the vocabulary of statesmen and militarists for four hundred years, they should be making renewed efforts to define more accurately the goals, objectives, and drives of nation-states in the international system.

My interest in the concept of national interest is traceable to the Vietnam war, which forced me to seek some better way to define the goals the United States should strive for in its foreign policy. The initial outcome of this search was *United States National Interests in a Changing World* (1973), which sought to devise a method that would enable U.S. policymakers to make wiser judgments about what the United States should, and should not, be willing to negotiate for or fight for. That book dealt exclusively with the United States, its experience in world affairs since World War II, and its dilemma in trying to define what its aims were in Vietnam. Since then, I have broadened the framework to include a comparison of the national interests of several nation-states involved in international issues, assuming that such comparison will lead to greater understanding of the policies states have adopted in past crises and may also suggest how they might respond in future ones. The earlier study contained only one case study of how national interests influenced policy decisions: the perceptions of six presidents were assessed on the question of Vietnam's importance for the United States. The present book contains more cases, covering both past conflicts in international politics and probable future crises that would affect the interests of major and superpowers.

I believe that the concept of national interest can, and should be, taken out of the "bottom drawer" of our file of knowledge and given a more prominent role in explaining state behavior. Integration theory and a number of other theories of international relations that have been in vogue for the past twenty years seem to be called into serious question today as the world moves into a new and more complex set of international relations, particularly between rich industrial states and the ever-increasing number of poor and undeveloped states. To explain why the Arab states imposed an oil embargo on the United States in 1973—and why the United States permitted them to do so without serious retaliation—requires a meaningful conceptual framework that takes account of the basic aspirations of the Arab nations as well as those of the United States. It should also be able to explain why this episode led not to war—as surely would have happened twenty years ago—but to negotiations in which the United States, in fact, capitulated to the weaker Arab states. By focusing on the values that serve as the underpinnings of state aspirations and by weighing them against the costs and risks that are inherent in the use of force or strong economic retaliation, I believe it is possible to ascertain with some accuracy the intensity with which nation-states will view specific threats to their security, economic well-being, and sense of justice (basic interests). It should, therefore, be possible to suggest the probable courses of action they will follow when these interests are at stake.

The first two chapters of this book present a conceptual framework for assessing the national interests of states. The methodology allows us to determine whether a *vital* interest is in question (i.e., whether a state may no longer be willing to negotiate and may be contemplating the use of force). The next three chapters are case studies of how four U.S. presidents—Wilson, Roosevelt, Truman, and Johnson—viewed U.S. national interests when they decided to take the nation to war in four crises outside the Western Hemisphere—the traditional sphere of U.S. interests. The comparison of their perceptions of U.S. interests in 1917, 1941, 1950, and 1965 helps us see what parallels exist in the way they handled the crises. Chapter 6 deals with Richard Nixon's perception of the national interest in 1970, when he decided to send U.S. forces into Cambodia, a choice not comparable in scope to the choices made by the other presidents, but one that nevertheless had great repercussions in the United States. Chapter 7 deals with the decision-making process of the National Security Council and the limitations imposed by Congress in 1973 on the president's war-making authority. The last three chapters are case studies of probable *future* crises in which the United States will have important interests. The purpose of these future scenarios is to assess how the United States and its principal antagonists are likely to view their national interests and to suggest the probable courses of action they would take to defend or promote those interests.

The value of this study lies not only in its definition of national interest and its usefulness as an analytical tool for illuminating state behavior in past international issues, but also in its potential for anticipating how major powers are likely to react to issues that are apparent at the present time, but have not yet reached the crisis point. It is not intended as a system for predicting state behavior in international crises; however, the methodology will make possible more accurate assessments of how states view their national interests—particularly vital interests—and thus more accurate projections of the kinds of policies and actions likely to be employed when those interests are challenged.

I also hope that this volume will provide the philosophical underpinnings for efforts by other scholars who wish to deal with the subject in greater depth, particularly on the quantitative side. My aim is to stimulate students, policymakers, and the informed American public to take a serious look at this important concept in international relations and to use it as an analytical tool in judging state behavior.

A number of friends from academia were kind enough to read parts of this manuscript and offer valuable suggestions: Tom Murphy and Ron Stupak at the Federal Executive Institute; Inis Claude, Norman Graebner, and Bob Wood at the University of Virginia; Mike McCann at Indiana University; Hedley Bull at Oxford University; and Ieuan John at the University College of Wales, where I spent 1976 as a Fulbright scholar. I am also indebted to a number of friends in government in Washington who contributed helpful suggestions on the later chapters of the study. My deep thanks go to Joyce Carter and Susie Houchens for their care in typing the manuscript, and to my family for being supportive during the year this project has been under way. Special appreciation goes to Millie, my wife, for all her work in reviewing the manuscript. The final product, of course, is solely my own responsibility.

D. E. N.
May 1978

National Interests
and Presidential Leadership

1. National Interest: What Is It?

Since the founding of nation-states, statesmen and scholars have used the term *national interest* to describe the aspirations and goals of sovereign entities in the international arena. Today foreign ministers, military strategists, and scholars discuss the vital interests of countries in ways that suggest everyone understands precisely what they mean and will draw the correct conclusions. In fact, the opposite is true: the study of international politics as well as the art of diplomacy suffer from widespread ambiguity about the meaning of national interest. As a result, many scholars and statesmen believe the term should be abandoned. Some even think that the very effort to identify the goals of nation-states is pointless because national leaders show no consistency in pursuing national goals. But the criticism is misplaced. Abandoning the concept of national interest would solve little. Whether we like it or not, the phrase is unlikely to be dismissed from our vocabulary simply because some critics find it useless. Rather than create more jargon in an attempt to find an alternative phrase, would it not be wiser to retain the term and provide a broader conceptual framework for discussing the interests of states? Scholars and statesmen might then be able to find some common ground in defining the issues, even though they do not reach agreement on what policies states ought to pursue to defend their interests. In a word, is it not time for serious students of foreign policy and international politics to agree on basic definitions regarding the goals of states so that we may get on with the job of better explaining state behavior?

1

This is no easy task. A major part of the difficulty is that *national interest* has become so closely associated with the "realist" school of thought in the 1940s and 1950s that it is difficult for many scholars to think of this concept without being heavily influenced by the interpretations of Hans Morgenthau, George Kennan, and the disciples of the realist cult. Even though other scholars have successfully challenged many of Morgenthau's views in the last twenty years, many students of foreign policy and international politics are still hung up on the idea that national interest is somehow synonymous with the acquisition of national power, especially military power. The realist school maintained that there was no room in their conceptualization for anything labeled idealism because they considered this to be the antithesis of realism—looking at the world the way it should be rather than the way it actually is. But why should the term *national interest* be defined so narrowly as to exclude all state aspirations except the acquisition of power? Why should not the pursuit of freedom of the individual and democratic government be considered a valid goal of U.S. foreign policy? Do we seriously believe that the pursuit of world socialism is *not* a national interest of the Soviet Union, one that goes beyond the interest of building a powerful Russian state?

Another problem we encounter in trying to construct a new and more useful conceptual framework for national interest is that the realists have convinced us that each sovereign state has an *objective* national interest. They also argue that defining this interest should be the responsibility of a select few experts who understand the world of international politics and are best able to divine the policies a state should follow to enhance its national interest vis-à-vis other states. This view has no room for public opinion of the nation, which would interfere in what these philosopher-kings decide; indeed, it has little room for a legislature either. The realist school would have us believe that the definition of national interests should be isolated from the political interplay in a democratic system of government; in their view, the president (read: a few principal foreign policy advisers) should have a free hand to make foreign policy, because petty politics and selfish interests ought not to influence a rational and impartial assessment of the nation's external needs. We continue to be influenced by this narrow view of foreign policymaking when we use the term *national interest;* and many scholars find it difficult to make the intellectual leap from this view to the one proposed here: that the determination of a nation's interests is the result of a political process in which conflicting private interests, bureaucratic politics, and the so-called totally dispassionate view of the facts by policy planners play a role—and should play a role.

Another difficulty is use of the word *rational.* The realists claim that to be rational about a nation's interests is to divorce oneself from all personal and political considerations. In this view, to think about foreign policy issues in political terms is somehow indecent. But why should this definition be so restricted? Is not the person who views national interests and foreign policy as separate from practical political considerations being rather idealistic, and perhaps naive?

Before attempting to redefine national interests in a broader context, therefore, certain qualifications must be made about the use of terms. First, it is assumed here that the leaders of nation-states act *rationally* in the pursuit of state objectives, i.e., that they follow policies they believe will enhance the well-being of their societies, whatever the constitutional system. It is not a question of whether the state actions are cost-effective, wise, or moral; we simply assume that foreign policy decisions are made with some degree of reasoning—that they are not purely the result of guesswork or chance. Second, it is assumed that the number of persons involved in deciding national interests will vary from state to state, depending on the type of government. In a free democratic society, many persons—both official and private—exert influence in deciding what issues are vital interests; in a totalitarian society, far fewer persons make this determination.

Let us then proceed to definitions. The *national interest* is the perceived needs and desires of one sovereign state in relation to the sovereign states comprising its external environment.[1] Several aspects of this definition require elaboration. First, we are talking about the perception of state needs, which suggests that decisions about the national interest are the result of a political process in which a country's leaders ultimately arrive at a decision about the importance of a given external event or crisis to the country's well-being. It is also clear that this definition pertains only to fully sovereign states, not to international organizations or dependent territories; for better or worse, we live in a world where decisions to use force, to impose trade restrictions, to enter alliances, and to provide foreign aid are made only by the governments of sovereign states. This definition also draws a distinction between the external and the internal environments of states; the way in which a government deals with the internal environment of the state is usually referred to as the *public interest,* but the way it deals with the external environment is the *national interest.* Finally, this definition implies that we are talking about the interests of the nation-state in its entirety, not the interests of private groups, bureaucratic entities, or political organizations within the state.[2]

Basic National Interests

Simply offering a definition of national interest does not, however, provide the scholar or policymaker with any guidelines to help identify such an interest. To do this, we need additional definitions of the *basic* interests of nation-states— those national needs that form the underpinnings of their foreign policies. They may be described as follows:

1. *defense interests:* the protection of the nation-state and its citizens against the threat of physical violence directed from another state or against an externally inspired threat to its system of government
2. *economic interests:* the enhancement of the nation-state's economic well-being in relations with other states
3. *world order interests:* the maintenance of an international political and economic system in which the nation-state may feel secure and in which its citizens and commerce may operate peacefully outside its borders

4. *ideological interests:* the protection and furtherance of a set of values that the citizens of a nation-state share and believe to be universally good.

Several things must be said about these basic national interests. First, the order in which they appear does not suggest any priority of one over another, although it may be argued that unless a nation-state can defend its territory and citizens— either through a strong defense or in alliance with a major power or both—none of the other three interests is likely to matter much. Second, it is obvious that these four basic interests are not mutually exclusive and that policymakers must accept trade-offs among them. For example, the economic interests of certain industries within a state may sometimes be sacrificed in order to enhance a world order interest involving another country whose friendship and cooperation are needed to enhance stability in an important part of the world. Japanese automobile and transistor radio exports to the United States are an example. Third, as used here, a nation's *ideology* is an important part of its national interest—although it may not be adhered to as strongly as the other three, it is nevertheless important in determining how a nation reacts to international issues. The charge made by critics of U.S. foreign policy in the post-1945 period that the government supported dictators instead of democratic forces in various allied countries is evidence of one kind of ideological view held by many Americans. Another kind is that the United States should withdraw support from countries even if they have democratic systems due to racial policies enforced by their governments. South Africa is an example.

The key point here is that sovereign states—particularly major powers—have interests that cut across all of the four elements listed above and that compete for attention and resources from their governments. Bureaucratic politics and pressure group politics within states center on questions of which basic national interest should receive priority and resources—often to the detriment of others. In the 1950s, when the United States seemed to have unlimited resources to devote to international activities, all of the four basic interests received strong support; in the 1970s, however, when the U.S. economy was strained by the Vietnam war and when its competitive advantage with Germany, Japan, and other countries was declining, the U.S. government had to give higher priority to economic interests and somewhat less to world order interests, as the Nixon economic "shocks" in 1971 dramatized.

One other point about the definition of basic national interests should be emphasized. Defense interests, as described here, entail only the protection of the homeland, the citizens, and the political system of the nation-state; they do *not* include alliances with other states, although they may include strategic bases whose primary function is the protection of the homeland. For example, Israel requires the strategically located Golan Heights for the defense of its territory; but its close political relationship with the United States is required for *world order* reasons—namely, to insure that the Soviets do not tip the military balance in the Middle East by intervening on the side of Israel's enemies. World order interests deal with a multitude of international issues, many of which are handled through international organizations; but insofar as political objectives are involved, a primary objective of world order interests is to maintain a balance of power favorable to one's own feeling of security. Before World War II, the United States did not pay much attention to world order interests because it thought it could be secure and prosperous without being actively involved in the League of Nations or in alliances. In the postwar era, it reversed field and decided it must pay far greater attention to world order interests because the old structure of international relations had been shattered by the war. Wilson's dream of 1918-1919, which Congress and the American people had rejected, was revived in the Truman period and resulted in such unprecedented actions as the Marshall Plan, the North Atlantic Treaty, and the Truman Doctrine of aid to Greece and Turkey to stem Soviet pressure in the Eastern Mediterranean. Not one of these three dramatic foreign policy moves between 1947 and 1949 was absolutely necessary for the protection of North America; indeed, several influential political leaders—among them Senator Robert Taft and former President Herbert Hoover—argued strongly that an alliance with Europe was not essential to the safety and well-being of the United States. This "Fortress America" concept did not prevail in postwar U.S. foreign policy, however, because public sentiment had shifted as a result of World War II and seemed ready to accept the necessity of giving high priority to world order interests as well as to strictly defense interests. Yet in the 1970s, largely as a result of the Vietnam experience, there is renewed questioning in Congress as to whether it is desirable to give such heavy emphasis to world order interests (some critics call it the "world policeman role") when both U.S. economic interests and ideological interests (support for freedom abroad) have suffered from an overemphasis on alliances and anticommunism.

In sum, the four basic national interests outlined above are dynamic factors conditioning the behavior of nation-states, and changes in priority among them are usually measured in years and decades, rather than in months. In democracies of the Western type, these changes in emphasis among the basic interests are decided after much debate in their legislative forums and information media, and they are usually sustained when new governments come to power. Again, drawing on twentieth-century American history, one may argue that during World War I there was little change in the United States' view of the priority among these basic national interests: even though Congress and the public supported Wilson's conclusion that the nation had to intervene in the European conflict, they did not share his view that the United States had to reorient its priorities and give far greater attention to world order interests. Americans fought in that war essentially for defense (German U-boat attacks on U.S. vessels) and ideological interests (to prevent autocracy from dominating European politics). But the idea that U.S. participation in the postwar world order was essential to ensure the benefits of military intervention did not inspire the American people, despite Wilson's heroic efforts. Thus, after World War I, the United States again concentrated its energies on economic and defense interests and rejected both world order and ideological interests as the forces of world totalitarianism gathered momentum in the 1920s and 1930s.

Intensities of Interest

Identifying the basic national interest, or interests, involved in foreign crises is only the first step in determining foreign policy. The next step is to assess the intensity of that interest, or stake, which the political leadership of a country believes is involved. For example, a government may be deeply concerned about a coup d'etat in a friendly country, but the intensity of its concern will depend on several factors, such as distance from its own borders, composition of its government, the amount of trade and investment that exists there, and historical relationships. Policymakers must also look at the potential costs of attempting to counter an unfavorable event or trend in another country—for example, the effectiveness of various policy options in changing the course of events, and risks of war.[3] Thus, the degree of interest the United States, or any major power, has in a specific international issue results from thinking through the values and costs perceived to be involved in coping with the issue. Ultimately, a government concludes what it should do and what policies it will adopt; but the process of deciding the degree, or intensity, of interest (concern) that the country should exhibit involves trade-offs among the four basic interests described above. For example, a change in government through a coup d'etat may be distasteful to the United States for both ideological and world order reasons, but if there are important economic ties with that country and if there is no threat to the United States itself, it is likely that ideological concerns and potential security problems will be subordinated to economic considerations.

In order to analyze the differing degrees of interest a government believes may be involved in international events, it is useful to categorize these intensities as follows:[4]

1. *Survival issues:* when the very existence of a nation-state is in jeopardy, as a result of overt military attack on its

own territory, or from the threat of attack if an enemy's demands are rejected. Hitler's ultimatums in the late 1930s are examples. The key to whether an issue is survival or vital on this scale is the degree to which it is an immediate, credible threat of massive physical harm by one nation-state to another. By this definition, probably no economic, world order, or ideological issues qualify; only defense interests, as defined above, would reach this level of intensity. The distinction becomes more meaningful if the use of strategic nuclear weapons is factored into the equation: only if the issue is sheer survival, i.e., only if the very existence of the state is in jeopardy, would a government be justified on any rational ground in using large nuclear weapons against an enemy. The Cuban missile crisis in 1962 was almost a survival interest.

2. *Vital issues:* when serious harm will very likely result to the state unless strong measures, including the use of conventional military forces, are employed to counter an adverse action by another state or to deter it from undertaking a serious provocation. In the long run, a vital issue may be as serious a threat to a country's political and economic well-being as a survival issue; but time is the essential difference, and a vital issue usually provides a state with sufficient time to seek help from allies, bargain with the antagonist about a solution to the dispute, or take aggressive countermeasures to warn the enemy that it will pay a high price unless it eases its political, economic, or military pressure. Unlike survival issues, a vital matter may involve not only defense interests but also economic, world order (alliance and national prestige), and in some cases ideological interests. For example, when the United States in 1971 imposed a 10 percent surcharge on all imports in order to force its trading partners to accept a devaluation of the dollar, it signaled that its growing balance-of-payments difficulties had become vital. Similarly, when the Soviet Union intervened in Czechoslovakia in 1968 to put down the Dubček regime, it had reached the point where its

ideological and world order interests were vitally affected
and strong measures were needed to cope with the
problem.

3. *Major issues:* when a state's political, economic, and
ideological well-being may be adversely affected by
events and trends in the international environment and
thus requires corrective action in order to prevent them
from becoming serious threats (vital issues). Most issues
in international relations fall into this category and
usually are resolved through diplomatic negotiations. It
is when diplomatic talks fail to resolve such disputes that
they can become dangerous. Governments must then
decide how deeply their interests are affected by the event
or trends in question; if in the final analysis a
government is unwilling or unable to compromise on
what it considers to be a fundamental question, it has
implicitly ascertained that the issue is a vital one. On the
other hand, if compromise is possible, then the issue is
probably a major one. Most economic problems between
states are major, not vital, issues; the same is true of
ideological issues, although states sometimes cloak other
issues in ideological garb in an effort to mobilize public
opinion at home and abroad. World order issues are
different, however, because these usually affect a
country's feeling of security and are more difficult to
compromise. Germany and France between the world
wars found it difficult to compromise on many issues
because of their deep feelings of insecurity. U.S.-Soviet
relations in the 1950s and 1960s suffered from similar
mutual suspicions, which made compromise on issues
involving arms limitations impossible.

4. *Peripheral issues:* when a state's well-being is not
adversely affected by events or trends abroad, but when
the interests of private citizens and companies operating
in other countries might be endangered. Obviously, a
parent nation-state usually gives its large and powerful
multinational corporations a higher priority because
their earnings and their taxes have a significant effect on
its economic well-being. When a major oil company's

assets are nationalized, for example, by Peru and Libya, the parent state treats this as a major issue, particularly if inadequate compensation is paid for the property. Each nation-state decides how greatly it values commercial enterprises operating abroad: for some states, these are major issues of national interest, but for others they are only of peripheral interest. Some economic issues that formerly were considered vital are no longer so: the willingness of the oil-importing countries to accept the oil-exporting countries' huge price increases in 1973, as well as their acquiescence in the nationalization of major oil companies, was a clear signal that these were no longer vital issues, but major ones to be negotiated.

The National Interest Matrix

To illustrate how policymakers may use these categories, I have devised a matrix that identifies degrees of national interest (see Chart 1.1). For example, in the Suez crisis of 1956, when the Eden government in Britain decided to use force against Nasser after his abrupt nationalization of the canal, British policy decisions on Suez might have been as follows: the Eden government decided that Britain's economic interests were so endangered by the potential closure of the canal that it could not compromise with Nasser on this issue. Therefore, it perceived the intensity of British interest to be a *vital economic* one and had to meet the threat with force because Nasser refused to negotiate suitable guarantees on use of the canal. But

CHART 1.1

Country:		Issue:		
Basic interest at stake		Intensity of interest		
	Survival	Vital	Major	Peripheral
Defense of homeland				
Economic well-being				
Favorable world order				
Ideological				

other British interests were involved: Nasser was seen as a threat to Western-oriented governments in the Middle East (world order interest), and he was clearly moving his country into a close relationship with the Soviet Union as well as following an antidemocratic course at home (ideological interest). Thus, world order and ideological interests, although not as intense as the economic interest, were also important. Eden therefore decided against compromise with Nasser and for the use of force to deal with the issue. We may therefore postulate how Britain viewed its interests in October 1956 (Chart 1.2) and from this conclude that it was likely to use force.

CHART 1.2

Country: Britain		Issue: Suez Canal, 1956		
Basic interest at stake		Intensity of interest		
	Survival	Vital	Major	Peripheral
Defense of homeland				X
Economic well-being		X		
Favorable world order			X	
Ideological			X	

The use of the matrix is more interesting when two or more countries' interests are compared in relation to the same issue. The Cuban missile crisis is a classic case of superpower confrontation, and the ways in which the the United States and the Soviet Union perceived their national interests in this issue in 1962 can, in retrospect, be postulated quite accurately.[5] One superpower was seeking to gain an ideological and probably a world order advantage over its rival by surreptitiously installing medium-range ballistic missiles with nuclear warheads on an island lying less than a hundred miles from its antagonist's shores. It appears that both countries' leaders miscalculated how the other would view its national interests, and the policies that the other would (or would not) adopt. Khrushchev clearly believed that Kennedy was a weak leader and would not take strong action when the missiles were discovered, any more than he did when the Berlin Wall was erected in 1961 or when the Cuban exiles faltered in their attempt to land at the Bay of Pigs earlier that year. Kennedy apparently underestimated the audacity of the Soviet leader, not believing that he would be so reckless as to put missiles on the doorstep of the United States. An observer of the way each power viewed its interests in 1962 on this issue might have used the national interest matrix in the manner shown in Chart 1.3.

CHART 1.3

Country: US USSR		Issue:	Cuban Missile Crisis, 1962	
Basic interst at stake		Intensity of interest		
	Survival	Vital	Major	Peripheral
Defense of homeland		US	USSR	
Economic well-being			US	USSR
Favorable world order		US	USSR	
Ideological		USSR	US	

The wise observer would also have known that Kennedy could not pass off so blatant a challenge to the Monroe Doctrine tradition one month before the 1962 congressional elections and that most Americans would see missiles in Cuba as a threat both to the defense of the country and to the political balance in the Caribbean and in Latin America generally (world order interest). He would also have known that none of the Soviet Union's basic national interests was vitally affected in this case, except perhaps for the ideological interest of keeping Castro in power at a time when some Soviet leaders believed the United States was preparing another invasion. In the end, Krushchev realized that Kennedy felt so strongly that he was prepared to go to war. Since Soviet interests did not warrant so high a level of confrontation, a face-saving compromise was therefore worked out, and war was averted. One lesson to be drawn from this crisis is that both Moscow and Washington miscalculated the stake and, therefore, the policies that the other side would adopt in seeking to enhance or defend its national interests. Some observers argue that the United States' clear strategic superiority at that time was the key factor in the Soviets' acceptance of a humiliating diplomatic defeat; however, it can also be argued that the American people would have forced a reluctant president to take action in the face of so clear a threat to the United States—or run the risk of impeachment—even if the nuclear balance had been in rough parity in 1962. The Cuban missile crisis should have proved to Moscow that the United States was at least as concerned about Soviet intervention in Cuba as the Soviet Union was about the possibility of U.S. intervention during the Hungarian revolution in 1956.

The two cases cited here—Britain at Suez in 1956 and the United States and Soviet Union at Cuba in 1962—were issues in which military force was used because the British and U.S. governments perceived a vital interest to be at stake. But many issues in international relations, even those bordering on crises, are not resolved through military force; rather, they are settled through negotiations. In most of these cases, none of the antagonists had a vital interest involved, or only one side did— e.g., the Arab oil embargo against the United States and Western Europe in 1973-1974.

The oil embargo in 1973 was precipitated by an Egyptian attack on Israeli forces stationed at the Suez Canal in October 1973. After a week of fighting, Israeli forces lost a large number of tanks, planes, and much ammunition, so much that the Israeli government made an urgent plea to the United States to airlift ammunition and other arms to its forces. After some delay, President Nixon ordered the Defense Department to organize the airlift and to give top priority to meeting Israel's military needs. The government of Saudi Arabia had warned Washington through diplomatic channels that in this situation it would regard U.S. aid to Israel as siding with Israel and that it would cut off oil shipments to the United States and possibly Western Europe—which it had done in the 1956 Suez crisis and again during the 1967 Arab-Israeli war. President Nixon disregarded this warning, and within a few days all the Arab oil-producing countries placed an embargo on shipments of oil to the United States and warned the European countries that they would be similarly treated if they took a pro-Israel stance. Not only did the Arabs cut off oil to the United States, but the Organization of Petroleum Exporting Countries (OPEC) raised the price of petroleum by 400 percent over the next six months. These bold actions by the Arab oil producers, particularly Saudi Arabia, caused much displeasure in the United States and brought forth some proposals for strong economic, and even military, action against the Arab countries—e.g., the sending of Marines to take control of the oil fields of Saudi Arabia if the embargo was not raised. By March 1974, however, Secretary of State Henry Kissinger's shuttle diplomacy had produced interim agreements on both the Israeli-Egyptian front and the Israeli-Syrian border. The Arab states then lifted the oil embargo. But the plain facts were clear for the world to see: the Arab states had successfully used the oil weapon against the United States to pry political concessions from Israel on the issue of returning the Arab lands Israel had seized during the 1967 war. It was a significant diplomatic victory, particularly for Saudi Arabia.

In terms of national interest, how should we assess the interests of the United States and Saudi Arabia—the two principal contestants in the oil embargo issue in 1973-1974?[6] Based on the facts currently available, Chart 1.4 seems to be a reasonable assessment.

CHART 1.4

Country: US Saudi Arabia		Issue: Arab Oil Embargo, 1973-74		
Basic interest at stake		Intensity of interest		
	Survival	Vital	Major	Peripheral
Defense of homeland			Saudi Arabia	US
Economic well-being			US Saudi Arabia	
Favorable world order		Saudi Arabia	US	
Ideological		Saudi Arabia	US	

As Chart 1.4 suggests, the United States did not have a vital interest at stake in the oil issue, but Saudi Arabia did. In the end, the Saudis' view prevailed. This conclusion is based on several considerations. (1) The United States had sufficient oil production of its own, as well as access to non-Arab sources, such as Venezuela and Canada, so that it could manage without Middle East oil during the embargo; therefore, unlike the interests of several West European countries, the U.S. economic interest in the embargo was major, not vital. (2) The degree of U.S. world order interest was contingent on two other factors—the security of Israel and noninvolvement by the Soviet Union in the war. Since neither of these contingencies occurred, the U.S. world order interest remained *major;* and Kissinger's diplomacy, rather than the introduction of U.S. forces, was the policy adopted by the Nixon administration to deal with the problem of ending the oil embargo. (3) Saudi Arabia, on the other hand, had a vital world order interest in preventing Israel from expanding its borders at the expense of its Arab neighbors. (4) Furthermore, Saudi Arabia, the most Muslim of all the Arab states and guardian of Islam's holy places, had a vital ideological interest in removing Israel's control over the Islamic shrines in Jerusalem—which the Saudi king had vowed to liberate before he died. (5) The United States had a major ideological interest in helping the Israelis gain recognition from the Arabs for an independent Jewish state, but this did *not* extend to the Israeli-occupied territories seized during the 1967 war. (6) The Israelis, for the most part, were at the mercy of President Nixon in October 1973, and he insured that they received sufficient military aid to prevent Egypt from winning a great victory in the Sinai.

The conclusion is inescapable: in 1973-1974 the United States was prepared to let the Arab oil-producing countries win their gamble of using oil as a political weapon in the confrontation between Israel and its neighbors so long as the existence of the state of Israel was not in question. As a result of this reassessment of U.S. national interests, the international financial world has been profoundly affected, and a new dialogue has been opened between the industrialized nations and the underdeveloped nations regarding the terms of trade for raw materials of many kinds—not just oil. In a word, the decision of the United States to acquiesce in the Arab oil embargo and the subsequent fourfold price rise for crude oil have profoundly altered international relations and have conferred major-power status on several countries—Iran and

Saudi Arabia, for example—that had no previous claim to such status. All this resulted from a decision in Washington, D.C., that the United States could live with higher oil prices and with Saudi demands for concessions from Israel on a Middle East peace settlement. This clearly meant that Middle East oil was a *major* U.S. interest, not a vital one. The primary interest for the United States continued to be achievement of a Middle East peace and the availability of Arab oil. Concessions to the Arabs, rather than a trade embargo or the use of force, seemed the best way of serving this interest.

To sum up, the leaders of nation-states are guided in their decisions about international relations by certain basic values that they and their people hold to be important to their national well-being; these values, or aspirations, are subsumed under the term *national interest.* However, states as well as individuals have more than one interest, and usually these interests are in competition and must be balanced by whatever political system the state has adopted. All of the interests of a nation-state may be subsumed under four *basic national interests:* defense of homeland, economic well-being, favorable world order, and promotion of the nation's ideology. The degree to which any or all of these basic interests are threatened by issues in the external environment determines the *intensity of interest,* which may be peripheral, major, vital, or survival. The intensity of interest, in turn, usually prescribes the policies that leaders of the state will adopt to meet the challenge; and when an interest is so deeply affected that national leaders conclude it should not be negotiated or compromised further, we may conclude that the issue is a *vital* interest and that the state may use force, or threaten to do so, in order to persuade an antagonist to alter its position. When two or more countries decide that their vital interests are at stake in a given issue—whether it be defense, economic, world order, or even ideological—one must assume that warfare may result, because neither side is prepared to compromise further to reach a settlement. The task of the policy planner and the scholar, therefore, is to assess whether and when a vital interest of a party to an international dispute is at stake and whether war is therefore likely to result. On strictly economic issues, which are few, economic warfare rather than military operations may be instituted by a government to protect its interest; but in the great majority of international crises, the basic interests involved are world order and defense matters—those that are political in nature and affect a society's feeling of security in its relations with other states.

The conceptual framework outlined above is not a scientific method for predicting state behavior in international crises, even though the methodology does lend itself to quantification. It suggests that scholars and policy planners can and must do a better job of analyzing the basic motivations of states, motivations that impel leaders occasionally to contemplate the use of force to deal with international problems. The thesis here is that if policy planners and scholars are more rigorous in their analysis of how states view their national interests and how they decide that an interest is *vital*, there are likely to be fewer miscalculations about state actions and, one hopes, fewer military confrontations between states. For this kind of analysis, a nation-state's values must be correctly assessed, and its willingness to run risks and pay costs must be reasonably calculated.

2. When Is an Interest Vital?

Vital interests, as defined earlier, entail the possibility that conventional warfare or economic sanctions may result from a crisis in which neither side is prepared to compromise further to achieve a solution. It is essential, therefore, that policymakers carefully calculate both their own country's stake in the issue and their antagonist's perception of its own national interest. But how do policymakers measure the *degree* of importance a given issue has for their country?

When policy planners in the State Department and Defense Department draw up recommendations for their secretaries to discuss with the president in a National Security Council (NSC) meeting, their staff studies take account of what might be called *value* factors and *cost* factors bearing upon the decisions to be made. Military planners in the Joint Chiefs of Staff usually do a threat analysis of the issue under consideration and estimate the costs, in military terms, that might have to be paid if the issue is important enough to require military action. State Department planners look primarily at political and economic factors involved and the political and economic costs that may be incurred if the issue cannot be settled by negotiations. Both seek to be systematic in their analysis of potential crises, and their recommendations attempt to take account of all relevant information. But in light of the serious miscalculations by both State Department and Defense Department planners in the period leading up to U.S. intervention in Vietnam in 1965, it is apparent that their analysis was not good enough and that some better way for determining vital interests—those for which the United States should be prepared to take strong economic or military action—must be developed and utilized to avoid such mistakes in the future.

Table 2.1 lists sixteen factors which are essential to a clear analysis of national interests—whether military, economic, or political interests—and to a decision of which issues should be considered vital. These factors are divided into value and cost/risk categories, and most of them apply to all four basic national interests: defense of homeland, economic well-being, favorable world order, and ideological aspirations. An explanation of each of these factors follows.[1]

TABLE 2.1

Essential Factors for Determining Vital Interests

Value factors	Cost/risk factors
Proximity of the danger	Economic costs of hostilities
Nature of the threat	Estimated casualties
Economic stake	Risk of portracted conflict
Sentimental attachment	Risk of enlarged conflict
Type of government	Cost of defeat or stalemate
Effect on balance of power	Risk of public opposition
National prestige at stake	Risk of UN opposition
Policies of key allies	Risk of congressional opposition

Value Factors

Proximity of the Danger

Distance from one's own borders remains an important factor in judging the importance of an international issue, primarily because people still think in geographical terms when viewing a foreign threat to the national interest. Even though intercontinental bombers and ICBMs can fly thousands of miles before reaching a target, public opinion still judges a threat from a neighboring country as more dangerous than one from a more distant country. For example, Americans reacted strongly to Soviet efforts to place nuclear missiles in Cuba in 1962, even though the Soviets probably had an ICBM capability that could threaten several U.S. cities from silos in the USSR.

Proximity of danger applies only to defense and world order interests, not to economic or ideological interests, because the latter have little to do with geographical limits. The United States and the Soviet Union, as well as other powers, are clearly more concerned with dangers in their immediate neighbor- hoods, as far as defense interests are concerned, than with those in distant areas. (Eastern Europe to the Soviet Union, and North America to the United States, are areas where the superpowers view their defense interests to be at least at the vital level.) The more difficult question is how superpowers and major powers view their world order interests when the threat is not to their homeland, but to their ally. Here the national interest is determined by other criteria, and a "domino effect" might well be a reason for dealing with a danger while it is still some distance from the homeland, rather than waiting until it comes closer. In 1941 President Roosevelt used this argument effectively to convince Americans that if Britain fell to Nazi Germany, the Nazi menace would eventually penetrate the Western Hemisphere and directly threaten the continental United States. President Johnson was not able to convince American opinion with similar arguments when he sought to justify U.S. intervention to stop North Vietnamese commu- nism from spreading throughout Southeast Asia.

Nature of the Threat

Here the problem may affect any of the four basic interests. For the United States, for example, the threat could be another Soviet threat in the Caribbean (defense), another Arab oil embargo (economic), the toppling of a friendly government in South America by communist groups (world order), or the flagrant disregard for human rights by a country allied to the United States (ideological). However, it is unlikely that any ideological interest would be so threatened that the United States would be willing to use force (vital); and until 1971, when President Nixon imposed import restrictions on all goods brought into the United States in order to force U.S. trading partners to agree to a devaluation of the dollar, no *economic* issue had yet become vital. Reaction in the United States to the Arab oil embargo in 1973 indicates that more economic issues in the future may be considered vital.

It is in the world order category that the "nature of the threat" is the most ambiguous for policy planners. This is because Americans and other peoples tend to distinguish between overt acts of aggression—such as the Korean case in 1950—and conflicts that are essentially internal—such as Chile and Angola. Much of the public dissatisfaction with President Johnson's definition of the national interest in Vietnam stemmed from Hanoi's care in using Viet Cong (South Vietnamese) to carry on the fight against the Saigon government until the introduction of large U.S. forces in 1965, when the North felt justified in openly sending its own forces southward. Americans tend to judge civil wars and domestic struggles as strictly internal conflicts and therefore as less worthy of U.S. involvement. The difference in U.S. political leaders' views in 1976 over the possibility that the Italian Communist Party might enter the Italian government is symptomatic of this dilemma.

The difficulty posed to Western democracies that distinguish between internal and external wars is apparent in the struggles for power in several countries in southern Africa. If the Soviet Union and its Cuban ally are able to discourage the United States and other powers from sending military assistance to pro-Western factions by claiming that these are *internal* struggles, Soviet influence will probably gain significantly in Africa, for the Soviet Union has no scruples about providing military aid—even Cuban mercenaries—to intervene on the side of leftist forces in the name of supporting "wars of national liberation." In this case, Soviet ideological interests clearly *encourage* intervention in internal struggles for power, but U.S. ideology *inhibits* such actions. This is one of the greatest problems U.S. presidents will have in defining national interests: if world opinion judges most international conflicts to be *internal* struggles for power and if the United States is unable to help pro-Western factions, the Soviets may well win the struggle for Third World resources without having to use their own forces.

Economic Stake

Investments, trade, and commerce are still important factors conditioning the interest the United States has in other states, but rarely have they alone caused the United States to resort to war in recent years. Radical historians have sought to prove that the United States has used its military power since World War II to support economic ends, but no one has argued convincingly that the two most costly U.S. interventions during this period—Korea and Vietnam—were decided upon because of economic factors. On the contrary, both Korea and Vietnam were a drain on the U.S. economy. Nevertheless, the worldwide investments and trade carried on by U.S. firms, and the effect this has had on various segments of U.S. society, make economic factors among the important considerations foreign policy planners must take into account when recommending policy. The United States' unwillingness to bar chromium imports from Rhodesia, despite a UN sanction against that state in the 1960s, resulted from strong lobbying in Congress by private U.S. groups. Conversely, the U.S. government has acquiesced in the nationalization of U.S. firms by many states so long as compensation was paid to the owners. Peru, Venezuela, and Saudi Arabia are recent examples where the U.S. national interest regarding private investments abroad was not very high and a compromise solution to these economic issues was found.

The economic stake clearly affects two of the basic U.S. national interests—economic and world order. For example, a vital economic interest seemed to be at stake in the Nixon "shocks" of 1971, when the United States took very strong economic measures against its trading partners, and in the U.S. reaction to the Arab oil embargo in 1973. Middle East oil has always been vital to Western Europe, but only in the 1970s has it become very important to the United States—because of the decline in U.S. production. Had the embargo continued a few more months into 1974, and had Europe been more cooperative with Washington in arriving at a joint policy, it is likely that strong economic countermeasures against Saudi Arabia would have been taken.

Sentimental Attachment

The United States, more than most states, is influenced in its attitudes toward other countries by the sentiments of the many immigrants who came to the United States before and after World War II. The "ethnic vote" seems to exert more influence on foreign policymaking than the numbers of voters involved. Historically, Americans have felt a sentimental attachment to the British people because both countries have had similar values and institutions. In World War I, however, President Wilson was well aware that there was strong pro-German and pro-Irish sentiment among recent immigrants from those countries, a sentiment that tended to cancel out pro-British sentiment until 1917. Similarly, the strong Jewish minority in the United States has had an overriding influence on U.S. policy in the Middle East. And Secretary of State Kissinger could not work out a solution to the Cyprus issue in 1974-1975 because Greek-Americans brought very strong pressure on Congress to punish Turkey for sending troops to Cyprus. Conversely, the lack of sentimental attachment to the Vietnamese and Laotian people made it more difficult for President Johnson to obtain a commitment from the American people to defend South Vietnam against communist insurgents determined to impose their own form of government.

Although it can be argued that sentiment should have no place in the formulation of national interest, democracies find it difficult to ignore this factor because their peoples have some voice in determining foreign policy. Even President de Gaulle, who excluded questions of sentiment from his thinking about France's national interests, nevertheless drew on the sentimental attachment to France in Quebec to stir up latent nationalist feelings there during a visit to Canada in 1967. When Brezhnev talks about fraternal ties with Fidel Castro, there is a certain sentimental tone struck there as well. Clearly, sentiment is still an important factor in determining U.S. national interests in the Middle East, and it probably will greatly influence U.S. policy toward Africa as well.

Type of Government

This factor is linked to sentimental attachment and flows from the ideological underpinnings of U.S. society, namely, belief in representative government, individual rights for citizens, religious freedom, etc. This factor also has posed a dilemma for U.S. policymakers: they have had to trade off world order interests and economic interests on the one hand and ideological interests on the other. For example, military assistance and economic aid to authoritarian Asian regimes during the 1950s and 1960s—South Korea, Republic of China, and Thailand—were justified on the grounds that U.S. support for these regimes was essential to the containment of the People's Republic of China, at a time when Peking was strongly anti-American and revolutionary vis-à-vis other Asian countries. A similar dilemma has existed in U.S. relations with many Latin American regimes, very few of which are democratic by American standards. Nevertheless, since the end of the Vietnam war, there has been increasing sentiment in Congress and in the public media for the U.S. government to give greater attention to the type of government when it gives aid and makes defense commitments. It is likely that the American people's historical interest in supporting freedom will receive greater attention in coming years, as President Carter's human rights policy shows.

Effect on the Balance of Power

This factor should be viewed on two levels: the strategic balance between the Soviet Union and the United States, and the regional balance of political forces in any part of the world. On the strategic level, the two superpowers are constantly measuring the effectiveness of their nuclear missile forces in order to assess whether the other side has gained, or will gain, an advantage and thus be in a position to intimidate the other side to make political concessions. In June 1961 Chairman Khrushchev thought he was in an advantageous strategic position when he met President Kennedy in Vienna and sought to force concessions from him on Berlin and elsewhere. The outcome of the Cuban missile crisis sixteen months later showed that the Soviet leader had overestimated his strategic position; as a result, Soviet planners launched a large military effort to gain strategic parity with the United States. The Strategic Arms Limitation Talks, which began in 1969 between the superpowers, were motivated in part by both sides' need to avoid mistakes and to keep a close watch on the other's technological developments.

The regional political balance of power is more difficult to assess. Unlike the strategic balance, which depends largely on the superpowers' decisions to produce or limit the weapons that maintain the balance, a regional political balance depends on the willingness of other countries to cooperate with one another and with the superpowers to insure that one country can never dominate the politics of a whole region. The second-level balance resembles the classical balance of power practiced by European statesmen in the eighteenth and nineteenth centuries, a practice that resulted in three great European wars between 1795 and 1945. Indeed, when European powers dominated world politics, Asia, Africa, and the Western Hemisphere were but bystanders to the balance-of-power politics played out among the British, French, Dutch, Germans, and Portuguese.[2] Today there are four or five regional balances, which gain added importance in international politics as the superpowers reach agreement not to use their strategic forces except for defense of their own territory or that of close allies. The struggle for a balance of power in Asia—of which the Vietnam war was a part—has now been altered by the outcome of that contest, but also by the bitter rivalry between China and the Soviet Union, a rivalry that works to the advantage of the United States and Japan. In South Asia and the Middle East, India and Iran are emerging as regional powers, and in Africa the new black countries' rivalry for influence has recently drawn the attention of the superpowers. Even in Latin America, where U.S. influence was dominant for most of this century, the regional balance is shifting as Brazil's economy grows remarkably and Venezuela uses its oil revenues to gain influence among the small countries of the Caribbean and the Third World.

It is the degree to which political changes in various parts of the world affect the feeling of security, economic well-being, and ideological aspirations of the superpowers that determines how much attention they give in terms of diplomatic support and economic and military equipment. After the Vietnam war, the focus of U.S. world order interest has shifted from the Far East to the Middle East, largely because Middle East oil has become a vital economic interest of the United States. Thus, what happens in the politics of Saudi Arabia, Iran, Syria, and Egypt is of immense importance to U.S. policy planners; and their perception of U.S. national interests in that area is heavily influenced by how they see the regional balance of power shaping up—whether these countries will be friendly or unfriendly to the United States, and the extent to which the Soviet Union or any other rival superpower in the future may take advantage of discord in that area.

National Prestige at Stake

All states are interested in the image they project to other states in the international system, but national prestige is more important to major and superpowers than to small states. President de Gaulle talked about the grandeur of France, and Secretary Rusk referred to the credibility of U.S. commitments abroad. Both were concerned with the respect that other countries showed their own countries and the esteem they were accorded in international organizations. This factor is no less true for communist powers: Soviet leaders have gone to great lengths to gain respectability in international organizations and are extremely sensitive to charges that the USSR has broken any international agreements.

Prestige is difficult to measure because it has to do with perceptions and subjective judgments about many questions. Does a country use its power wisely? Does it respect the legal rights of other states? Does it aid its allies when they need help? Does it achieve domestic support for its foreign policy? Is it realistic in the pursuit of goals? Nations lose prestige when they take a stand on an international issue but do not carry through to a successful outcome—e.g., Britain's humiliation in the Suez crisis of 1956, the Soviet Union's retreat in the Cuban missile crisis of 1962, and the United States' ignoble helicopter withdrawal from Vietnam in 1975. On the other hand, nations usually gain prestige when they win wars, bring peace to a troubled area, or achieve significant gains from diplomatic negotiations. The prestige of the United States and that of its secretary of state, Dr. Kissinger, gained significantly in 1974 when his "shuttle diplomacy" was able to produce an interim peace settlement in the Middle East. Prestige often becomes a personal matter with heads of government because of the attention given to summit meetings and because most government leaders are deeply involved in foreign policy issues. A U.S. president's political prestige at home may be significantly affected by his prestige abroad, as was the case during the first year of the Kennedy administration and the last year of the Nixon administration. Policy planners are constantly reminded that maintaining credibility with allies and enemies abroad is an important value in deciding foreign policy issues, and this factor bears on their perception of the nation's interest in a given case. In the wake of the Vietnam experience, it is unlikely that the United States' prestige will again be so committed to an issue whose real value to this country is so questionable.

Policies of Key Allies

Most states, including the superpowers, have allies whose loyalty is highly valued and whose views are usually considered before a decision is made to take strong action against a third state. This factor is less relevant when a defense or ideological interest is at stake than when an economic or world order issue is under consideration. For example, when the United States was threatened by Soviet efforts to place missiles in Cuba, President Kennedy advised his NATO allies of his actions but did *not* consult with them in advance. On the other hand, when the Nixon administration was formulating a policy to deal with the Arab oil embargo in 1973-1974, the unwillingness of the NATO countries to go along with strong retaliatory measures was an inhibiting factor in U.S. policy. On world order interests, Presidents Truman and Eisenhower were always concerned about obtaining British and, they hoped, French support in cases where it seemed likely that U.S. forces would have to be used outside North America to defend a world order interest. Lebanon in 1958 and Korea in 1950 are examples. Presidents Kennedy and Johnson, however, paid less attention to their NATO allies in deciding when to use U.S. forces abroad, particularly in Asia, where British and French unwillingness to become involved in the Vietnam struggle was clear from the beginning. Presidents Nixon and Ford seemed to give greater attention to NATO's views before taking military actions, but on economic matters President Nixon ignored both the NATO allies and Japan when he imposed economic sanctions in 1971 against their exports.

The policies of allies can be expanded as a consideration in determining national interest by including world opinion, or more particularly the United Nations. To what degree should policymakers be concerned about the reactions of all other states in the international system when they calculate national interests and recommend policy actions? The answer probably lies in the degree to which a country's leaders believe that they *need* support of allies or of world opinion when deciding a national interest. Superpowers probably have less need of world support than other powers because they have other sources of strength.

Cost/Risk Factors

Economic Costs of Hostilities

If an economic or world order issue is so important that hostilities could result, such hostilities may take several forms, including trade embargoes, economic sanctions, and limited armed intervention. In all such instances, the state taking such measures will incur economic costs. When the United States imposed a trade embargo on Cuba, this affected U.S. business and shut off the supply of Cuban sugar to U.S. markets. When Britain decided to use force against Nasser in 1956, there were financial consequences for sterling, and British shipping interests were affected.

Of the two major U.S. interventions since World War II— Korea and Vietnam—the economic costs of intervening in Korea were more accurately calculated, and President Truman did not hesitate to ask Congress to raise taxes. Nor did he delay in imposing wage and price controls on the economy. In the Vietnam case, President Johnson greatly underestimated the costs of the war—which led to huge budget deficits and inflation by the end of the decade. In the Arab oil embargo of 1973, the economic consequences of a trade war or military intervention appeared to be very great for all Western countries, and the latter did not retaliate. The probable costs of intervention or of embargoes on trade must be carefully calculated in advance and weighed against the value factors cited above.

Estimated Casualties

If armed intervention is considered a likely consequence of "no compromise" on a vital issue, policymakers should be reasonably clear about the likely manpower needs for a limited war, the likely level of hostilities, and the probable casualties. In advising the president what the manpower needs would be for armed intervention in Vietnam, Secretary of Defense Robert McNamara grossly underestimated the size of the force needed to contain North Vietnamese–sponsored warfare in South Vietnam. Conversely, when the Soviets intervened to put down the Hungarian freedom fighters in 1956, they used massive force and quickly ended the insurrection. In a free society, the size of the force used and the potential casualties must be assessed correctly because they are crucial in calculating public reaction to an intervention. U.S. intervention in the Dominican Republic in 1965 did not result in widespread opposition in the United States, in large part because the force employed was modest and casualties were small.

If a local conflict could involve a direct confrontation between the superpowers, policymakers would also have to estimate the civilian casualties that might result if the local conflict escalated into a nuclear exchange. President Kennedy had to consider this risk when he decided how to deal with the Soviet move to put offensive missiles in Cuba in 1962. As more and more countries are now acquiring nuclear weapons, the risk of civilian casualties is important to all powers. Terrorist raids on civilian airliners and ground installations are also a new danger to free societies.

Risk of Protracted Conflict

Unless a country is fighting for its own homeland (defense interest), it is probably reluctant to use its military forces to fight for world order or economic interests unless it believes such conflicts will be of reasonably short duration. This is more true for free societies than for totalitarian or authoritarian ones because public opinion is likely to play a larger part in the determination of how long the country's armed forces should fight for an interest that is not close to home. It is probably universally true that a nation believing it can accomplish its objectives through the limited use of force for a short period of time is more likely to undertake such action than if it knows in advance that the conflict will be long and costly. Both President Truman and President Johnson were supported by the American people when they intervened in Korea and Vietnam, respectively; and had these conflicts been ended satisfactorily within six months to a year, both would have been cheered. As it was, neither of them could end the war before he left office, and each saw his party defeated in the ensuing general election. The lesson in both cases is that U.S. policymakers should have prepared the country for long and costly conflicts instead of misleading the public to believe the wars would be of short duration. In Korea and Vietnam, the American people became disillusioned when the wars dragged on without a decision.

Risk of Enlarged Conflict

This point is always considered when limited military force is contemplated, but it is not always correctly calculated. In large measure, it is a matter of good intelligence—to clearly understand the concerns and intentions of *all* nation-states affected by a planned intervention. The miscalculations flowing from misperceptions of other states' intentions have too often resulted in unwanted and costly wars. Had Stalin known in 1950 that Truman would intervene to repel an attack on South Korea, would he have given his blessing to North Korea's plan to unify the country by force? Conversely, had Truman known that China would intervene in that war if U.S. forces were permitted to move to the Yalu River, would he have given General MacArthur the authority to take his forces north of the thirty-eighth parallel?

Many military leaders and some politicians have charged that the Vietnam war could have been "won" in the first six months if President Johnson had been willing to use enough force quickly to prevent North Vietnam from adjusting its economy and supply lines to the South. On strictly military grounds, this thesis is debatable, but more important for this discussion is the likelihood that massive U.S. intervention in Vietnam—both South and North—in 1965 would have triggered a Chinese intervention, just as moving U.S. forces to the Yalu in 1950 brought in Chinese troops—much to the surprise of U.S. intelligence officials. In 1965 President Johnson wanted no repeat performance because his war aims were limited to South Vietnam. That he failed in this objective was due less to his limited use of forces than to the extraordinary tenacity of the North Vietnamese.

Cost of Defeat or Stalemate

This factor is closely linked to the previous considerations but adds one element: even if the issue is deemed so important that it cannot be compromised and is, therefore, thought to be vital, will the limited use of conventional force bring about the desired result? This is an extremely difficult question: on the one hand, the value attached to the issue may be very high, but on the other hand, the potential level of warfare may also be high, thus raising the question whether the objective is important enough to risk the use of tactical nuclear weapons. It is clear that if the basic interest involved is "defense of homeland," the likelihood of taking that risk is higher than it would be in the case of defending an ally far removed from the homeland (world order interest). When China intervened in Korea in 1950, President Truman publicly speculated about using the atomic bomb to halt the Chinese drive, but was persuaded both by his European allies and domestic opinion that this would not be a wise move. Thus, the conventional Korean conflict then continued for three more years. The record shows that the Soviet Union threatened Britain and France with a large war in November 1956 only after it was sure that the United States would not support their invasion of Egypt.

Risk of Public Opposition

An open democratic society must always calculate this cost, and it is probably a general rule that public opinion supports limited wars when they commence but loses patience when they are not brought to a speedy conclusion. Although public opinion does not generally operate as a brake in communist or other totalitarian states, the leadership of a communist government must take into account the views of party members even though the party is far more tightly controlled than in freely elected representative governments.

In the late 1970s, this factor has assumed very large proportions for the leading Western countries, including the United States, and it is likely to be exploited by the Soviet Union for its worldwide purposes. Britain, which was the world's policeman for over one hundred years, is no longer willing even to send peacekeeping forces to southern Africa to prevent a race war in its former colony of Rhodesia. France has no interest in using its forces for anything other than defense of its own territory. The United States was so bruised by the Vietnam experience that Congress blocked President Ford from sending any kind of aid to noncommunist forces in Angola in 1976. Recent polls show that American public opinion would not be in favor of defending any country in the Middle East and that many Americans would question even the defense of Europe. In these circumstances, President Carter will have some difficulty convincing the USSR that he will be tough in countering its moves—with either Soviet forces, or with proxy forces in Africa, the Middle East, or even in Latin America—to turn the world order to its advantage.

Risk of United Nations Opposition

Condemnation by other states, particularly if the issue is taken to the United Nations, is a cost that decision makers must calculate when contemplating whether an issue is worth fighting for. Major powers and superpowers often ignore international opinion when the issue is a vital one, as

Czechoslovakia was to the USSR in 1968, Tibet was to China in 1958, and East Pakistan was to India in 1971. In such cases, however, the state doing the intervening gives greater attention on the value scale to the attitude of allies and friends. There is usually a trade-off here: for lesser powers, the attitude of the United Nations and world opinion might have a greater influence on their decisions.

The consistent opposition of Third World countries in the United Nations to policies that Washington feels are responsible has greatly reduced the esteem Americans hold for this international organization. Therefore, UN opposition is likely to be viewed as acceptable when policymakers calculate the costs of taking strong action to protect U.S. economic and world order interests. It is also likely that the United States will keep reminding the Third World and the Soviet bloc that it stands for individual freedoms for all people and that most of their countries deny individual rights to their citizens and continue to hold political prisoners. This reiteration of American ideological interests may not change any votes in the United Nations, but it will keep the United States on the offensive in one area where it has justice on its side.

Risk of Congressional Opposition

In a Western democratic system, the party in power always takes into account the political price that will have to be paid if an armed intervention turns out to be unpopular. Political leaders usually try to obtain nonpartisan support for decisions involving the use of forces, in order to share responsibility for costs. Truman and Eisenhower were especially diligent in seeking support from congressional opposition parties. This is not always true, however; Eden did not consult his opposition before launching the Suez expedition, and Lyndon Johnson did not get a vote of support from Congress for his massive intervention in Vietnam. In the Soviet Union, China, and other totalitarian states, the leadership also struggles to convince the opposition that its policy is right; but in these systems, far fewer leaders participate than in a western system. If the leadership in a communist state pursues a course that turns out to be disastrous, it is likely to be replaced—as Khrushchev was after his debacle in Cuba in 1962, and as Brezhnev might have been had the intervention in Czechoslovakia in 1968 proved counterproductive.

In the U.S. context, the political risk to a president who adopts a policy of confrontation with an adversary is far greater if the opposition party controls Congress. This was the case in both the Nixon and Ford presidencies, and Congress resisted both of them in foreign as well as domestic policy. When President Johnson was in the White House, several important congressional leaders expressed strong reservations in private about his plan to intervene in Vietnam; but for reasons of party unity, they did not publicly protest his policies until the public became aroused. It will be interesting to see whether a Democratic-dominated Congress enforces the "War Powers Act" on President Carter as it did on President Nixon.[3]

Assessing Values and Costs/Risks

To make this discussion of values and costs meaningful to policy planners, it is desirable to have each of the sixteen factors evaluated in terms of its importance to a specific foreign policy issue. The issue may affect any of the four basic national interests, and the level of interest would vary from one issue to another. For example, an Arab oil embargo against the United States would be evaluated differently from a threatened communist takeover in Guatemala, or an attack by Iraq on Syria. These criteria may be evaluated in several ways, including the following three:

1. Each factor may be rated by the adjectives *low, medium, high,* and *very high.* If most of the value factors are "high" and the cost-risk factors are "low," the issue is probably a *vital* interest.
2. The terms *survival, vital, major,* and *peripheral* might be attached to each factor. If the value factors are averaged out to be "major" and the cost-risk factors appear to be "vital," the issue is probably a *major* interest.

3. A numbering scale may be used, with "1" representing a
low value or cost, and "10" representing a very high stake
or risk. If the value numbers add up to 40 and the costs
reach 50, the issue is probably a *major* interest.

This evaluation can be done with a questionnaire like the
one in Figure 2.1.

FIGURE 2.1

```
Questionnaire:
Determination of Vital Interests


        Values                              Costs/Risks
___ Proximity of the danger        ___ Economic costs of hostilities

___ Nature of the threat           ___ Estimated casualties

___ Economic stake                 ___ Risk of protracted conflict

___ Sentimental attachment         ___ Risk of enlarged conflict

___ Type of government             ___ Cost of defeat or stalemate

___ Effect on balance of power     ___ Risk of public opposition

___ National prestige at stake     ___ Risk of UN opposition

___ Policies of key allies         ___ Risk of congressional opposition



    NOTE: You may indicate the degree of concern each of the value
    and cost/risk factors holds for you by using any of the following
    ranking systems:

        (a)                    (b)                     (c)
    Very high              Survival               9 - 10

    High                   Vital                  6 - 8

    Medium                 Major                  3 - 5

    Low                    Peripheral             1 - 2
```

The factor evaluation method is not intended to produce
precise computations of the degree of national interest involved
in a specific international issue: rather it is hoped that a
systematic measuring of the principal factors that policymakers ought to consider will produce better decisions and
help us avoid serious mistakes in judgment. It is *not* suggested
as a scientific method for making foreign policy decisions,

because the making of foreign policy remains an art, not a science. Yet it ought to be possible to find a more rigorous means of sorting out the crucial question: when does an economic issue, or a world order issue, or threat to national defense become so important that the president should consult with Congress as well as cabinet members about the probability that the use of economic or military force (or both) will have to be threatened to convince an adversary that the issue cannot be compromised further?

3. Wilson's and Roosevelt's Perceptions of National Interest

When Woodrow Wilson entered the White House in 1913 and Franklin Roosevelt did the same twenty years later, neither man was aware that a general European war would erupt during his presidency and eventually pull the United States into a major conflict outside North America. Both presidents came to power following a long period of Republican rule in Washington, and both saw their major task to be initiating major domestic reforms to deal with the nation's pressing economic problems. Although Europe had been through several minor crises in 1911 and 1912, Wilson remained true to the traditional U.S. attitude that Europe's power struggles were of no concern to the United States. In March 1933 Roosevelt faced the most serious economic crisis the United States had ever known, and he did not become aware until several years later that Adolf Hitler's accession to the chancellorship of Germany in January 1933 would eventually pose an even greater threat to the future of democratic government. In sum, both of these remarkable men came to the White House convinced that their principal task would be to deal with the *public* interest of the United States, but they ended their terms totally absorbed in defending the country's *national* interest.

Many biographers and historians have commented on the process by which Wilson and Roosevelt turned their attention from domestic to foreign affairs and the steps each took to prepare the country for war. These authorities do not agree, especially in Wilson's case, on why these presidents took so long to ask Congress to declare war on Germany. Rather than seek to provide new insights on that question, the objective of this discussion will be to assess how Wilson viewed U.S.

interests vis-à-vis the European war in the period 1916-1917, and how Roosevelt viewed U.S. interests vis-à-vis Germany in the period June 1940 to December 1941. Specifically, what was the basis for each president's decision that *vital* U.S. interests were at stake in these European wars and that U.S. forces would eventually have to be used to defend those interests?

During the periods under review, Wilson and Roosevelt made major public addresses about U.S. objectives in Europe and the world. Roosevelt also held many press conferences on these subjects. Although the public statements and private views of presidents often do not coincide, there is good reason to believe that Wilson's principal speeches to Congress early in 1917 and Roosevelt's statements to Congress and to the American people during 1941 were reasonably accurate reflections of their moods and of their thinking about the U.S. stake in the great European conflicts. Although historians may disagree on *why* Wilson did some of the things he did, there is little dispute over the point that Wilson *believed* what he said at the time he said it. Likewise, there is little doubt that Roosevelt's postelection statements in 1940-1941 were an accurate reflection of his deep concern over the dangerous situation in Europe.

The public statements of these wartime presidents strongly suggest that each had a keen perception of U.S. national interests in the periods leading up to U.S. involvement in World Wars I and II. Furthermore, both were realistic in their attempts to persuade a reluctant nation to accept and support their perceptions. To measure the validity of this conclusion, the following questions, based on the framework outlined in Chapter 1, may be posed:

1. How did these presidents view the military threat to North America and to American lives? *(defense interest)*
2. How did they view the impact of a German victory on U.S. trade and commerce? *(economic interest)*
3. How did they assess the effect of a German victory on the world balance of power and on future peace? *(world order interest)*

4. How did they perceive the threat to fundamental American values? *(ideological interest)*

So long as the president believed that answers to those questions did not suggest a serious challenge to the country, the interest remained at the *major* level. However, when the president believed that the situation in Europe had gone beyond the point of compromise (as it did for Wilson early in 1917), then we may conclude that his perception of the national interest moved to the *vital* level (as Roosevelt's did in June 1940, after the fall of France). The problem of convincing the nation that a vital interest was at stake was a different question; of primary concern here is the *basis* on which Wilson and Roosevelt decided that the United States had no alternative but to enter these European wars.

Wilson and World War I

Woodrow Wilson, by all accounts, fervently desired to keep the United States out of the European conflict that started in the summer of 1914. He pursued this objective with vigor (his critics said humiliation) up until about two weeks before delivering his war message to Congress on April 2, 1917. Observers differ on why Wilson followed this course so stubbornly and for so long. Some, such as Patrick Devlin, believe that Wilson was guilty of self-deception from 1914 to 1916 and that he cloaked a giant ego in idealism and morality.[1] Others, such as former President Theodore Roosevelt and a number of Republican senators, believed that Wilson was weak and unmanly. Most writers are more charitable toward Wilson, however, even though they disagree about why it took him so long to make up his mind for war. Newton Baker, Wilson's secretary of war, summed up his impression with this interesting observation: "The President believed that Providence had set the United States apart as a mediating nation, and that the day would certainly come when the exhausted European powers would turn to him, as our representative, to use our great spiritual and material power to aid them in constructing a plan of life which they could accept from us as a disinterested friend but which they would be unable to find for themselves, blinded by passion and grief and disappointment."[2] In this view, Wilson's idealism was authentic, not a mask for other motives.

A more pragmatic view of Wilson's behavior is offered by Arthur Link: "All the evidence of Wilson's thinking since the summer of 1916 about long-range American national interests in the outcome in Europe leads to the conclusion that he believed that American interests, to say nothing of the interests of mankind, would be best served by a draw in Europe. He not only thought that a peace without victory offered the best hope for the right reconstruction of the world order, but he also now feared destruction of German power and an absolute Anglo-French-Russian military hegemony in Europe."[3] According to this view, Wilson was well aware of balance-of-power politics and had a realistic view of the U.S. interest vis-à-vis the European power centers.

However, Wilson's concept of what constituted a suitable world order was *not* a new balance of power, but a system of collective security based on international law. Thus, Germany should not be defeated but should look to the United States as an impartial arbiter of the ghastly European conflict in which no victor and no loser would emerge. In a word, Wilson thought there was a better chance of restructuring the postwar world order if there was no decisive victory by either side in the war and if the United States remained a nonbelligerent. In 1916 that may have been a naive view of the world, but it was a *rational* view held by a sincere and dedicated man groping for the basis of a lasting peace.

By the beginning of 1917, time was running out for Wilson and for Germany. British domination of the high seas insured that the Allies were getting essential food and war materials from North America, and the Allied blockade of the Central Powers was beginning to have a serious effect on Germany. At the end of 1916, German military leaders forced a decision to resume unrestricted submarine warfare in order to impose a counterblockade on Britain and France. This was a sharp reversal of promises the Germans gave Wilson earlier that year that unarmed vessels of nonbelligerent states would not be attacked by U-boats. It clearly was a shock and a severe challenge to Wilson, as well as to U.S. shipping. To make matters worse, Berlin rejected his latest peace effort. Wilson's great dream of bringing both sides to a conference table now had vanished. The fact that neither Britain nor France was any more interested than Germany to accept a negotiated peace was not lost on Wilson; the blunt truth he had to accept was that, despite all his efforts, both sides in the European holocaust still believed it was possible to achieve a military victory. Since Europe was determined to fight to the finish in 1917, Wilson had to decide whether his desire to keep the United States out of war overrode his equally strong hope of building a more durable peace when the fighting was finally over. Wilson's desire to be a principal, not an observer, at the peace table won out, because he perceived that U.S. national interests in the twentieth century would not permit the luxury of continued isolation, protected by the British fleet. He would have to be at the peace conference as a full participant if he hoped to have any influence in shaping future world events. Link subscribes to this view: "Then there was a final tempting thought. It was that American belligerency would enhance his own ability to force an early settlement. He would continue as a neutral to be frustrated by both sides in his efforts for peace. He would have more influence with the Allies as a belligerent and, finally, some bargaining power with Germany."[4]

Gilbert Fite and Norman Graebner have a different view of why Wilson decided to join the Allies against Imperial Germany. They argue that Wilson was guided, whether he knew it or not, by America's historic interest in a balance of power in Europe. By 1917 Germany threatened to destroy this balance through submarine warfare, which would not only threaten Britain's ability to continue in the war but also seriously hurt U.S. commerce. In their view, Wilson's reasons for going to war were too legalistic and, for the American public, too misleading about the reality of the U.S. national interest.[5]

This criticism may be too strong, however. Wilson's own statements, contained in four speeches to Congress between

January 22 and April 2, 1917, provide a reasonably clear picture of why he believed that the United States must enter the war on the side of the Allies. A careful reading of these speeches shows that he was influenced in one degree or another by all four of the basic U.S. national interests discussed above. In the first address, on January 22, he laid out his concept of what constituted a just peace in Europe, and he suggested that the American people could render a "great service" if they decided to add their power and authority to that of other countries "to guarantee peace and justice throughout the world." Regarding a final peace treaty to be drawn up by the warring nations, Wilson asserted: "The question upon which the whole future peace and policy of the world depends is this: Is the present war a struggle for a just and secure peace, or only for a new balance of power? If it be only a struggle for a new balance of power, who will guarantee, who can guarantee, the stable equilibrium of the new arrangement? Only a tranquil Europe can be a stable Europe. There must be, not a balance of power, but a community of power; not organized rivalries but an organized common peace." It was in this speech that Wilson referred to "a peace without victory," a peace that would allow both sides to come to the peace table as equals. "Only a peace between equals can last," he asserted.

This was Wilson's vision of a new world order, one in which the United States could join with other nations to preserve the peace. But was this world order interest worth the price of U.S. military intervention in the European war, i.e., was it a *vital* interest? Wilson did not suggest this. He merely laid out for Congress and the American people his view of what a just peace should entail, a view that could command the support of the United States if intervention became inevitable.

Wilson also talked about ideological interests in this January 22 address: "No peace can last, or ought to last, which does not recognize and accept the principle that governments derive all their just powers from the consent of the governed." He then advanced this startling idea: "I am proposing, as it were, that the nations should with one accord adopt the doctrine of President Monroe as the doctrine of the world, that no nation should seek to extend its policy over any other nation or people, but that every people should be left free to determine its own polity, its own way of development, unhindered, unthreatened, unafraid, the little along with the great and powerful."[6] He made no mention in this address of any U.S. defense and economic interests affected by the European war—that would come later. Here the president chose the high idealistic ground of the new world that *ought to be*. In retrospect, Wilson was no doubt carefully laying the groundwork for U.S. military intervention if circumstances made it impossible to remain aloof; by January 22, 1917, therefore, Wilson probably knew in his heart that war was coming whether he wanted it or not. In that case, would it not be prudent for him to begin educating both the American people and the belligerents—so that they would understand his long-range objectives?

Two weeks later, on February 3, Wilson again went before Congress, this time to announce that he was breaking diplomatic relations with Germany because it had resumed unlimited submarine warfare. In this address, he concentrated on the U.S. defense interest—i.e., the threat to lives of U.S. citizens—and suggested that this could become a *vital* issue for the government: "I think that you will agree with me that, in view of this declaration, which suddenly and without prior intimation of any kind deliberately withdraws the solemn assurance given in the Imperial Government's note of the 4th of May, 1916, this Government has no alternative consistent with the dignity and honor of the United States but to take the course. . . ." He warned that if German submarines did in fact carry out the threat of their government, "I shall take the liberty of coming again before the Congress to ask that authority be given to me to use any means that may be necessary for the protection of our seamen and our people in the prosecution of their peaceful and legitimate errands on the high seas. I can do nothing less. I take it for granted other governments will take the same course."[7]

In a third message to Congress three weeks later, on February 26, Wilson asked for authority to arm U.S. merchant ships, although he believed he had inherent powers to do so without a vote of support from Congress. In this speech, he referred for the first time to issues relating to the nation's *economic* interests. Admitting that the number of ships sunk by German submarines had not increased substantially since early February, Wilson called attention to "the tying up of our shipping in our own ports because of the unwillingness of our shipowners to risk their vessels at sea without insurance or adequate protection, and the very serious congestion of our commerce which has resulted, a congestion which is growing rapidly more and more serious every day." Later in this address he asserted: "No one doubts what it is our duty to do. We must defend our commerce and the lives of our people in the midst of the present trying circumstances, with discretion but with clear and steadfast purpose. Only the method and the extent remain to be chosen, upon the occasion, if the occasion should indeed arise."[8] Was the president suggesting that protection of U.S. commerce was a *vital* interest, to be protected by force if necessary? This was one of the very few references Wilson made to the economic aspects of the war, indicating he was not unmindful of the manufactured goods and food being produced in the United States and shipped to Britain and other belligerents.

At the conclusion of this February 26 address, the president sought to summarize his thinking about the basis for U.S. intervention in the war if events made that necessary:

> I have spoken of our commerce and of the legitimate errands of our people on the seas, but you will not be misled as to my main thought, the thought that lies beneath these phrases and gives them dignity and weight. It is not of material interests merely that we are thinking. It is, rather, of fundamental human rights, chief of all the right of life itself. I am thinking not only of the rights of Americans to go and come about their proper business by way of the sea, but also of something much deeper, much more fundamental than that. I am thinking of those rights of humanity without which there is no civilization. My theme is of those great principles of compassion and of protection which mankind has sought to throw about human lives. We are speaking of no selfish material rights but of rights which our hearts support and whose foundation is that righteous passion for justice. I cannot imagine any man with American principles at his heart hesitating to defend these things.

Here Wilson touched on all four basic national interests: protection of American lives (defense); protection of U.S. shipping (economic); protection of humanity and civilization (world order); and protection of fundamental human rights (ideological). It is difficult to tell from this speech which of the four he considered to be the most important, i.e., whether any was yet *vital*. But the thrust of his idealism indicates that he put the greatest value on world order and ideological interests. If the United States was forced to intervene in a dreadful European war, he seemed to be saying, it would not be for self-interest only, but for the interests of humanity, and of liberty, and justice. This was Wilsonian idealism in full bloom.

Wilson's message on April 2, 1917, one of the greatest ever delivered by a U.S. president, was a brilliant argument for the United States' entry into the war against Germany. In this message, he justified his decision for war primarily on grounds of defense. He also covered world order and ideological interests. But he de-emphasized the economic factor. Wilson's statements about the national interests were as follows:

Defense interest: "There is one choice we cannot make, we are incapable of making: we will not choose the path of submission and suffer the most sacred rights of our nation and our people to be ignored or violated. The wrongs against which we now array ourselves are no common wrongs: they cut to the very roots of human life."

Economic interest: "I am not now thinking of the loss of property involved, immense and serious as that is. . . . Property can be paid for; the lives of peaceful and innocent people cannot be."

World order interest: "Our object now, as then, is to vindicate the principles of peace and justice in the life of the world, as against selfish and autocratic power, and to set up amongst the really free and self-governed peoples of the world such a concert of purpose and of action as will henceforth ensure the observance of those principles."

Ideological interest: "We are glad, now that we see the facts with no veil of false pretense about them, to fight thus for the ultimate peace of the world and for the liberation of its peoples, the German peoples included: for the rights of nations great and small and the privilege of men everywhere to choose their way of life and of obedience. The world must be made safe for democracy. Its peace must be placed upon the tested foundations of political liberty."[9]

Wilson's war message was greeted with relief by most members of his cabinet and by leaders of both political parties, many of whom had criticized him sharply during preceding months for being timid in the face of blatant German provocations. There had been growing public sentiment that only U.S. intervention could end the European holocaust, and Congress voted overwhelmingly to declare war. Why did Wilson wait so long to decide that war was unavoidable, that *vital* interests were at stake that could not be compromised further? What had changed between the autumn of 1916 and the spring of 1917 to lead Wilson to conclude that at least one of the United States' basic interests was being *vitally* affected by a continuation of the war?

Wilson's view of U.S. world order interests probably changed significantly in the first months of 1917. Namely, it rose from major to vital intensity, for two major reasons: (1) Germany had all but won the war on the Russian front, and the Czar's abdication early in 1917 signaled that German armies might be diverted to the western front, where the battered British and French armies might not be able to continue the fight without U.S. reinforcements;[10] (2) the reimposition of German submarine warfare signaled that Imperial Germany was not interested in negotiating with Wilson but was determined to deliver a knockout blow against Britain by preventing commercial ships from landing there. In this new situation, Wilson had to conclude that continued U.S. aloofness might result in a German victory in 1917 and that it would then probably be impossible for the United States to work out a reasonable peace with a victorious Germany. This is not to denigrate Wilson's idealism nor his apparently sincere hope that the United States could be spared the casualties that war would bring. It does suggest that Wilson was also a realist, that he knew when his peace track had run out, and that he was enough of a political leader also to know that he needed to educate the public about his aims before moving the nation to war. As a result of his four superb speeches to Congress, and with help from an inept German Foreign Office (the Zimmermann cable) and brilliant British propaganda, Wilson was able finally to lead a reasonably united country into war in April 1917. Three months earlier, the country would have been sharply divided had he recommended this course.

In sum, Wilson's assessment of the threat to national interests in 1917, as conveyed in his own speeches to Congress, was realistic; and his timing of the movement toward a declaration of war was excellent in terms of public reaction. His longer-term problem was that his *reasons* for going to war differed from those held by many U.S. political leaders. Wilson favored entering the war primarily for world order and ideological reasons, but many senators and other leaders favored war for economic and anti-German reasons. These diverse perceptions would plague Wilson in the postwar period and lead to the ruin of his great dream of establishing a new world order based on collective security. His difficulty was not that he *misled* the country by his idealism; he was unable to *convince* the country of its merits.

A word needs to be said about Wilson's handling of relations with Congress and with the American people in the three months preceding the April 2 speech. It seems clear that he acted wisely on both counts and was able to convince the country that it indeed had to enter the war. Walter Millis, in his study *Road to War,* gave particular attention to press and public opinion during this period. He came to the conclusion that Wilson managed the situation so well that by April 2 the public was ready for a declaration of war. Of course, the famous Zimmermann telegram helped, as did the sinking of three U.S. ships in March. But Millis gives Wilson credit for adroit handling of public opinion on the war issue, with the result that antiwar sentiment, which had been so strong only six months earlier, was melting away by March 1917. Ross Gregory, in his *Origins of American Intervention in The First World War,* concludes that "from all appearances most of the American people approved of Wilson's performance" in his decision to break diplomatic relations with Germany. Although the interventionists were deeply frustrated that he did not move quickly to a declaration of war, and although German-American groups demanded that U.S. ships be kept out of the war zone, the bulk of the population seemed willing to follow Wilson's judgment of what was best for the country, "some because they believed and trusted him, many because in this bewildering time they did not know what else to do."[11] Above all, Wilson maintained his own credibility with the American public.

In his relations with Congress, Wilson also showed very good judgment. Not only did he appear personally before joint sessions four times in ten weeks to present his views on the deteriorating European situation, but he also conferred at the Capitol on February 2 with the chairman of the Senate Foreign Relations Committee and fifteen other members of Congress about the wisdom of breaking diplomatic relations with Germany. Link believes that the senators stiffened Wilson's resolve to be tough with the Germans. But the noteworthy aspect of this episode, from the vantage point of the 1970s, is that the president went to the Capitol to meet with key senators on a crucial foreign policy issue; he did not invite a group of them to sit with him in the Oval Office. Although a number of Republicans, notably Senator Lodge of Massachusetts, were no admirers of Wilson or his handling of relations with Germany in this period, most of them gave him their unrestrained support after he finished his moving war speech to a joint session. The vote in the Senate was 82 to 6 in favor of war, and in the House 373 to 50. This was an overwhelming vote of confidence for a president who only six months earlier, during the election campaign, was called the man "who kept us out of war."

Roosevelt and World War II

Franklin Roosevelt's perception of the danger to U.S. national interests from a German victory in Europe was considerably different from Wilson's in World War I, for two major reasons: first, Nazi Germany appeared far more powerful and menacing, particularly after the fall of France in 1940, than did the Kaiser's Germany in 1914; and second, Roosevelt had a deeper and more realistic grasp of international politics than the idealistic Wilson did. Roosevelt had been assistant secretary of the navy during World War I and had seen firsthand the tragedy of Wilson's postwar efforts to persuade the American people to abandon isolationism. Unlike Wilson, Roosevelt never believed that he could be an impartial mediator between the warring powers because Nazi Germany, Fascist Italy, and Imperial Japan presented so potent a threat to the global balance of power that the United States was not permitted the luxury of stepping in only after the other powers were exhausted. This became a harsh reality for Roosevelt in June 1940, when Hitler crushed France and was then supreme in Western Europe. The question for Roosevelt and his cabinet was whether Britain could hold out against Germany. Or would Hitler accomplish what Napoleon had failed to do and then pose a direct threat to North America?[12]

Roosevelt's position differed from Wilson's in another important respect. Wilson in April 1917 had a Congress and a public that was ready to accept war, and he himself appeared to be cast in the role of "reluctant dragon." But in 1940-1941, until the Japanese attacked Pearl Harbor in December 1941, both the Congress and the American people were opposed to a U.S. entry into the war against Hitler. Roosevelt's problem was not in making up his own mind about U.S. interests; rather, it was in persuading a reluctant Congress that *his* perception of those interests was correct and ought to be accepted. Roosevelt's task was one of educating the public, of alerting it to the dangers of neutrality and isolationism, while at the same time providing sufficient hope to the beleaguered British (and after June 1941, also the Russians) to persuade them to continue to resist Hitler even though the United States was not in the war. It was a most difficult task, certainly more challenging than the one Wilson faced early in 1917.

The crucial period in determining U.S. national interests in Europe began in June 1940 and ended eighteen months later when the Japanese attacked Pearl Harbor and brought a German declaration of war on the United States. However, when Congress passed Roosevelt's Lend-Lease legislation in March 1941, permitting him to send large quantities of war material to Britain, this set in motion the events that brought the United States into the war against Germany. It is of particular interest, therefore, to study Roosevelt's public statements during the nine months between June 1940 to March 1941 to determine how he analyzed U.S. interests and why he concluded that the nation must enter in the European war.

Roosevelt had sought to warn the nation of the dangers of totalitarian governments in his so-called "quarantine" speech in Chicago in October 1937, but the isolationist reaction was so strong that he remained relatively quiet on the subject for several years. However, after the Germans swept into Scandinavia and the Low Countries in 1940 and France was on the verge of collapse, Roosevelt made a remarkably strong statement at the University of Virginia on June 10, 1940. He emphasized U.S. ideological and world order interests, and to a lesser extent the U.S. defense interests that were involved in the European struggle. Referring to the contempt that "irresponsible European conquerors" had for the moral values to which Americans had been dedicated for more than three hundred years, Roosevelt asserted: "Surely the new philosophy proves from month to month that it could have no possible conception of the way of life or the way of thought of a nation whose origins go back to Jamestown and Plymouth Rock. . . . This perception of danger has come to us clearly and overwhelmingly; and we perceive the peril in a worldwide arena—an arena that may become so narrowed that only the Americans will retain the ancient faiths." Then, this challenge to isolationism: "Let us not hesitate—all of us—to proclaim certain truths. Overwhelmingly we, as a nation—and this applies to all the other American nations—are convinced that military and naval victory for the gods of force and hate would endanger the institutions of democracy in the western world, and that equally, therefore, the whole of our sympathies lies with those nations that are giving their life blood to combat against these forces."[13]

Three months later, while Britain fought for its survival

against German bombing and impending invasion, Roosevelt announced the transfer of fifty old U.S. destroyers to the British government in exchange for base rights in the Caribbean islands. In his letter to Congress advising of this agreement, the president justified the action wholly on grounds of national defense interest: "Preparation for defense is an inalienable prerogative of a sovereign state. Under present circumstances, this exercise of sovereign right is essential to the maintenance of our peace and safety. This is the most important action in the reinforcement of our national defense that has been taken since the Louisiana Purchase. Then as now, considerations of safety from overseas attack were fundamental."[14] His unilateral action produced howls of protest from Congress, which felt it should have been consulted in a matter of such importance to U.S. foreign policy. However, by basing his decision squarely on the defense interests of the nation, Roosevelt argued that he had the power to make this decision without the assent of Congress. Implicit in his handling of the case was the certainty that had he submitted a treaty to the Senate for ratification, it would have been rejected. Therefore, for what he perceived to be valid reasons of national defense, Roosevelt set a precedent for several subsequent presidents to take crucial foreign policy actions without the formal advice or consent of Congress.

Roosevelt also took a major political risk in transferring these warships to Britain because he was on the eve of launching an election campaign for a third term as president. Isolationist Republicans used the destroyer deal to warn the country that Roosevelt intended to take the nation into war if reelected, charges that stung the president and caused him in his first major speech of the campaign, in Philadelphia on October 23, to deny the charge and reassert his dedication to the cause of peace:

> To Republicans and Democrats, to every man, woman, and child in the nation I say this: Your President and your Secretary of State are following the road to peace. We are arming ourselves not for any foreign war. We are arming ourselves not for any purpose of conquest or intervention in foreign disputes. I repeat again that I stand on the Platform of our Party: "We will not

participate in foreign wars and we will not send our army, naval
or air forces to fight in foreign lands outside of the Americas
except in case of attack." It is for peace that I have labored, and it
is for peace that I shall labor all the days of my life.[15]

His promise not to send U.S. forces abroad unless the United
States was attacked caused Roosevelt much difficulty in 1941,
when pressures on him to intervene in the war grew steadily
within his own cabinet. He had been convinced in October
1940 that U.S. isolationist sentiment was so strong that he
needed specifically to reassure the public of his peaceful
intentions or else risk defeat in his bid for reelection in
November.[16]

After Roosevelt won reelection to an unprecedented third
term, he set about seriously to find a way short of war to provide
significant military and economic aid to help Britain
withstand the continuous German bombing and threat of
invasion. Finding the formula to do this and overcoming the
power of the isolationists in Congress was one of Roosevelt's
greatest political achievements, and it may well have made the
difference between Britain's fighting on in 1941 or surren-
dering to Hitler. During a postelection cruise in the Caribbean,
the president received a long and sobering cable from
Churchill, which presidential adviser Harry Hopkins said
"had a profound effect" and led him to devise the Lend-Lease
plan for aiding Britain "short of war."[17] His first public
statement on this subject came at a press conference on
December 17, 1940, in which he set forth his view that the
survival of Britain as a democracy had now become a *vital*
interest of the United States: "It is possible—I will put it that
way—for the United States to take over British orders, and,
because they are essentially the same kind of munitions that we
use ourselves, turn them into American orders. . . . That would
be on the general theory that it may still prove true that the best
defense of Great Britain is the best defense of the United States,
and therefore, that these materials would be more useful in the
defense of the United States if they were used in Great Britain,
than if they were kept in storage here." Roosevelt went on to
cite the "garden hose" analogy to underline his point that the

war against Britain was like a neighbor's house catching
fire: "If he can take my garden hose and connect it up with his
hydrant, I may help him to put out his fire" without his having
to pay for it in advance.[18]

On December 29, 1940, the president made a radio address to
the nation, an address that might be characterized as a "call to
arms short of war." In it he took the offensive and challenged
the voices of despair and isolationism who were insisting that
there was no hope and no sense in giving U.S. aid to Britain.
Nearly a year before the United States was officially at war, this
speech was a clear warning of the vital threat to U.S. world
order interests. Roosevelt's arguments about U.S. basic
national interests were as follows:

Defense interest: "Germany has said that she was occupying
Belgium to save the Belgians from the British. Would she then
hesitate to say to any South American country, 'We are
occupying you to protect you from aggression by the United
States?' Belgium today is being used as an invasion base against
Britain, now fighting for its life. Any South American country,
in Nazi hands, would always constitute a jumping-off place for
German attack on any one of the other Republics of this
hemisphere." Later on he asserted: "Even today we have
planes that could fly from the British Isles to New England and
back again without refueling. And remember that the range of
the modern bomber is ever being increased."[19]

Economic interest: "If Great Britain goes down, the Axis
powers . . . will be in a position to bring enormous military and
naval resources against this hemisphere. It is no exaggeration
to say that all of us, in all the Americas, would be living at the
point of a gun—a gun loaded with explosive bullets, *economic*
as well as military." (emphasis added)

World order interest: "The Nazi masters of Germany have
made it clear that they intend not only to dominate all life and
thought in their own country, but also to enslave the whole of
Europe, and then to use the resources of Europe to dominate
the rest of the world. . . . In other words, the Axis not merely
admits but proclaims that there can be no ultimate peace
between their philosophy of government and our philosophy

of government." Further on he states: "Some of our people like to believe that wars in Europe and in Asia are of no concern to us. But it is a matter of most vital concern to us that European and Asiatic war-makers should not gain control of the oceans which lead to this hemisphere."

Ideological interest: "The history of recent years proves that shootings and chains and concentration camps are not simply the transient tools but the very altars of modern dictatorships. They may talk of a 'new order' in the world, but what they have in mind is only a revival of the oldest and the worst tyranny. In that there is no liberty, no religion, no hope. The proposed 'new order' is the very opposite of a United States of Europe or a United States of Asia. It is not a government based upon the consent of the governed. It is not a union of ordinary, self-respecting men and women to protect themselves and their freedom and their dignity from oppression. It is an unholy alliance of power and pelf to dominate and enslave the human race."

Remarkably, Roosevelt's radio address of December 29, 1940, did *not* ask for a declaration of war on Germany. When this address is compared with Wilson's war message of April 2, 1917, one finds a striking similarity in the arguments about the defense, world order, and ideological interests that would be at stake if the Germans dominated Europe. Yet, having issued this stark warning of the danger threatening U.S. interests—including the very existence of its own form of government—Roosevelt stated categorically that U.S. troops would *not* be required: "The people of Europe who are defending themselves do not ask us to do their fighting. . . . There is no demand for sending an American Expeditionary Force outside our own border. There is no intention of any member of your Government to send such a force. You can, therefore, nail any talk about sending armies to Europe as deliberate untruths. Our national policy is not directed toward war. Its sole purpose is to keep war away from our country and our people."[20]

Why did he make such an assertion if the danger was so real? A reasonable explanation is that, whereas in April 1917 Wilson had the full support of Congress and most of the public for his estimate of the danger to the United States, Roosevelt in

December 1940 faced an isolationist Congress and a deeply divided electorate—despite his recent reelection—and felt he could not go further than to ask for war supplies for the British.

In his annual State of the Union message to Congress on January 6, 1941, Roosevelt reiterated some points made in his December 29 fireside chat but attacked even more strongly the appeasers and isolationists who opposed his policies. He made a strong plea for the Lend-Lease legislation, shortly to be submitted to Congress, and repeated his view that a *vital* world order interest of the United States was at stake in Europe: "Let us say to the democracies: 'We Americans are vitally concerned in your defense of freedom. We are putting forth our energies, our resources and our organizing powers to give you the strength to regain and maintain a free world. We shall send you, in ever-increasing numbers, ships, planes, tanks, guns. This is our purpose and our pledge.' "[21]

The Lend-Lease Bill was thoroughly and hotly debated in the Congress and in the U.S. press for two months and finally passed both houses of Congress in March by majorities of 60 to 31 in the Senate and 317 to 171 in the House. It marked a turning point in Roosevelt's effort to subdue the isolationists in Congress. It is noteworthy that this legislation and a subsequent bill to establish priorities for aid to foreign governments specifically gave the president authority to determine which countries' defense is "vital to ours"; Congress retained the authority to appropriate the necessary funds to implement the program for each country, but the president was given the power to decide which countries were vital to U.S. national interests.

There has been much discussion and some criticism of Roosevelt's unwillingness to move the nation into war against Germany following his congressional victory on the Lend-Lease legislation. Secretary of the Treasury Morgenthau and Secretary of War Stimson, the principal "war hawks" in his cabinet, called on the president to take bolder actions against Hitler in 1941 and to speak out plainly to the American people about the urgent necessity for the United States to enter the war, particularly after Hitler attacked the Soviet Union in June 1941 and appeared to be well on his way to knocking another major country out of action before the end of the year.[22] A key factor in Roosevelt's calculations, however, was the persistence of a virulent isolationism in Congress and his strong desire to have a united country behind him when he finally went to war. According to his biographer, James McGregor Burns, he feared that a military response to anything short of an unprovoked attack would be used by his enemies in Congress to hinder the war effort.[23]

By the fall of 1941, Churchill began to doubt that the United States would ever enter the war; Hitler seemed determined not to give Roosevelt the pretext he sought to obtain a declaration of war from Congress. However, as incidents occurred in the North Atlantic and U.S. warships were fired upon by German submarines, Roosevelt seized these as a basis for additional steps toward open hostilities. On September 11, he addressed the nation in a long and impassioned speech precipitated by a German submarine attack on the U.S. destroyer *Greer*. Warning the American people that Hitler was determined to deny the United States freedom of the seas and that the nation must abandon its illusions about being able to live in peace with totalitarian dictatorships, Roosevelt asserted that "when you see a rattlesnake poised to strike, you do not wait until he has struck before you crush him."[24] He warned the Axis powers that U.S. naval vessels would protect themselves if they found hostile submarines in waters that were "necessary for American defense," and on October 9 he asked Congress to repeal the Neutrality Act of 1939, to permit the arming of U.S. flag vessels.

Meanwhile, relations with Japan had so deteriorated in the autumn of 1941 that it seemed only a matter of time before Tokyo would force the issue by an attack in Southeast Asia. When the Japanese attacked Pearl Harbor on December 7, 1941, the only surprise was where they struck and the extent of the damage they inflicted on the U.S. Pacific Fleet. The president's war message to Congress on December 8 shifted the focus away from his previous warnings about the threat to U.S. world order and ideological interests, and he hammered on the issue of an attack on the homeland. Referring to this "date which will live in infamy," he told the American people that "there is no blinking at the fact that our people, our territory, and our interests are in grave danger." Congress declared war, unanimously in the Senate and with only one dissenting vote in the House.

On December 9, Roosevelt addressed the American people on radio about the long and difficult times that lay ahead as the nation mobilized to deal with the "powerful and resourceful gangsters [who] have banded together to make war upon the whole human race." He referred to the steps the government had taken to prepare for the situation and sought to vindicate the controversial actions he had taken:

> Now a word about the recent past—and the future. A year and a half has elapsed since the fall of France, when the whole world first realized the mechanized might which the Axis nations had been building for so many years. America has used that year and a half to great advantage. Knowing that the attack might reach us in all too short a time, we immediately began greatly to increase our industrial strength and our capacity to meet the demands of modern warfare. Precious months were gained by sending vast quantities of our war material to the nations of the world still able to resist Axis aggression. Our policy rested on the fundamental truth that the defense of any country resisting Hitler or Japan was in the long run the defense of our own country. That policy has been justified. It has given us time, invaluable time, to build our American assembly lines of production.[25]

The irony of the situation on December 9, 1941, was that the United States was at war with a country Roosevelt had not been primarily concerned about during those eighteen months. Hitler had refused to be provoked into launching an all-out attack on U.S. shipping during the fall of 1941, so the president found himself at war in the Pacific, not in the Atlantic and Europe, where the main threat to U.S. interests lay. Fortunately, Hitler resolved this dilemma for him by honoring Germany's alliance with Japan: on December 11, Germany declared war on the United States. The isolationists were finally quiet, although many of them believed that Roosevelt had tricked the nation into war. In a few hours over Pearl

Harbor, the Japanese did what the president had been unable to do in eighteen months—convince the American people that *vital* interests were at stake in Germany's grand design to establish a new world order dominated by Berlin and Tokyo.

The controversy surrounding Woodrow Wilson's apparent indecisiveness in 1917 about moving the nation toward war has no parallel in Roosevelt's actions during the months before December 7, 1941. The recent publication of British secret files shows conclusively that Roosevelt knew that the United States must intervene in the war against Germany and that he took many kinds of covert actions to support the British war effort until he could mobilize U.S. public opinion to accept his policies. He knew that if his secret dealings with Churchill were revealed, he might be impeached by Congress. Yet his determination to keep Britain afloat during the dark days of 1940-1941 was based on a deep conviction, formed at the time of France's collapse, that the survival of Britain was a *vital* national interest of the United States. The Japanese grab for Indochina in 1941 was a sideshow for Roosevelt, except to the extent that Japan might help awaken the American people and Congress to the worldwide danger that the Axis powers presented.

At another level, however, a parallel does exist between Wilson and Roosevelt: their appreciation of congressional and public opinion as the nation drifted closer to war. Both showed a deep awareness of the need to achieve as much national consensus as possible *before* recommending to Congress that U.S. military forces be sent overseas. Roosevelt, in particular, believed that the United States could not sustain the long, costly war effort unless the vote for war in Congress represented a clear national mandate. For Wilson, that mandate emerged without the shock of an attack on U.S. territory; for Roosevelt, the isolationists in Congress could not be subdued without an overt attack against the United States. Indeed, there was concern in Roosevelt's administration that if the attack had been on the Philippines rather than on Hawaii, Congress would not have voted for war against Japan. The Japanese attack on Pearl Harbor accomplished what Roosevelt wanted: it awakened the country to the peril he knew it faced.

In sum, in June 1940 Roosevelt perceived vital national interests to be at stake and probably knew that the United States would eventually have to go to war to save Britain (world order interest) and to insure the survival of freedom and democracy (ideological interest). The Japanese attack dramatized a vital defense interest as well, the only interest that could mobilize American public opinion for war in 1941. It is tempting to speculate what a different course history might have taken in the early 1940s if a less tenacious man had been in the White House. There is good reason to believe that if a man of Woodrow Wilson's outlook had then been president, Britain would not have survived the punishment it received from German planes and submarines in 1940-1941, the Soviet Union would not have turned back the German armies in 1941-1942, and the United States would have faced Germany and Japan alone.

4. Truman's and Johnson's Perceptions of National Interest

World War II shattered the Americans' traditional view of their role in the world. Although a few isolationists remained in influential positions in 1945, the intensity of the war and the unconditional surrender of both Germany and Japan caused a great majority of the American people to conclude that the United States had the power and the obligation to insure that the new order was maintained in the postwar period. U.S. participation in the United Nations was seen as a way to avoid the mistakes of the post–World War I period, and massive aid to help Europe rebuild was viewed as a means of helping that war-torn continent to regain its political balance and to work out a rapprochement between Germany and France, thus avoiding the folly of the Versailles Treaty. There was much optimism and idealism in American thinking in the early postwar period, which translated itself into a belief that American leadership could produce a safer and more prosperous world. American self-confidence was at its height.

President Harry Truman prided himself on being a realist in international affairs, and he soon came to the conclusion that the country's dream of a peaceful and prosperous world could be shattered by the Soviet Union's ideology, which, he believed, Stalin was prepared to impose wherever possible, even by force of arms. Soviet behavior in Eastern Europe in the period 1945-1947, culminating in the ouster of the democratic Beneš government in Czechoslovakia in February 1948, convinced Truman that the United States could not rely merely on goodwill to create a favorable world order in Europe and

elsewhere and that only the United States could organize the
West to resist Soviet pressures on Europe and the countries
along the periphery of the USSR. The "containment policy"—
authored in 1947 by George Kennan, a State Department expert
on Russia—became Truman's bible for dealing with Soviet
leaders and accounted for such U.S. foreign policy initiatives as
the Truman Doctrine, the Marshall Plan, the North Atlantic
Alliance, and the Point Four program. In Truman's approach
to international politics, the United States must be prepared to
resist Soviet-inspired communism *everywhere* in the world if
it was to be successful in defeating it *anywhere*. It was the
beginning of globalism in U.S. foreign policy, and its first real
test in Korea in 1950 marked the beginning of U.S. police
action outside North America.

By 1964, when Lyndon Johnson was president, the
globalism of Truman's era had become the imperialism of
Kennedy and Johnson—whereby America was prepared to
"pay any price in the cause of freedom," to paraphrase
Kennedy's inaugural address in January 1961. In both Korea
and Vietnam, the question for U.S. leaders was whether these
seemingly internal struggles in Asian countries were serious
threats to U.S. interests in Asia and around the world and
should thus be viewed as a *vital* national interest (see Chapter
1). Unlike the threats posed by Germany in 1917 and in 1940-
1941, the fighting in Korea and in Vietnam did not involve a
major world power and was clearly not a direct threat to the
security of North America.[1] But now that the United States had
forsaken isolationism and had taken responsibility under the
United Nations to help maintain peace everywhere in the
world, could it be argued that aggression in a small Asian
country was not important enough to warrant the use of force?

This dilemma faced Presidents Truman and Johnson as they
grappled with the United States' responsibilities in a new
world order, one that the United States had helped to create and
by 1950 had assumed large responsibilities for defending. The
key question was whether the president's perception of U.S.
interests—and responsibilities—would be matched by the
perceptions of other U.S. political leaders, who in turn
reflected the sentiments of the U.S. electorate. If the United

States was to take up the mantle the British had had during the nineteenth and early twentieth centuries and become a policeman for the world, would the American people sustain this role when the costs became high? In short, had American opinion about national interests changed sufficiently since 1941 to permit postwar presidents to use armed forces outside North America for what were clearly *local* conflicts, not world conflicts?

Truman and the Korean War

When the North Korean army attacked South Korea on June 24, 1950, President Truman saw this as a direct and serious Soviet attack on the very basis of postwar U.S. foreign policy. By 1950, the United States under Truman's leadership had completely reversed the prewar isolationist foreign policy and had assumed the leadership of a Western alliance system whose purpose was to contain communist power within the Soviet Union and its Eastern European satellite states. In 1949, China had emulated the Soviet Union by bringing a communist government to power through revolution, and in February 1950 its leader, Mao Tse-tung, had signed a military alliance with the Soviet Union. Therefore, when the attack occurred four months later in Korea, Truman saw this as a clear threat from Moscow and Peking to U.S. world order interests and was determined to meet the challenge with U.S. power. As he returned to Washington from Missouri by plane, the president thought about the implications of the crisis and came to the conclusion that it was a *vital* world order interest:

> I had time to think aboard the plane. In my generation, this was not the first occasion when the strong had attacked the weak. I recalled some earlier instances: Manchuria, Ethiopia, Austria. I remembered how each time that the democracies failed to act, it had encouraged the aggressors to keep going ahead. Communism was acting in Korea just as Hitler, Mussolini and the Japanese had acted ten, fifteen and twenty years earlier. I felt certain that if South Korea was allowed to fall, Communist leaders would be emboldened to override nations closer to our own shores. If the Communists were permitted to force their

way into the Republic of Korea without opposition from the
Free World, no small nation would have the courage to resist
threats and aggression by stronger Communist neighbors. If
this were allowed to go on unchallenged it would mean a third
World War, just as similar incidents had brought on the Second
World War. It was also clear to me that the foundations and the
principles of the United Nations were at stake unless this
unprovoked attack on Korea could be stopped.[2]

Secretary of State Dean Acheson had more influence on
presidential decisions than Lansing had had in 1917 or Hull
had had in 1940-1941. Acheson's memoirs reveal his thinking
about the U.S. national interests at stake in the Korean crisis:

Plainly, this attack did not amount to *casus belli* against the
Soviet Union. Equally plainly, it was an open, undisguised
challenge to our internationally accepted position as the
protector of South Korea, an area of great importance to the
security of American-occupied Japan. To back away from this
challenge, in view of our capacity for meeting it, would be
highly destructive of the power and prestige of the United
States. By prestige I mean the shadow cast by power, which is of
great deterrent importance. Therefore, we could not accept the
conquest of this important area by a Soviet puppet under the
very guns of our defensive perimeter with no more resistance
than words and gestures in the Security Council. *It looked as
though we must steel ourselves for the use of force.*[3]

In this succinct statement of his own thoughts on the Korean
crisis, Acheson clearly concluded that a *vital world order*
interest of the United States was at stake.

Although both the president and his secretary of state had a
predisposition to believe that the issue in Korea was vital,
would other top executive officials—civilian and military—
share this view? In describing the discussion that took place
among his principal advisers on the evening of June 25, 1950,
Truman recalls two key impressions: "One was the complete,
almost unspoken acceptance on the part of everyone that
whatever had to be done to meet this aggression had to be done.
There was no suggestion from anyone that either the United
Nations or the United States could back away from it. This was

the test of all the talk of the last five years of collective security."
The other point was whether air power alone could turn the
tide in Korea, or whether ground forces would have to be used if
the South Korean Army were defeated. After hearing the
chairman of the Joint Chiefs of Staff argue that a line would
have to be drawn somewhere against Soviet pressure and that it
ought to be drawn in Korea, Truman agreed most emphatically
and said that "the Russians were trying to get Korea by default,
gambling that we would be afraid of starting a third World War
and would offer no resistance."

Thus, the executive branch seemed to be united from the
beginning in favor of confronting the Soviets on the issue of
Korea. But what about the Congress? Was there to be a
declaration of war, or a joint resolution of support for the
president's position?

Truman decided not to ask for a formal vote of support for
his proposed course of action, but instead invited several
groups of congressional leaders to the White House for
discussions about his intended course of action. Acheson
recalls that when the president met on June 30 with a large
group of congressional leaders, one of them questioned his
legal authority to take armed action. Another senator suggested
a congressional resolution approving the president's course,
but a third, a Republican, commented that Congress was
"practically unanimous in its appreciation of the President's
leadership." The president agreed to consider a congressional
resolution in support of his actions, but Acheson later
recommended that he only make a report to Congress, not seek
a resolution of approval, and rest on his constitutional
authority as commander in chief of the armed forces. Truman
then decided to put off a decision, apparently believing that
under authority of the United Nations he needed no authority
from Congress to use U.S. military forces in Korea. In
discussing the wisdom of this decision, Acheson later wrote:

> To have obtained congressional approval, it has been argued,
> would have obviated later criticism of "Truman's war." In my
> opinion, it would have changed pejorative phrases, but little
> else. Congressional approval did not soften or divert the antiwar

critics of Presidents Lincoln, Wilson and Roosevelt. What inspired the later criticism of the Korean war was the long, hard struggle, casualties, cost, frustration of a limited and apparently inconclusive war. . . . Nevertheless, it is said, congressional approval would have done no harm. True, approval would have done none, but the process of gaining it might well have done a great deal. . . . Congressional hearings on a resolution of approval at such time, opening the possibility of endless criticism, would hardly be calculated to support the shaken morale of the troops or the unity that, for the moment, prevailed at home. The harm it could do seemed to me far to outweigh the little good that might ultimately accrue.[4]

In sum, to avoid open criticism from a minority group in Congress and thus risk stirring up doubts about the nation's resolve, Truman decided to take the nation into war on his *own* authority.

Truman's perception of the U.S. national interests in Korea is contained in his reports to the American people and in his messages to Congress. These clearly support the view suggested in his memoirs that the United States fought in Korea for world order and ideological interests. On July 19, 1950, the president sent a special message to Congress asking for funds and other legislation to support the war effort, and he addressed the American people on radio and television the same day. In his message to Congress, he justified the intervention as follows:

World order interests: "If this challenge had not been met squarely, the effectiveness of the United Nations would have all but ended, and the hope of mankind that the United Nations would develop into an institution of world order would have been shattered." "The attack upon the Republic of Korea makes it plain beyond all doubt that the international communist movement is prepared to use armed invasion to conquer independent nations. We must therefore recognize the possibility that armed aggression may take place in other areas." "The free world has made it clear, through the United Nations, that lawless aggression will be met with force. This is the significance of Korea—and it is a significance whose importance cannot be over-estimated."

Ideological interests: "It should be made perfectly clear that the action was undertaken as a matter of basic moral principle. The United States was going to the aid of a nation established and supported by the United Nations and unjustifiably attacked by an aggressor force." "We are determined to maintain our democratic institutions so that Americans now and in the future can enjoy personal liberty, economic opportunity and political equality. We are concerned with advancing our prosperity and our well-being as a nation, but we know that our future is inseparably joined with the future of other free peoples." (This latter statement might be interpreted to mean that Truman also had an economic interest in mind, namely, continued American prosperity at home; but it is more likely, from the context, that he meant prosperity in the generic sense—not in the sense that war would benefit the U.S. economy.) At the end of this message, the president asserted: "The Congress of the United States, by its strong, bi-partisan support of the steps we are taking and by repeated actions in support of international cooperation, has contributed most vitally to the cause of peace. The expressions of support which have been forthcoming from the leaders of both political parties for the actions of our Government and of the United Nations in dealing with the present crisis, have buttressed the firm morale of the entire free world in the face of this challenge."[5]

It is curious that Truman should have complimented Congress on its support of his war policies when Congress had not formally concurred. However, he chose to accept congressional approval of increased defense expenditures and of controls on the economy as evidence of Congress's support for the decision to enter the war. No doubt this was valid politically. But from a constitutional as well as an historical standpoint, it is dubious whether the president was correct in saying that he had the firm support of Congress without having obtained a joint resolution of Congress on the specific question of sending troops to fight in Korea.

In his address to the nation on July 19, 1950, Truman repeated many of his earlier arguments but emphasized the ideological interests of the nation: "We know that the cost of freedom is high. But we are determined to preserve our freedom—no matter what the cost. . . . Our country stands before the world as an example of how free men, under God, can build a community of neighbors, working together for the good of all. That is the goal we seek not only for ourselves, but for all people. We believe that freedom and peace are essential if men are to live as our Creator intended us to live."[6] Here Truman sounded much like Wilson in his addresses to Congress in 1917, taking the high moral ground and appealing to the nation on the basis of principle, not selfish interest.

By the end of November 1950, it was all too clear to the Truman administration that its earlier hopes for a quick end to the Korean war had vanished, despite the brilliant landing of MacArthur's forces at Inchon in September and the near rout of the North Korean army. As MacArthur's forces drove north of the thirty-eighth parallel in pursuit of the retreating North Korean army, Chinese forces entered the war and soon engaged American forces, inflicting serious casualties and forcing them into a humiliating retreat. MacArthur and his supporters in the United States urged Truman to enlarge the war by bombing China and threatening the Soviet Union. The whole face of the war had suddenly changed, and Truman now had to explain to the nation why it was necessary to prepare for a long and more costly war. He sought to do this by sending a special message to Congress on December 1, asking for even greater military appropriations and additional controls on the economy, and by declaring a national emergency. He also made a radio and television appeal to the nation to support his policies. Now the president sounded a shriller note than he had during the summer regarding the degree of national interest at stake in Korea. In addition to world order and ideological interests, cited in July, he now included defense interests as well. On December 15, Truman explained his declaration of a national emergency: "Our homes, our Nation, all the things we believe in, are in great danger. This danger has been created by the rulers of the Soviet Union. . . . Then in November, the Communists threw their Chinese armies into the battle against the free nations. By this act they have shown that they are now willing to push the world to the brink of a general war to get what they want. This is the real meaning of the events that have been taking place in Korea. That is why we are in such grave danger. The future of civilization depends on what we do—on what we do now, and in the months ahead." Regarding world order interests, Truman shifted the focus from a threat in Asia to one in Europe: "There is actual warfare in the Far East, but Europe and the rest of the world are also in very great danger. The same menace—the menace of Communist aggression— threatens Europe as well as Asia.... The defense of Europe is of the utmost importance to the security of the United States." Finally, Truman appealed to the nation's ideological interests: "Our freedom is in danger. Sometimes we may forget just what freedom means to us. It is as close to us, as important to us, as the air we breathe. Freedom is in our homes, in our schools, in our churches. It is in our work and our Government and the right to vote as we please. Those are the things that would be taken from us if communism should win."[7]

It is astonishing that in his appeal to the nation in December 1950, Truman did not ask Congress for a declaration of war, or at least for a joint resolution of support for his course of action; rather, he asked the nation to respond to his declaration of a national emergency and took upon himself full responsibility for pursuing a long, bloody war. In the same speech, he called attention to a rail strike that was then in progress and called upon the union, "as Commander-in-Chief," to return to work immediately. Was Acheson correct that the cost of asking Congress for a vote of support would be greater than the gain? Considering the political price that Truman paid for this decision, one may argue that it was not a wise one, even though his constitutional right to do so was clear. Even though Acheson may have been correct that the limited war to restore the status quo ante in Korea did not justify going to Congress for a vote of support, it can surely be questioned whether by December—when the introduction of large Chinese forces enlarged and changed the whole nature of the war—Truman would have been on stronger ground politically had he asked for a full congressional debate, and won a vote of support for the war with China. Had he done so, the political effects could have been no worse and probably would have proved better.

Johnson and the Vietnam War

Much has already been written—both scholarly and unscho-
larly—about Lyndon Johnson's decision to take the nation
into war in Vietnam in 1965. Most are critical of his judgment
and handling of congressional and public opposition to the
war. The purpose here is not to judge whether the president's
decision to go to war in Vietnam was right or wrong, but rather
to ascertain his perception of U.S. national interests in
Southeast Asia in 1965 and to see whether Congress shared his
perception.

The record seems to show that although Johnson knew less
about, and was less interested in, foreign policy than Wilson,
Roosevelt, and Truman, he nevertheless had very strong views
on aggression and the need for opposing it wherever it
occurred. His biographer, Eric Goldman, describes his view as
follows: "Aggression is when one country won't let another
one alone. Everybody knows when that is happening.
Aggression was the nub of the world problem in the twentieth
century, and a series of aggressions had turned into tragedies
because the United States did not sufficiently make plain that
its interest—peace—was threatened by aggression and that it
would do something about it. His foreign policy attitude could
be summed up in the phrase: 'No More Munichs.' "[8]

Unlike his predecessors, Lyndon Johnson apparently had
made up his mind four years *before* the United States actually
sent large ground forces to Vietnam. In the spring of 1961,
President Kennedy sent his vice-president on a fact-finding
mission to Asia, with particular focus on what the United
States should do about the deteriorating situation in Laos and
Vietnam. In a powerful memorandum to the president,
Johnson asserted: "The battle against Communism must be
joined in Southeast Asia with strength and determination to
achieve success there or the United States, inevitably, must
surrender the Pacific and take up our defenses on our own
shores." Johnson did not then think U.S. ground forces would
be necessary to save Southeast Asia, and he thought a statement

to that effect by the president would allay concerns in Congress and elsewhere about the danger of greatly increasing military aid to Vietnam: "But the present probability of open attack seems scant, and we might gain much needed flexibility in our policies if the spectre of combat troop commitment could be lessened domestically." But the vice-president seemed to contradict himself later in the report: "This decision must be made in a full realization of the very heavy and continuing costs involved in terms of money, of effort, and of United States prestige. It must be made with the knowledge that at some point we may be faced with the further decision of whether we commit major United States forces to the area, or cut our losses and withdraw should our other efforts fail. We must remain the master in this decision."[9] For Johnson, Vietnam was a *vital* U.S. interest in 1961.

The Pentagon Papers reveal that the Kennedy administration decided in 1961 to introduce limited numbers of combat forces into Vietnam to help the Saigon government cope with the growing insurgency sponsored by North Vietnam. When Johnson assumed the presidency in November 1963, there were about 16,000 U.S. servicemen in Vietnam performing various missions, including combat. By the early part of 1964, it was clear that a limited U.S. involvement could not help Saigon win against the communist forces and that the spectre of sending in U.S. combat troops, which Johnson had mentioned in 1961, was fast becoming a reality. If Vietnam was a *vital* world order interest, how could he convince Congress of that and avoid doing what he had described in 1961, namely, to "throw in the towel in the area and pull back our defenses to San Francisco and a Fortress America concept"?[10] Johnson's decision, unlike Truman's, was to seek a joint resolution of support from Congress and then use that resolution as a de facto declaration of war if the situation warranted it. As Johnson maintains in his memoirs: "I was determined, from the time I became President, to seek the fullest support of Congress for any major action that I took, whether in foreign affairs or in the domestic field. I believed that President Truman's one mistake in courageously going to the defense of South Korea in 1950 had been his failure to ask Congress for an expression of its backing. . . . I had made up my mind not to repeat that error, but always to follow the advice I myself had given President Eisenhower."[11] The result was the Southeast Asia Resolution of Congress, usually referred to as the Gulf of Tonkin resolution, approved on August 7, 1964, and signed by the president on August 10. This declaration was precipitated by two incidents in the Gulf of Tonkin, off the North Vietnamese coast, in which U.S. destroyers were attacked by North Vietnamese torpedo boats. There has been much dispute about whether the second attack actually took place, but the president claimed to have incontrovertible evidence that the second attack had taken place and that it was part of a specially designed provocation by North Vietnam.

During the Vietnam war, much controversy arose over the intent of Congress in passing the Tonkin Gulf resolution. There is little doubt about what President Johnson asked for: "I recommend a Resolution expressing the support of the Congress for all necessary action to protect our armed forces and to assist nations covered by the SEATO Treaty. . . . Hostile nations must understand that in such a period the United States will continue to protect its national interest and that in these matters there is no division among us."[12] The text of the resolution, passed *unanimously* in the House of Representatives and in the Senate by a vote of 88 to 2, gave the president sweeping authority to use the armed forces to defend the nations of Southeast Asia. The pertinent passage of this short document is: "Resolved by the Senate and House of Representatives of the United States of America in Congress assembled, that the Congress approves and supports the determination of the President, as Commander-in-Chief, *to take all necessary measures* to repel any armed attack against the forces of the United States and to prevent further aggression." The key paragraph on the importance of Southeast Asia to U.S. national interests was the following:

> The United States regards as *vital* to its national interest and to world peace the maintenance of international peace and security in Southeast Asia. Consonant with the Constitution of the United States and the Charter of the United Nations and in

accordance with its obligations under the Southeast Asia Collective Defense Treaty, the United States is, therefore, prepared, *as the President determines,* to take all necessary steps, including the use of armed force, to assist any member or protocol state of the Southeast Asia Collective Defense Treaty requesting assistance in defense of its freedom.[13]

The resolution specified that it would expire either when the president determined that peace and security were assured, or through a concurrent resolution (with or without presidential consent).

In President Johnson's mind, there was no ambiguity about what Congress intended. In a statement released after the congressional vote, he said: "The 414-to-nothing House vote and the 88-to-2 Senate vote on the passage of the Joint Resolution on Southeast Asia is a demonstration to all the world of the unity of all Americans. They prove our determination to defend our own forces, to prevent aggression and to work firmly and steadily for peace and security in the area." In his memoirs, Johnson cites an exchange of views during the Senate debate between Senator Fulbright, chairman of the Foreign Relations Committee, and Senator Cooper, who wanted to know if the resolution gave the president advance authority to use the armed forces in a way that could lead to war. Fulbright replied: "That is the way I would interpret it. If a situation later developed in which we thought the approval should be withdrawn, it could be withdrawn by concurrent resolution." Cooper then commented: "I ask these questions because it is well for the country and all of us to know what is being undertaken." President Johnson used this exchange of views to support his position: "I wanted the Congress and the country to know what was being, or might have to be undertaken. The resolution served that purpose. I also hoped this strong congressional endorsement would help influence North Vietnam to refrain from accelerating aggression."[14]

The conclusion seems inescapable that in the summer of 1964, President Johnson believed that war in Southeast Asia was inevitable if the North Vietnamese did not stop their attacks on South Vietnam and on U.S. forces stationed there.

He had already determined that Vietnam was a vital interest of the United States, and he had sought a congressional vote of support for his perception of the national interest as well as for his use of the armed forces to defend it. Congress had given him an overwhelming affirmative vote, which he hoped would dissuade North Vietnam, as well as China and the Soviet Union, from pushing forward with the insurgency in South Vietnam. But if the North did not stop its aggression, Johnson now felt he had full congressional approval to use whatever force was required to defend South Vietnam. According to later statements by Senator William Fulbright and others, congressional leaders had been persuaded by the White House that voting for the resolution would make the use of U.S. forces in Vietnam unnecessary because the communists would be impressed by such a show of national solidarity and would not push a full confrontation with the United States. Nevertheless, if Congress had a serious doubt about giving the president such broad authority to make war, it could have made the resolution valid for six months or for a year and thus have kept the matter under review. But it did not qualify its support of the president in 1964, and in so doing it probably committed a major constitutional blunder.

The Tonkin Gulf resolution gave the president *authority* to use the armed forces in Southeast Asia to repel communist aggression, but left open the question whether and when to use them, especially ground forces. Twice during the latter months of 1964, the Viet Cong attacked U.S. installations in South Vietnam, and the president chose not to respond with air strikes against North Vietnam, even though many of his advisers urged him to do so. In February 1965, however, the communists attacked a U.S. barracks at Pleiku, killing nine Americans and wounding more than a hundred. This attack occurred within two weeks of the time that Johnson had received a memorandum from his national security adviser, McGeorge Bundy, and his secretary of defense, Robert McNamara, warning that the military situation in South Vietnam was deteriorating rapidly and that stepped-up military action against North Vietnam was necessary unless the United States was prepared to see South Vietnam defeated.

After a long and detailed discussion at a National Security Council meeting on February 6, following the attack on Pleiku, the president authorized retaliatory air strikes against North Vietnam and ordered the evacuation of all U.S. dependents from Vietnam. Thus began the gradual escalation of U.S. military involvement in Vietnam.

According to his own account, President Johnson did not make the final decision to intervene in Vietnam with ground troops until the latter part of July 1965. This followed a visit to Vietnam by Secretary of Defense McNamara, who reported to the president that the military situation in South Vietnam was worse than it had been a year earlier and that North Vietnamese forces were fully supporting the Viet Cong to dismember the South and bring about the collapse of the Saigon government. McNamara outlined three alternatives: (1) a graceful exit from Vietnam; (2) some enclave strategy, whereby a limited number of U.S. forces would protect key areas in South Vietnam, leaving the South Vietnamese to fight the Viet Cong; or (3) use of U.S. combat forces to bring about the communists' defeat and a settlement that preserved the independence of South Vietnam. McNamara recommended the third, which he thought had a reasonable chance of success: "This alternative would stave off defeat in the short run and offer a good chance of producing a favorable settlement in the longer run." But he also warned of the costs of following this course: "It would imply a commitment to see a fighting war clear through at considerable cost in casualties and material and would make any later decision to withdraw even more difficult and even more costly than would be the case today."[15]

The McNamara report gave rise to several long and tense NSC meetings in July 1965, where the overwhelming sentiment seemed to be that the situation in Vietnam was nearly hopeless unless the United States committed sizable ground forces. According to President Johnson, only two of his senior advisers opposed this course of action: Under Secretary of State George Ball, and the chairman of the President's Foreign Intelligence Advisory Board, Clark Clifford. Both expressed grave doubts that even the introduction of U.S. ground forces could turn the tide in Vietnam, and they believed that the United States would eventually suffer a "catastrophe," as Clifford put it. Ultimately, the president decided in favor of the military alternative: "I had listened to and weighed all the arguments and counterarguments for each of the possible lines of action. I believed that we should do what was necessary to resist aggression but that we should not be provoked into a major war. . . . We would not make threatening noises to the Chinese or the Russians by calling up reserves in large numbers. At the same time, we would press hard on the diplomatic front to try to find some path to a peaceful settlement."[16] According to Johnson's account, no one present at this large NSC meeting dissented on this compromise course of action—including Clifford and Ball. He therefore felt he had a consensus.

The president met with a group of Senate and House leaders before announcing his decision and outlined all the alternatives. He then asked for their views. Of this group, only Senator Mansfield opposed enlarging the war and felt the United States should seek a negotiated settlement on the best terms it could get. When the meeting closed, the president felt he had the support of the congressional leadership for the course he had decided on. Even Senator Mansfield said he would go along, albeit reluctantly, according to the president's account.

Looking back on his fateful decision to take the nation into a large and costly war in Vietnam, Lyndon Johnson listed five reasons for his actions, which also indicate the basic national interests he sought to defend:

1. "From all the evidence available to me it seemed likely that all of Southeast Asia would pass under Communist control, slowly or quickly, but inevitably, at least down to Singapore but almost certainly to Djakarta. . . . The evidence before me as President confirmed the previous assessments of President Eisenhower and of President Kennedy." (*world order interest*)

2. "I knew our people well enough to realize that if we walked away from Vietnam and let Southeast Asia fall, there would follow a divisive and destructive debate in our country. This had happened when the Communists

took power in China." *(ideological interest)*

3. "Our allies not just in Asia but throughout the world would conclude that our word was worth little or nothing. Those who had counted so long for their security on American commitments would be deeply shaken and vulnerable." *(world order and ideological interest)*

4. "Knowing what I did of the policies and actions of Moscow and Peking, I was sure as a man could be that if we did not live up to our commitments in Southeast Asia and elsewhere, they would move to exploit the disarray in the United States and in the alliances of the Free World." *(world order interest)*

5. "As we faced the implications of what we had done as a nation, I was sure the United States would not then passively submit to the consequences. With Moscow and Peking and perhaps others moving forward we would return to a world role to prevent their full takeover of Europe, Asia, and the Middle East—*after* they had committed themselves." *(defense interest)*

On this last point, the president implied that such a situation would involve nuclear war and that "I did not want to lead this nation and the world into nuclear war or even the risk of such a war" by doing nothing about the challenge until it was too late.[17]

In his announcement to the nation on July 28, 1965, that he was committing large ground forces to Vietnam and thereby greatly expanding the war, the president justified his action almost solely on the grounds of U.S. *world order interests*. He did not cite, as Presidents Wilson, Roosevelt, and Truman had, a grave peril to U.S. territory if he failed to take action; nor did he mention any imminent danger that necessitated this action. He asserted that the people of South Vietnam should be given the right to choose their own form of government without being intimidated from the outside. He also appealed to the American people to have the courage to fight for freedom wherever it was challenged so that they would not eventually lose it by default (ideological interests). But the major thrust of his argument, as it had been four years earlier, was that Vietnam was a *vital* world order interest of the United States and the noncommunist nations and that this challenge could not be ignored. On the question, "Why are we in Vietnam?" he stated in a press conference on July 28, 1965: "The answer, like the war itself, is not an easy one, but it echoes clearly from the painful lessons of half a century. Three times in my lifetime, in two World Wars and in Korea, Americans have gone to far lands to fight for freedom. We have learned at a terrible and a brutal cost that retreat does not bring safety, and weakness does not bring peace. It is this lesson that has brought us to Viet-Nam."[18] Johnson thus admitted that he was strongly influenced by the actions of three of his predecessors.

In the summer of 1965, some public opposition was expressed over the U.S. large-scale entry into the Vietnam war, and some members of the Congress publicly aired their misgivings about the use of ground troops. But there is no evidence that the large majority of the public, or of the Congress, opposed the president's perception of Vietnam as a vital U.S. interest or his decision to make a stand on Vietnam. It is a matter of conjecture, however, whether Johnson would have been wiser in the summer of 1965 to seek a reaffirmation of the Tonkin Gulf resolution rather than move ahead on the authority of the 1964 declaration, in light of the failure of the North Vietnamese to heed the earlier warning. Had Johnson gone back to Congress in July 1965, one may argue, and asked for a vote of support for sending large ground forces to South Vietnam to prevent its collapse, he would have received a majority vote in both houses favoring his course. He could then have dealt better with opponents of the war in 1966 and 1967. The opposite view also has merit, however. It holds that no matter what Congress decided in the summer of 1965, the war was bound to become unpopular with the American people when casualties mounted and there was no "light at the end of the tunnel"; the country simply could not be persuaded that Vietnam was a *vital* interest to the United States. According to this view, Johnson's only chance for achieving his objective in Vietnam—an independent South Vietnamese state recognized by Hanoi—was to convince North Vietnam's leaders at an early stage of the U.S. intervention that the war was hopeless from their point of view. This he clearly failed to do, despite tremendous bombing, and with this failure also went his hope of preventing the ultimate collapse of the Saigon regime.

5. Comparing Presidential Decisions in Four Foreign Wars

The decisions made by four U.S. presidents to take the country to war outside North America may be compared, but only tentatively because the circumstances—both international and domestic—surrounding their assessment of U.S. national interests varied. Roosevelt, for example, faced far more domestic opposition to his conviction that the United States must go to war than did Wilson, Truman, or Johnson—even though the United States faced a much greater danger in 1940-1941 than it did in the other cases. Nevertheless, two areas do lend themselves to such comparison, both of them of fundamental importance to the functioning of the U.S. constitutional system: (1) the process by which the president evaluates threats to U.S. national interests in time of crisis, and (2) the way he goes about obtaining congressional and public support for his assessment of the threat and for his course of action. Specifically, why did these presidents decide that sending U.S. troops to fight in four wars in Europe and Asia was a vital interest of the United States, and how did they carry out their constitutional obligation to obtain the consent of Congress?

The data included in the two previous chapters show that all four presidents had a keen understanding of U.S. national interests, even though Wilson tended to talk about them in more idealistic terms. Although public speeches do not necessarily reflect the true beliefs of presidents in foreign policy, a careful analysis of the public statements of these presidents shows that they were reasonably accurate in their appraisals of the danger to the country as they moved toward war.[1] If there was an ambiguity in their public statements, it had more to do with their efforts to persuade (or manipulate) public opinion in order to gain congressional support than it did with deciding what the threats to U.S. interests were.

First let us compare the basis for the presidents' decisions to go to war. For this purpose, we may employ a national interest matrix (see Chapter 1) to measure the intensity of concern for each of the four basic national interests—defense of homeland, economic well-being, world order and ideological.

Presidential Perceptions of Interest

Using the data in Chapter 3, it is clear that Woodrow Wilson, in the early part of 1917, looked at the level of U.S. interests at stake in Europe as shown in Chart 5.1. In my view, Wilson perceived that vital ideological interests were at stake long before he saw that the vital world order interests of the United States would also be deeply affected by a German military victory. It is unlikely that he would have been able to move the country toward war in 1917 if *only* an ideological interest had been affected; in the end, what profoundly shook Wilson was the prospect that renewed German submarine warfare and a possible Russian withdrawal from the war would put British and French *survival* in question. For the United States, that threat constituted a *vital* world order interest, and for Wilson, it tipped the scales in favor of war. Much of the country was ahead

CHART 5.1

Country: US		Issue: World War I		
Basic interest at stake		Intensity of interest		
	Survival	Vital	Major	Peripheral
Defense of homeland			X	
Economic well-being			X	
Favorable world order		X		
Ideological		X		

of him in perceiving this threat, however, and his war speech of April 2, 1917, was not controversial. Some members of Congress certainly believed that vital economic interests were also at stake, but nothing in Wilson's speeches or biographies suggests that he shared that view. The same was true for defense of homeland: the Germans could do little physical damage to the United States, although they could and did kill Americans at sea through submarine warfare. In sum, President Wilson took the nation to war for reasons of world order and ideological interest, and the country supported him in his decision.

In June 1940, Franklin Roosevelt came to the conclusion that Nazi Germany posed a vital world order and ideological threat to the United States, and potentially a vital defense threat as well. Unlike Wilson, he could not persuade the country and Congress of this until Japan attacked Pearl Harbor eighteen months later, thereby moving "defense of homeland" interest to the vital level. For Roosevelt, the matrix would be as shown in Chart 5.2. The difference between Wilson's and Roosevelt's situations was that although the threat to U.S. interests was far greater in 1940 and 1941 than it had been in 1917, the country was not willing to accept Roosevelt's judgment of the level of U.S. interest at stake. Public disillusionment with U.S. participation in World War I had nurtured an intense isolationist sentiment two decades later, which Republican leaders championed in the Congress. Thus, because Roosevelt had not been able to quickly persuade the nation to accept his

CHART 5.2

Country: US		Issue: World War II		
Basic Interest at stake		Intensity of interest		
	Survival	Vital	Major	Peripheral
Defense of homeland		X		
Economic well-being			X	
Favorable world order		X		
Ideological		X		

perception of the danger in 1940-1941, postwar presidents were in a dilemma: should they take independent action when they cannot persuade a reluctant Congress that the national interest requires the use of U.S. armed forces abroad?

In 1950 Harry Truman dealt with this problem by *not* asking Congress for a resolution of support—either on his initial decision to resist the North Korean attack or on his subsequent decision to carry the war to North Korea despite Chinese threats of intervention. In the first instance, Truman saw U.S. interests jeopardized primarily by a threat to world order, an order heavily tied to the desires of the United Nations at that time. Truman's view of the situation may be summarized as shown in Chart 5.3.

CHART 5.3

Country: US		Issue: Korea, June 1950		
Basic interest at stake		Intensity of interest		
	Survival	Vital	Major	Peripheral
Defense of homeland			X	
Economic well-being				X
Favorable world order		X		
Ideological			X	

Nothing in the public record indicates that Truman thought any U.S. economic interest was at stake in Korea, and as his actions and statements showed, he believed that only major defense and ideological interests were involved in resisting the North Korean invasion. His ideological arguments were nearly all anticommunist in nature, for it would have been difficult to convince the American public that U.S. forces were defending freedom and democracy in South Korea. But his primary emphasis was on working within the United Nations framework to restore the thirty-eighth parallel as a border between North and South Korea. This touched a responsive chord in the American public, even when it looked as if General MacArthur's forces might be driven off the Korean peninsula in July-August 1950. In sum, Truman could justify American fighting in Korea only so long as it involved a UN police action within Korea itself. The interest was not sufficient to support a war with China.

By December 1950 it was clear that the United States was no longer in a police action simply to restore order in Korea: it was now engaged in a large war with China and North Korea, with the possibility of war also with the Soviet Union, in Europe if not in the Far East. Truman's perception of the threat to U.S. national interests then changed, as shown in Chart 5.4.

CHART 5.4

Country: US		Issue: Korea/China, December 1950		
Basic interest at stake		Intensity of interest		
	Survival	Vital	Major	Peripheral
Defense of homeland			X	
Economic well-being			X	
Favorable world order		X		
Ideological		X		

Truman's problem was that Congress and a large segment of the public did not share his and MacArthur's perceptions of U.S. interests at stake in this new situation. Although the American people were strongly anticommunist at this time,[2] most of them did not perceive any *vital* defense of homeland interest or world order interest that required them to go to war with Peking. A police action to restore order in Korea was one thing; a large-scale war with the People's Republic of China was something else. Truman had blundered into war with China by permitting MacArthur to attempt a unification of Korea by force, and he would spend two frustrating years in the White House in a vain effort to convince the country that a vital U.S. interest was at stake in North Korea.

Ten years later, in 1961, another administration faced a similar dilemma in another divided Asian country—Vietnam. President Kennedy died before the final decision had to be made about sending large U.S. combat forces into South Vietnam to prevent its collapse under pressure from the North, but the fateful decision to do so if necessary was made in the fall of 1961. The question for the new president, Lyndon Johnson, was whether to honor that previous decision or renounce it in favor of a compromise peace with North Vietnam. In 1964 Johnson reluctantly came to the conclusion that a vital world order interest was at stake in Vietnam and that he would use U.S. combat forces to defend it, when that became necessary. His perception of interests may be summarized as in Chart 5.5.

CHART 5.5

Country: US		Issue: Vietnam, 1965		
Basic interest at stake		Intensity of interest		
	Survival	Vital	Major	Peripheral
Defense of homeland				X
Economic well-being				X
Favorable world order		X		
Ideological			X	

It was clear to the Johnson administration that the case for going into Vietnam could not be made on either defense of homeland or economic grounds—there simply was nothing of strategic or economic importance to the United States in Indochina. But there were important world order and ideological reasons why the United States should not be driven out of Vietnam, just as there had been in Korea. On the ideological side, the forces of Ho Chi Minh were dedicated communists who practiced total state control and followed the "wars of national liberation" doctrine developed by Mao Tse-tung and Ho. If successful in Indochina, this guerrilla warfare could be applied elsewhere throughout Southeast Asia, giving rise to a "domino effect" wherein the fall of Vietnam would push neighboring states into accepting communist governments. This seemed a real threat to the balance of power in East Asia (world order interest), and a U.S. failure to react would work to the advantage of China, North Korea, North Vietnam, and Indonesia (which, under Sukarno, had formed a tacit alliance with Hanoi and Peking to help oust British and U.S.

influence from Southeast Asia). Johnson became convinced
that Japan and the Philippines, two vital base areas for U.S.
military power in the western Pacific, could not survive as U.S.
allies if Hanoi and Peking were permitted to bring off their
grand design.

Even though Lyndon Johnson could make a case for a vital
world order interest in Vietnam, it was difficult to do so also on
ideological grounds—there was no way that individual
freedom and democratic government could be transplanted
into South Vietnam. What Johnson and his administration
tried to argue was that South Vietnam's freedom to choose its
own destiny was also an ideological interest, just as self-
determination had been a key theme espoused by Wilson after
World War I. But the repressive and corrupt nature of a
succession of South Vietnamese governments, combined with
their inability to rally their own people to fight against the Viet
Cong, made the ideological argument seem spurious to most of
the American public. Therefore, Johnson had to justify this
war primarily on the ground that a vital world order interest
was at stake in the outcome of the struggle in Southeast Asia. As
the war dragged on, even that basis for going into Vietnam was
called into question because China was plunged into its
cultural revolution and Sukarno was ousted by the Indonesian
military after an abortive communist coup in October 1965.
Once China and Indonesia became preoccupied with internal
problems, the threat to U.S. world order interests in Southeast
Asia seemed considerably reduced.

Assessing Value and Cost/Risk Factors

Another way of looking at the presidential perception of
national interests is to calculate how they might have viewed
the values and risks involved in the crises they faced (see Table
2.1, page 20).[3] In Woodrow Wilson's case, it is reasonably clear
that early in 1917 he was heavily influenced by the following
value factors: nature of the threat (submarine attacks on U.S.
shipping), effect on balance of power (if Germany defeated the
Allied powers), and national prestige (if the United States were
excluded from the peace conference). Of the *cost* factors,

Wilson probably gave greatest attention to: estimated casualties (if the United States sent an army to Europe), risk of public
opposition (there was still strong anti-British sentiment early
in 1917), and risk of congressional opposition (Wilson wanted
an overwhelming majority in favor of war).

For Franklin Roosevelt, *all* of the value factors were
important, especially the nature of the threat, type of
government, and effect on the balance of power (German
victory). On the cost/risk side, Roosevelt's only real concern
was public opposition and the virulence of the isolationist
sentiment in Congress; all the other costs were acceptable. For
Wilson and Roosevelt, the value factors clearly outweighed the
cost/risk questions in the months preceding the U.S. entry into
war, but both felt it imperative to give public opinion time to
catch up with that judgment.

In the cases of Truman and Johnson, the dilemma was
greater and the results less satisfactory. This is because the
value factors were not clearly apparent to the Congress and the
public, and the potential costs and risks were high for both
Korea and Vietnam. In Truman's case, the initial decision to
send U.S. forces into Korea risked a UN military defeat in the
summer of 1950 as well as substantial casualties. However, the
values Truman perceived seemed overriding: the blatant
aggression of North Korea (nature of threat), the prestige of the
United Nations and the United States, and the probable
disastrous political effect on Japan if the whole Korean
peninsula came under communist control (effect on balance of
power).

Truman's decision to let MacArthur send his forces
northward to unite Korea under a pro-Western government
was quite another matter. Here Truman sought to tip the
balance of power in northeast Asia in favor of the West without
looking carefully enough at the risks and costs of such action.
Specifically, he discounted the risk of an enlarged conflict,
even though Peking had warned against sending U.S. troops to
the Yalu River. He also minimized the risk of protracted
conflict, thereby underestimating U.S. casualties and, ultimately, the disenchantment of the American public with that
brutal war. Truman probably did not risk strong public

opposition so long as his war aims remained limited, i.e., restoring the thirty-eighth parallel under UN sponsorship. The real risk he took was in assuming that he could unite Korea by force (even with the UN's blessing) without triggering an enlarged war, which he clearly did not want. That was the tragedy of Truman's Korean policy.

As for Lyndon Johnson, only two value factors in Vietnam could remotely qualify as vital considerations: effect on the balance of power in Asia, and U.S. credibility and prestige. None of the other value factors mattered much: the danger was far removed from the United States, the threat was essentially a civil war supported from the outside, Vietnam was a huge economic drain on the United States, Americans felt no historical or sentimental attachment for these Asian people, the government there was corrupt and authoritarian, and U.S. policies were not supported by the NATO allies. Thus, Johnson's and Rusk's claim that Vietnam was *vital* rested on balance of power and prestige factors alone. As for costs and risks, Johnson probably knew that they would be high if he could not end the war within one year because a protracted conflict would increase both the casualties and the economic drain on the United States. Since he, like Truman, wanted to avoid an enlarged war with China and the Soviet Union, Johnson carefully avoided a military solution in North Vietnam, which in turn made stalemate inevitable. And a stalemate was certain to turn U.S. public opinion and congressional opinion against the war, just as had occurred in Korea. Johnson's only hope of avoiding a political disaster was to arrange a negotiated settlement favorable to the West within a reasonably short period of time, but Hanoi refused to cooperate despite the massive punishment heaped on the North by U.S. air power. Therefore, the war dragged on without solution. In sum, the costs of Vietnam far outweighed the values involved, and when this became apparent to the American people and to Congress, the war had to be ended.

Comparative Interests among Antagonists

This leads to a final way of viewing the decisions of these

four U.S. presidents who took the nation to war: when they made their decisions for war, how realistically did they perceive the national interests of the United States' principal adversaries? In World Wars I and II, there is not much dispute about the degree of interest involved for the major belligerents: for Germany, France, Russia, and Great Britain, their defense interests were at the *survival* level because losing the war would mean political domination and probably occupation by a foreign power. British and French survival was perceived by Wilson—and British and Soviet survival was seen by Roosevelt—to be a *vital* U.S. world order interest; and this assessment justified the massive introduction of U.S. forces into Europe. In 1914 all the European powers knew that the survival of their political systems was at stake; but in World War II this did not become crystal clear to Britain and France until the spring of 1940, or to the Soviet Union until June 1941. Wilson probably underestimated the Germans' determination to win a military victory until their resumption of submarine warfare in 1917; and when he realized the depth of Berlin's interest, it speeded his decision to intervene. Roosevelt, on the other hand, never underestimated Nazi Germany's intentions, and his realistic appraisal led to his demand for an unconditional surrender rather than a negotiated settlement of the European war.

The Korea and Vietnam cases were different, and it is useful to utilize the national interest matrix (Chapter 1) to illustrate why. In Korea the principal antagonists from December 1950 on were the United States, North Korea, and the People's Republic of China. Judging by their statements and actions, their interests in that conflict were as shown in Chart 5.6.

As this evaluation implies, Truman and his advisers completely misjudged the intensity of interest felt by Peking vis-à-vis the U.S. decision to permit General MacArthur to move his forces into North Korea. When the North Koreans launched their attack in June 1950, both the United States and China had important interests at stake. When the United States intervened, China's interest increased as U.S. troops moved closer to its own border. The fact that Truman and MacArthur chose to discount Chinese warnings was a blunder of major proportions and caused the war to last three years longer than it

CHART 5.6

Issue: Korea, December 1950				
Basic interest at stake		Intensity of interest		
	Survival	Vital	Major	Peripheral
Defense of homeland	North Korea	China	US	
Economic well-being		North Korea	US China	
Favorable world order		US China North Korea		
Ideological	North Korea	US China		

should have once the thirty-eighth parallel had been restored in September 1950. For the North Koreans, their original interest when planning the attack on the South may have been only *major*—certainly no higher than vital; they probably calculated that the U.S. interest was only a major one and that Truman would not intervene. But after MacArthur's brilliant landings at Inchon cut off a large part of the North Korean army and moved the war into North Korea, the interest for Pyongyang quickly became survival. If North Korea had foreseen that Truman would then send U.S. forces to defend South Korea, would it have launched its attack in June? The answer probably is "no"—because it would have seen the costs as too high.[4] Thus, there were two great miscalculations of interest in Korea: first, the North underestimated Truman's perception of the U.S. and UN stake in Korea; and second, Truman miscalculated China's interest when U.S. forces approached its border in November 1950.

In Vietnam the principal antagonists were the United States, North Vietnam, China, and the Soviet Union, even though the last two did not send troops. In 1965, their perceived national interests in that crisis were as shown in Chart 5.7. According to this assessment, North Vietnam had a survival defense interest at stake once the United States entered the war,

CHART 5.7

Issue: Vietnam, March 1965			
Basic interest at stake		**Intensity of interest**	
	Survival	Vital	Major	Peripheral
Defense of homeland	North Vietnam		China	US USSR
Economic well-being		North Vietnam	China	US USSR
Favorable world order		US North Vietnam	China USSR	
Ideological	North Vietnam	US	China USSR	

even though President Johnson proclaimed that he had no intention of invading the North or forcing a change in its regime. North Vietnam also had a survival ideological interest in uniting all Vietnamese under its control, since faltering in that goal might have resulted in its own demise. The Soviet Union had, at best, only a major interest in the conflict so long as there was no threat to the Ho Chi Minh regime in Hanoi. The same was true of China so long as its border was not threatened. In 1965 the United States thought it had a vital world order interest in Vietnam and probably a vital ideological one as well. But it underestimated North Vietnam's interest in uniting that whole peninsula and the enormous price Hanoi was willing to pay. Johnson correctly judged Moscow's interest in Vietnam (he probably misjudged China's once that country plunged into its cultural revolution), but he grossly misjudged Hanoi's. That cost him the war and another term in the White House. Hanoi probably assessed the intensity of the U.S. interest to be no more than major, even though President Johnson and other U.S. leaders talked in terms of vital interests and the falling domino theory. Hanoi probably concluded that if the war lasted longer than a year without a U.S. victory, Washington would eventually negotiate on terms acceptable to Hanoi. If that was Hanoi's plan, it was correct for one overriding reason: its own interest was far deeper than was the U.S. interest in South Vietnam. In the end, the imbalance in the comparative interest led to a U.S. withdrawal from South Vietnam and to the eventual achievement of Hanoi's objectives in the South.

An important conclusion should be drawn from this. Namely, the United States ought to have more than one of its basic national interests rooted at the *vital* level before its leaders contemplate using military force outside North America again. In World War I, Wilson persuaded the country that both world order and ideological interests were at stake in the European conflict. In December 1941, Roosevelt had no difficulty convincing the nation that vital defense, world order, and ideological interests were being threatened by Hitler in Europe and by Japan in Asia and the Pacific. Before Pearl Harbor, Roosevelt had hesitated on mobilizing the country because the defense interest was not clearly threatened. Conversely, Truman and Johnson took the country to war on the basis of their perception that a vital world order interest was sufficient, even though they tried to sell the ideological interest as well. Neither Truman nor Johnson was able to persuade American opinion that vital ideological interests—political rights, democratic government, religious freedom—were at stake in either Korea or Vietnam. In Truman's case, the UN charter and UN vote to send troops helped justify the war. But the only plausible case Johnson could make was the threat to the Asian balance of power (world order); and that was not enough to persuade the American people to continue the war when the casualties mounted.

The President and Congress: Constitutional and Political Questions

In a constitutional system such as that of the United States, the president has the primary responsibility for identifying those interests that we define here as *vital,* but he clearly does not have the exclusive responsibility. The framers of the U.S. constitution were clear on the Senate's right to ratify treaties and the Congress's right to declare war—both of which are demonstrations to the world that a U.S. vital interest is involved. However, in neither the Korean war nor the Vietnam conflict did a treaty obligate the United States to defend those countries; in neither case was there a declaration of war. Although the United States had no treaty of alliance with Britain or France at the beginning of World War I or II, Congress declared war in both cases, thereby confirming that the stakes were vital. The issue here is whether any president is politically justified in using large U.S. combat forces outside North America unless he has the explicit authority of Congress to do so. When enacting the War Powers Act of 1973, Congress decided that he could do so only for sixty days; after that he must withdraw the forces unless Congress expressly approves their continued use.[5]

In comparing Wilson, Roosevelt, Truman, and Johnson on their dealings with Congress on this important constitutional issue, it seems evident that each of them had the legal power to do what he did. The more difficult question is whether it was *politically* wise for them to use that power as they did.

In the case of Wilson, his problem with a large segment of Congress and the Eastern press was that, by the end of 1916 and early 1917, he was doing too *little* to prepare the country for war and being too conciliatory toward Imperial Germany in what many saw as his vain hope to bring about a negotiated peace in Europe. By March 1917, most of Wilson's cabinet as well as a majority in the Senate worried whether Wilson could face up to the reality of the European war—that unless the United States joined the Allies, they probably could not hold out. In short, Congress, the Eastern press, and probably a majority of the American people were convinced by the beginning of 1917 that the war in Europe had become a *vital* interest of the United States, but Wilson still clung to the view that it was only a *major* interest and did not require U.S. intervention. When Wilson finally went before Congress to propose a declaration of war, he received overwhelming support.

Roosevelt's problem was far more difficult. Congress was heavily influenced by isolationists who were determined to keep the United States out of the European war at almost any cost. Moreover, Hitler had so swiftly overwhelmed Denmark, Norway, the Low Countries, and France in the spring of 1940;

unlike Wilson, who observed a stalemated war in Europe for more than two years, Roosevelt was faced in the summer of 1940 with a German fait accompli on the continent, with the grim prospect that if Britain succumbed to Hitler's bombing attacks there would be nothing left in Europe for the United States to defend. To make matters worse for Roosevelt, he was obliged in this awesome situation to wage an election campaign for an unprecedented third term in the White House, against charges from the isolationists that he planned to involve the nation in war if reelected. Thanks only to his unique political sagacity and his remarkable ability to communicate with the American public, Roosevelt persuaded Congress to provide Lend-Lease supplies to Britain in March 1941. But he also believed that Congress either would not vote for a declaration of war against Germany or that the vote would be so close that the country could not enter the war as a united nation. Therefore, he chose to wait until the situation was right, much to the despair of Churchill and the British government and of some members of his own cabinet. In the fall of 1941, Roosevelt took some military actions in the Atlantic that were clearly provocative, and he used the sinking of U.S. ships as justification for taking even more belligerent actions. On each occasion, there were howls of protest from the isolationists, who simply did not share his perception that a vital U.S. national interest was at stake in Europe. Only when the Japanese attacked U.S. territory were these voices stilled, because the defense of *American* territory was a vital interest to Roosevelt as well as to large segments of the American public. By waiting for the enemy to strike, Roosevelt insured that when the United States finally went to war, it would do so as a nation united in its war aims.

Truman's handling of Congress was totally different from that of his two predecessors. He was probably influenced by Roosevelt's inability to persuade Congress during 1939 and 1940 that there was a vital U.S. interest involved in resisting Hitler's design to take over the continent bit by bit. From his own account, Truman never had any doubt that the North Korean attack in 1950 was a vital world order interest of the United States; his dilemma was in obtaining congressional support, thereby convincing the country that this tiny peninsula in northeast Asia was worth the lives of American soldiers. His decision not to ask Congress for a vote of support on the specific question of sending U.S. troops into combat, and instead to base this action on the UN Charter and the vote in the UN Security Council, was doubtless a reasonable decision so long as the UN's war aims were to restore order in Korea, i.e., to reestablish the thirty-eighth parallel as the administrative boundary between north and south. But when Truman acquiesced in MacArthur's plan to pursue the North Korean army northward and destroy it, that was a significant change in war aims for both the United Nations and the United States. Here Truman was certainly on more dangerous political ground: he did not ask Congress for a specific vote of confidence for his plan to unite the two Korean zones, yet he was risking Chinese and possibly Soviet intervention.

In other words, Truman was probably justified in using U.S. forces under UN authority so long as the Korean episode remained a "police action." When in the fall of 1950 it ceased to be a police action and became a major military effort to change the government of North Korea, Truman needed the specific support of Congress—not on legal grounds but because of the political risks he was undertaking in North Korea. The Chinese intervention and the shrill tone of Truman's rhetoric in December 1950, when he asked Congress for increased military appropriations, were surely evidence that the war in North Korea was something more than a local military operation. In his own political interest, Truman could not hope to gain public support for two and a half more years of war without obtaining a vote of confidence from Congress. The price he paid for his decision to avoid the issue was to leave the White House two years later an embittered and unpopular man, with the Republicans in control of the presidency.

Lyndon Johnson tried to avoid Truman's mistake by getting a congressional vote of confidence in the form of the Tonkin Gulf resolution in the summer of 1964. But again, most members of Congress saw this resolution as permitting the president to use U.S. combat forces for a "police action" in Southeast Asia, not for the massive introduction of U.S. power there. Had Johnson been able in the spring of 1965 to persuade Ho Chi Minh to negotiate a settlement of the war in the South—after the bombing had begun and the Marines had gone in—he would have had no further need for congressional support. Or, had Hanoi refused to enter negotiations and had U.S. military strategy been to introduce only as many troops as were needed to maintain security in the principal populated areas of South Vietnam and start a massive training program to build up the South Vietnamese army into an effective fighting force,[6] Johnson might not have needed the additional political support from Congress in the form of another joint resolution. When he agreed with the Joint Chiefs of Staff in July 1965 that U.S. forces would have to do most of the fighting in order to prevent a North Vietnamese victory, Johnson walked on weak political ground; that is, he did not go to Congress for a vote of support for what would now be a U.S. war against North Vietnam, not simply U.S. military support for a South Vietnamese fight for survival against the North.

Had Lyndon Johnson asked Congress for a resolution of support for the war in July 1965, he no doubt would have gotten a favorable vote in both houses because of the overwhelming Democratic majorities. The opposition vote might have been substantial, but there would have been a majority vote in favor of an enlarged war, the kind that the president now intended to wage, not the police action or show of force that was anticipated when Congress voted for the Tonkin resolution in 1964. With a new resolution of support, Johnson would still have had public opposition; but he could have argued effectively that his authority to fight a major war in Southeast Asia was clear and that the minority in Congress, such as Senator Fulbright, should either find a majority to discontinue the war or stop talking about a "credibility gap" insofar as the president's actions were concerned. Whether the outcome of the Vietnam war would then have been different is not possible to say, because so many other variables contributed to the war's outcome. But on this specific question—the president's political judgment in sending a large U.S. fighting force to Vietnam without the specific authority of Congress— his case would have been far stronger if he had gotten a vote of confidence in 1965.

In the longer run, this may be the most important heritage of the Vietnam episode: the credibility gap that grew between the presidency and the public because of the way in which Johnson "manipulated" the war, instead of "leveling" with Congress and the American people about the values and the costs. His successor, Richard Nixon, only made matters worse by his decision to send U.S. forces into Cambodia in May 1970 without so much as consulting with Congress in advance—or even with his own administration, for that matter. Thus, the tragic legacy of Vietnam is not only that the United States lost a war in which it expended large numbers of men and vast stores of equipment, but also that it left a weakened presidency. Gerald Ford did his best to restore faith in the office during his two years as president; but it remains for another president, Jimmy Carter, to try to put back together the prestige and authority of the presidency at a time when the external environment in which the United States will operate calls for strong and wise presidential leadership.

6. Nixon's View of the U.S. National Interest in Cambodia

Richard Nixon came to the White House in January 1969 determined to end U.S. military involvement in Vietnam. His problem was to devise a way to withdraw U.S. troops from that quagmire in a manner that would not seriously damage America's prestige as a world power while retaining a foreign policy consensus at home. During 1969 he laid the groundwork for the withdrawal by instituting a "Vietnamization" of the war, putting heavy emphasis on training the South Vietnamese army to take over from departing Americans the responsibility for defending their own country. Nixon began the military withdrawal in 1969, and in the spring of 1970 he initiated plans to withdraw another 150,000 troops. Then came Cambodia. On April 30, the president announced that he had authorized U.S. forces, along with Vietnamese troops, to cross the eastern Cambodian border and destroy North Vietnamese military bases and supplies and to attack enemy troop concentrations. His action stirred up violent protests in the United States, resulting in a massive student march on Washington, D.C., and a tragedy at Kent State University in which four students were killed. Why was tiny Cambodia, which had tried to maintain its neutrality throughout the Vietnam war, now invaded by U.S. forces? How did a U.S. president justify such an enormous gamble with his country's prestige and his own political future?

Throughout the 1960s, while the United States escalated its military involvement in Vietnam, Cambodia remained staunchly neutral under the leadership of a flamboyant leader,

Prince Norodom Sihanouk. Cambodian neutrality had been guaranteed by an international agreement signed in Geneva in 1954, and Sihanouk had walked a tight rope of diplomatic maneuverings for the next fifteen years in order to avoid having Cambodia drawn into the developing struggle between North and South Vietnam. When the United States intervened militarily in Vietnam in 1965, Sihanouk broke relations with the United States and drew closer to Moscow and Peking, in part in an effort to prevent his country from being drawn into war, in part because North Vietnamese troops had begun using Cambodian territory to extend the Ho Chi Minh trail and thus supply Viet Cong forces operating in the areas adjacent to Saigon. Sihanouk believed he would have more influence over Hanoi's policies about using Cambodian territory if his foreign policy were anti-American; he also seemed convinced that the United States would not attack Cambodia if he stoutly defended his nation's neutrality before the world and posed as a defenseless neutral surrounded by hostile forces.[1]

From 1965 to the spring of 1969, Sihanouk's diplomacy was successful in persuading the United States and its allies not to violate Cambodian territory, even though all concerned knew that North Vietnamese forces were increasing their penetration of the eastern provinces of Cambodia and establishing supply depots and base camps for communist forces operating in South Vietnam. The Johnson administration carefully considered bombing these sanctuaries, but it came to the conclusion that the political risks of doing so outweighed the military advantages. That remained U.S. policy until the beginning of the Nixon presidency in January 1969.

Private citizen Nixon had concluded already in 1967 that the massive U.S. military intervention in Vietnam was counterproductive to worldwide U.S. interests and had to be ended in the least painful way. In 1967, he gave a prophetic analysis of the impact of the Vietnam war on the United States:

> One of the legacies of Vietnam almost certainly will be a deep reluctance on the part of the United States to become involved once again in a similar intervention on a similar basis. The war has imposed severe strains on the United States not only

militarily and economically but socially and politically as well. Bitter dissension has torn the fabric of American intellectual life, and whatever the outcome of the war the tear may be a long time mending. If another friendly country should be faced with an externally supported communist insurrection—whether in Asia, or in Africa or even Latin America—there is serious question whether the American public or the American Congress would now support a unilateral American intervention, even at the request of the host government.[2]

Nixon did not criticize Johnson's decision to send U.S. forces into Vietnam: in fact, he asserted that U.S. intervention was "a vital factor in the turnaround in Indonesia" and that it had "diverted Peking from such other potential targets as India, Thailand and Malaysia." It had bought "vitally needed time for governments that were weak or unstable," he observed.[3] But the thrust of his argument was that Asian countries must not become dependent on a U.S. military presence to solve their problems and must form new collective relationships among themselves and bear more of the burden of their defense in the future. Nixon thus laid the groundwork in 1967 for his Guam doctrine of 1969—later to be known as the Nixon doctrine—which put limits on the future use of U.S. ground forces in local wars, even when an ally was concerned. It is noteworthy that in this article Nixon also laid the basis for his later "opening to Peking": "Any American policy toward Asia must come urgently to grips with the reality of China. . . . Taking the long view, we simply cannot afford to leave China forever outside the family of nations, there to nurture its fantasies, cherish its hates and threaten its neighbors. There is no place on this small planet for a billion of its potentially most able people to live in angry isolation."[4]

Given these sensible statements about U.S. national interests in Asia, why was Richard Nixon as president willing to disregard U.S. and world opinion when he sought to translate these objectives into policies, notably in Cambodia? Part of the answer lies in Nixon's negotiations with the Joint Chiefs of Staff over how to accomplish his stated intention of withdrawing U.S. forces from Vietnam. When he came to office, more than half a million U.S. military forces were tied down in Vietnam; despite President Johnson's bombing of the North, instituted in 1968, the ground war in South Vietnam continued. How, therefore, could U.S. forces be withdrawn "honorably" without bringing about the collapse of the South Vietnamese government and without also endangering the lives of remaining U.S. servicemen? His answer was "Vietnamization of the war"—an admission that the war had been an American show for four years and that a serious effort must now be made to train Vietnamese to assume the responsibility of defending their country, at least on the ground. Thus, a massive training program commenced to get the South Vietnamese army into the war and to reduce the combat missions (and casualties) of U.S. units. It was a sensible objective, which should have been implemented in 1965 and 1966. The key question in 1969 and 1970 was whether there would be enough time to do this and also get U.S. forces out of Vietnam during Richard Nixon's first term as president.

On February 18, 1970, in his first "State of the World" report to Congress, the president cited three reasons why he had decided on a gradual U.S. withdrawal from Vietnam, rather than on an immediate evacuation of U.S. forces:

1. "When it comes to peace, 'prestige' is not an empty word. . . . I speak, rather, of the respect that one nation has for another's integrity in defending its principles and meeting its obligations. If we simply abandoned our effort in Vietnam, the cause of peace might not survive the damage that would be done to other nations' confidence in our reliability."

2. "If Hanoi were to succeed in taking over South Vietnam by force—even after the power of the United States had been engaged—it would greatly strengthen those leaders who scorn negotiation, who advocate aggression, who minimize the risks of confrontation with the United States. It would bring peace now but it would enormously increase the danger of a bitter war later."

3. "Less attention had been given to another important consequence of our decisions—within the United States itself. When the Administration took office, Vietnam

had already led to a profound national debate. In considering our objectives there, I could only conclude that the peace must not intensify the bitter recrimination and divisions which the war had already inflicted on American society. Were we to purchase peace in Vietnam at the expense of greater suffering later, the American people would inevitably lose confidence in their leaders—not just in the Presidency or in either political party, but in the whole structure of American leadership."[5]

In these statements, Nixon sought to justify a gradual withdrawal from Vietnam in terms of three value factors discussed in Chapter 2: the prestige of the United States as a world power; the effect on the balance of power in Asia and elsewhere if the leaders of hostile countries decided that the United States would not resist aggression; and the impact on American society if the administration simply abandoned Vietnam after supporting it for nearly ten years through heavy economic and military involvement. Although stressing that he planned to continue efforts toward negotiating a reasonable settlement with Hanoi, Nixon was not optimistic about the prospects. Therefore, he argued, Vietnamization was the means by which the South Vietnam government could continue military resistance to the North without the direct participation of U.S. forces. Taking account of Lyndon Johnson's expectations of an early conclusion to the war, Nixon said: "Claims of progress in Vietnam have been frequent during the course of our involvement there—and have often proved too optimistic. However careful our planning, and however hopeful we are for the progress of these plans, we are conscious of two basic facts: We cannot try to fool the enemy, who knows what is actually happening. Nor must we fool ourselves. The American people must have the full truth. *We cannot afford a loss of confidence in our judgment and in our leadership.*"[6]

The Cambodian Incursion

Three months after submitting this report to Congress, the

president ignored his own wise judgment about not risking "a loss of confidence in our judgment and in our leadership" and ordered U.S. as well as Vietnamese forces to cross the border into Cambodia. He did so without consulting Congress or most segments of his own administration, and over the objections of key members of the National Security Council.[7] Why did he take this risk? Part of the answer is that he had decided a year earlier, in April 1969, to permit the U.S. Air Force to bomb Vietnamese military supply lines and bases in Cambodia, but to keep this operation highly classified. Thus, Nixon had already taken the air war into Cambodia as a means of disrupting the continuing North Vietnamese buildup of supplies and forces for operations inside South Vietnam; and sending U.S. and Vietnamese forces a few miles across the Cambodian border to complete the job did not therefore seem such a great escalation of the war—especially if he insured that it was only a "temporary" incursion aimed at the North Vietnamese, not at the Cambodians. Nixon later claimed that Prince Sihanouk was aware of the bombing in Cambodia and approved of it secretly, as a way of putting pressure on Vietnamese forces operating in his country.[8]

Another reason why Nixon and his national security adviser, Henry Kissinger, approved the military incursion into Cambodia was that a new government had come to power there in March 1970 and had reversed Prince Sihanouk's anti-American foreign policy. The Lon Nol regime in Phnom Penh pleaded for U.S. military assistance to help it oust North Vietnamese troops from Cambodia. And there was clear evidence that Hanoi had reacted to the change of government by sending more forces into Cambodia and by expanding their area of control to provinces near the Cambodian capital. This was the situation that faced the U.S. president late in April 1970.

Nixon's radio and TV address to the nation on April 30, his press conference statements on May 8, and subsequent reports on the Cambodian operation provide good insights into his perceptions and the reasoning that lay behind his decision to go into Cambodia. It is important to recall that Nixon carefully laid the groundwork for a decision to send troops into

Cambodia when he announced on April 20 that he had authorized the withdrawal of an additional 150,000 U.S. troops from Vietnam, to be completed during the coming year. "The timing and pace of these new withdrawals," he said, "will be determined by our best judgment of the current military and diplomatic situation." Referring to North Vietnam's stepped-up attacks in Laos, Cambodia, and South Vietnam during the previous month, Nixon admitted that his decision "clearly involves risks." He warned Hanoi that "while we are taking these risks for peace, they will be taking grave risks should they attempt to use the occasion to jeopardize the security of our remaining forces in Vietnam by increased military action." To be sure that Hanoi got his message, he made this threat: "If I conclude that increased enemy action jeopardizes our remaining forces in Vietnam, I shall not hesitate to take strong and effective measures to deal with that situation."[9]

Ten days later, when he again addressed the nation on radio and television and this time announced his decision to send U.S. forces into Cambodia, the president recalled the April 20 statement: "Despite that warning, North Vietnam has increased its military aggression in all these areas, and particularly in Cambodia." He said he had consulted fully with his National Security Council, Ambassador to Vietnam Ellsworth Bunker, U.S. Military Commander in Vietnam General Creighton Abrams, and other advisers; he had come to the conclusion that "the actions of the enemy in the last 10 days clearly endanger the lives of Americans who are in Vietnam now and would constitute an unacceptable risk to those who will be there after withdrawal of another 150,000." In announcing this course of action, Nixon based his decision on U.S. *defense interests* (protection of American lives) and on U.S. *world order* interests: "To protect our men who are in Vietnam and to guarantee the continued success of our withdrawal and Vietnamization programs, I have concluded that the time has come for action."[10]

For Nixon, it was not enough simply to withdraw U.S. forces with minimum casualties from Vietnam—Hanoi would have agreed to these terms at any time. What was at issue was his determination to withdraw those forces in an *orderly* manner while South Vietnam was being prepared to handle the job on its own. That made Nixon's decision a world order case: he wanted to retain a semblance of balance of power in Southeast Asia and did not believe this would be possible if Hanoi came to dominate the Indochina peninsula. But U.S. ideological interests also figured large in his decision.

It is useful to analyze Nixon's April 30 address in some detail to grasp fully his view of U.S. interests at stake in Cambodia. He first asserted that the United States had provided no military equipment to Cambodia for five years, even though North Vietnam had occupied sanctuaries on Cambodian soil along the South Vietnamese border. He also asserted that "neither the United States nor South Vietnam has moved against these enemy sanctuaries, because we did not wish to violate the territory of a neutral nation." This statement, of course, was not true, as subsequent revelations of U.S. bombing in Cambodia during the previous year eventually showed. Nixon might have argued this point, saying that violation of such sanctuaries from the air was not the same as "moving against" them on the ground. However, he went on to assert that the North Vietnamese had expanded their operations in Cambodia during April 1970 and that "they are encircling the Capital of Phnom Penh." In this situation, Nixon said, the Cambodian government called on several nations for assistance. Refusal to aid Cambodia would mean that "Cambodia would become a vast enemy staging area and a springboard for attacks on South Vietnam along 600 miles of frontier, a refuge where enemy troops could return from combat without fear of retaliation." To underline the seriousness of the situation, he said that some of the sanctuaries were as close to Saigon as Baltimore is to Washington, D.C.[11]

In his April 30 address, Nixon touched on three basic national interests:

Defense interests: "A majority of the American people want to keep the casualties of our brave men in Vietnam at an absolute minimum. The action I take tonight is essential if we are to accomplish that goal."

World order interests: "If, when the chips are down, the

world's most powerful nation, the United States of America, acts like a pitiful, helpless giant, the forces of totalitarianism and anarchy will threaten free nations and free institutions throughout the world."

Ideological interests: "We will not react to this threat to American lives mainly by plaintive diplomatic protests. If we did, the credibility of the United States would be destroyed in every area of the world where only the power of the United States deters aggression. . . . The action that I have announced tonight puts the leaders of North Vietnam on notice that we will be patient in working for peace, we will be conciliatory at the conference table, but we will not be humiliated. We will not be defeated. We will not allow American men by the thousands to be killed by an enemy from privileged sanctuaries."

The following statement best illustrates Nixon's perception of a vital ideological interest at stake:

> It is not our power but our will and character that is being tested tonight. The question all Americans must ask and answer is this: Does the richest and strongest nation in the history of the world have the character to meet a direct challenge by a group which rejects every effort to win a just peace, ignores our warning, tramples on solemn agreements, violates the neutrality of an unarmed people, and uses our prisoners as hostages? If we fail to meet this challenge, all other nations will be on notice that despite its overwhelming power the United States, when a real crisis comes, will be found wanting."[12]

Nixon assured the nation that "this is not an invasion of Cambodia. . . . Our purpose is not to occupy the areas. Once enemy forces are driven out of these sanctuaries and once their military supplies are destroyed, we will withdraw." He also reassured other powers that U.S. action did not endanger their security interests, and he repeated several times that he had taken this action so that the United States could proceed with its troop withdrawal from Vietnam. Finally, he took account of the political risks involved in his bold action. Citing a "Republican Senator's" statement that his action would negate all chances of a Republican victory in the congressional elections in November and others' predictions that it would make him a one-term president, Nixon stated:

> No one is more aware than I am of the political consequences of the action I have taken. It is tempting to take the easy political path: to blame this war on previous administrations and to bring all of our men home immediately, regardless of the consequences, even though that would mean defeat for the United States . . . to get peace at any price now, even though I know that a peace of humiliation for the United States would lead to a bigger war of surrender later. *I have rejected all political considerations in making this decision. . . .* I would rather be a one-term President and do what I believe is right than to be a two-term President at the cost of seeing America become a second-rate power and to see this nation accept the first defeat in its proud 190-year history.[13]

A careful reading of Nixon's announcement of his decision to send U.S. troops across the Cambodian border reveals his strongly held view that the stakes in Vietnam were so high that he could not risk withdrawing U.S. forces while North Vietnam expanded its bases on Cambodian territory and threatened a military disaster for U.S. and South Vietnamese troops in the area around Saigon. In fact, Nixon believed the stakes were so high that he was willing to lay his political career on the line at home. His perception of the threat to U.S. national interests in Cambodia was stated primarily in terms of defense and world order interests, but his April 30 address strongly suggests that his real concern was the ideological interest—he did not want the United States to be humiliated as it withdrew from Vietnam.

Some writers and commentators have claimed that Nixon grossly underestimated the political impact of his decision at home and have suggested that he might not have taken this action in Cambodia had he known what would occur on U.S. campuses during the next few weeks. This conjecture is not supported by a careful reading of Nixon's April 30 address to the nation: here he is a determined president who has overruled the counsel of key cabinet members and accepted the military view that it was "vital" to attack the Cambodian sanctuaries before withdrawing any more U.S. forces from Vietnam—*regardless* of domestic political costs.[14]

In subsequent weeks, while U.S. campuses closed down under the pressure of student demonstrations against the Cambodian "invasion," Nixon sought to defend his actions: Cambodia had been a brilliant military success that had allowed the withdrawal of U.S. forces from Vietnam to continue. His approach was to show that without the limited Cambodian incursion, he could not insure the safe withdrawal of U.S. forces and success of his Vietnamization program, both of which were campaign promises he wanted to keep. Thus, withdrawal with honor, meaning an independent South Vietnam, was a goal he had pledged to achieve even if it cost him a high political price at home.

On May 8, Nixon held a news conference dominated by the Cambodia issue. The first questioner asked whether he had been "surprised by the intensity of the protest against your decision . . . and will these protests affect your policy in any way?" Nixon's response was: "No. I have not been surprised by the intensity of the protests. I realize that those who are protesting believe that this decision will expand the war, increase American casualties, an increase of American involvement. Those who protest want peace. They want to reduce American casualties and they want our boys brought home. I made this decision, however, for the very reasons that they are protesting. As far as affecting my decision is concerned . . . I know that what I have done will accomplish the goals that they want."[15]

After responding to another question about what the students were trying to say to him, Nixon said: "I would add this: I think I understand what they want. I would hope they would understand somewhat what I want. When I came to the Presidency, I did not send these men to Vietnam. There were 525,000 men there. And since I have been here, I have been working 18 or 20 hours a day, mostly on Vietnam, trying to bring these men home." Answering another question about whether the North Vietnamese would not be able to reestablish their sanctuaries in six months or less, the president replied:

At the present time, I will say that it is my belief, based on what we have accomplished to date, that we have bought at least six months and probably eight months of time for the training of the ARVN, the Army of South Vietnam. We have also saved, I think, hundreds if not thousands, of Americans. . . . Rockets by the thousands and small arms ammunition by the millions have already been captured and those rockets and small arms will not be killing Americans in these next few months. And what we have also accomplished by buying time, the means [*sic*] that if the enemy does come back into those sanctuaries next time, the South Vietnamese will be strong enough and well trained enough to handle it alone.[16]

Another questioner asked the president what would be Cambodia's future after U.S. forces were withdrawn. He replied that the Guam Doctrine, which he had enunciated the previous year, meant that the United States "cannot take the responsibility and should not take the responsibility in the future to send American men in to defend the neutrality of countries that are unable to defend themselves." In response to another question on whether Secretary of State Rogers and Presidential Assistant Kissinger had opposed the incursion in Cambodia, Nixon dodged the question by stating:

Every one of my advisors, the Secretary of State, the Secretary of Defense, Dr. Kissinger, Director Helms, raised questions about the decision, and believe me, I raised the most questions, because I knew the stakes that were involved. I knew the division that would be caused in this country. I knew also the problems internationally. I knew the military risks. And then after hearing all of their advice, I made the decision. Decisions, of course, are not made by vote in the National Security Council or in the Cabinet. They are made by the President with the advice of those, and I made this decision. I take the responsibility for it, I believe it was the right decision. I believe it will work out. If it doesn't then I am to blame. They are not.[17]

In an interim radio and television report to the nation on June 3 from the White House, the president stated categorically that "based on General Abrams's report, I can now state that this has been the most successful operation of this long and very difficult war." He reported that 43,000 South Vietnamese and

31,000 Americans took part in the operations, in which "in the month of May, in Cambodia alone, we captured a total amount of enemy arms, equipment, ammunition, and food nearly equal to what we captured in all of Vietnam in all of last year." He revealed that 17,000 U.S. forces had already been withdrawn from Cambodia and that the rest would be out by the end of June: "The only remaining American activity in Cambodia after July 1 will be air missions to interdict the movement of enemy troops and material where I find that is necessary to protect the lives and security of our men in South Vietnam." In fact, these air missions had been going on secretly since April 1969, not from April 30, 1970, as Nixon well knew. After praising the conduct of South Vietnamese troops and their demonstration that the "Vietnamization program is succeeding," Nixon turned again to the storm of protest that his action had generated in the United States:

> As all of you know, when I first announced the decision on Cambodia, it was subjected to an unprecedented barrage of criticism in this country. I want to express tonight my deep appreciation to the millions of Americans who supported me then and who have supported me since in our efforts to win a just peace. But I also understand the deep division in this country over the war. I realize that many Americans are deeply troubled. They want peace. They want to bring the boys home. Let us understand once and for all that no group has a monopoly on those concerns. Every American shares those desires; I share them very deeply. Our differences are over the best means to achieve a just peace. As President, I have a responsibility to listen to those in this country who disagree with my policies. But I also have a solemn obligation to make the hard decisions which I find are necessary to protect the lives of 400,000 American men remaining in Vietnam. . . . Ask yourselves this question: If an American President had failed to meet this threat to 400,000 American men remaining in Vietnam, would those nations and peoples who rely on America's power and treaty commitments for their security—in Latin America, Europe, the Mideast, or other parts of Asia— retain any confidence in the United States? That is why I deeply believe that a just peace in Vietnam is essential if there is to be a lasting peace in other parts of the world.[18]

In his final report on the Cambodian operation, issued on June 30, 1970, Nixon reported that all U.S. troops had been withdrawn from Cambodia and stated categorically: "It is vital to understand at the outset that Hanoi left the United States no reasonable option but to move militarily against the Cambodian base areas." He attempted to gain support for his decision by citing "four basic facts [that] must be remembered":

1. "It was North Vietnam—not we—which brought the Vietnam war into Cambodia."
2. "It was the presence of North Vietnamese troops on Cambodian soil that contributed to the downfall of Prince Sihanouk," a coup he asserted the United States knew nothing about.
3. "It was the government appointed by Prince Sihanouk and ratified by the Cambodian National Assembly—not a group of usurpers—which overthrew him with the approval of the National Assembly."
4. "It was the major expansion of enemy activity in Cambodia that ultimately caused allied troops to end 5 years of restraint and attack the Communist base areas. The historical record is plain."

But the question of the cost to American society reappeared, and the president took account of it in this way: "Although there remains disagreement about its long-term significance—about the cost to our society of having taken this action—there can be little disagreement now over the immediate military success that has been achieved. With American ground operations in Cambodia ended, we shall move forward with our plan to end the war in Vietnam and to secure the just peace on which all Americans are united."[19]

Nixon thus conceded that the U.S. political climate had been damaged by his sending U.S. forces into Cambodia, an action he felt was totally justified on political grounds within Cambodia and on military grounds in terms of North Vietnamese activities inside Cambodia. He seemed to leave it to historians to decide the wisdom of his course; but in his own mind, the political costs at home apparently were worth paying—because, in his view, the costs of *not* acting would have been even greater and would have hindered his plan of withdrawal from Vietnam—an objective he was pledged to accomplish in his first term. The Joint Chiefs of Staff, the only major element in the National Security Council system to support military action in Cambodia, apparently had convinced the president that the risks of withdrawing additional U.S. troops in 1970-1971 were very high unless the U.S. commander was given permission to hit North Vietnamese base camps in Cambodia. It was a military argument, which few U.S. presidents in wartime find easy to withstand. Richard Nixon, like Lyndon Johnson before him, decided not to resist the pressure.

Nixon and the National Interest

This account of Richard Nixon's public justification for sending U.S. forces into Cambodia indicates that it was a difficult decision to make and that he was aware when he did so that it would cost him politically at home. How large a cost may not have been clear at first; moreover, the severe congressional reaction during May and June probably was greater than anticipated—particularly the threat of a congressional cutoff of funds for all operations in Cambodia.[20]

From the perspective of the United States, Nixon calculated that an orderly withdrawal of U.S. troops from Vietnam with the fewest casualties was a *major* and perhaps a vital interest— if Vietnamese troops operating from Cambodian sanctuaries severely hindered their withdrawal. From an economic standpoint, however, Cambodia was but a peripheral interest of the United States. It would have been a drain on U.S. economic resources if Nixon had planned to bolster the Lon Nol government with economic and military assistance, which he apparently did not contemplate. But the world order interest and the ideological interest of the United States were *vitally* affected, in Nixon's view, for two important reasons: first, there would be little hope of South Vietnam's defending itself if North Vietnamese troops occupied Cambodian territory and could bring supplies to within thirty-five miles of Saigon without challenge (world order); second, Nixon was convinced that Hanoi not only wanted the United States out of South Vietnam, but also was determined to inflict a humiliating withdrawal on Washington so that it would have no credibility anywhere in Asia. Nixon was determined that American *honor* had to be protected in Southeast Asia so that it could retain credibility with allies and foes elsewhere in the world (ideological).

Nevertheless, Nixon's perception of the national interest at stake in Cambodia forced him to the conclusion that he must take large risks or face even greater ones later on. Chart 6.1 is a reasonable assessment of how the president saw the problem.

Cambodia's very survival, of course, was at stake: it was defending its homeland against invaders, particularly the North Vietnamese, whose forces had been there for five years and who, in the spring of 1970, began to expand their area of control. North Vietnam clearly had a *vital* world order and a *vital* ideological interest in Cambodia: it needed Cambodian soil to carry out its design to take over South Vietnam by force,

CHART 6.1

Issue: Cambodia, 1970				
Basic interest at stake	Intensity of interest			
	Survival	Vital	Major	Peripheral
Defense of homeland	Cambodia		North Vietnam China US	
Economic well-being	Cambodia		North Vietnam	China US
Favorable world order		Cambodia US North Vietnam	China	
Ideological		North Vietnam Cambodia US	China	

and it strongly opposed the Lon Nol regime, which had ousted Sihanouk in March 1970 and began to ask the United States and other nations for help in ousting Hanoi's troops from its soil. China's interest in Cambodia was *major* on all counts except economic, because its vital interests would be affected only by what happened in North Vietnam—on its own borders; Cambodia, like South Vietnam, was not that close to the Chinese homeland. Nevertheless, China had a major interest in seeing Hanoi win in South Vietnam and in having a neutralist or communist regime reinstalled in Cambodia.

Assessing the Cambodia Gamble

Nixon's perception of the U.S. interest is the crucial one for our purposes, however. Why did he take such a risk in the spring of 1970 when the American people and the South Vietnamese government finally seemed convinced that the United States would withdraw all its forces from Vietnam? How did he calculate the costs and benefits of this risky military operation, override the objections of his key advisers, and justify expanding the war at a time most Americans thought it was being wound down? Here it is useful to look at the value and cost/risk factors outlined in Table 2.1 (page 20) and try to assess how the president might have viewed them in April 1970 as the crisis in Cambodia unfolded.

As Nixon thought about these questions, he probably rated such value factors as "national prestige of the United States," "balance of power in Southeast Asia," and "nature of the threat" very highly. He probably placed less value on such factors as "type of government in Cambodia" (although it was better than the previous Sihanouk regime), "policies of key U.S. allies," and "sentimental attachment." On the cost side, Nixon probably calculated that it would be a short operation, that it would be successful in destroying the sanctuaries and perhaps capturing some North Vietnamese forces, that U.S. casualties would be small, and that the economic cost would be minimal. He clearly calculated strong opposition from the press and public opinion and from some sectors of Congress. He may not have appreciated, however, the *degree* of opposition from the public and the way this would trigger congressional efforts to limit his authority to use troops in Vietnam. Public opposition would eventually cause Congress to pass legislation over his veto in 1973 restricting presidential authority to use U.S. forces *anywhere* outside the United States without the consent of Congress.

Nevertheless, Nixon would in all likelihood have permitted his military commanders to invade Cambodian soil even if he had known all the consequences of his action. As his public statements show, he was prepared to take very large political risks in order to prevent the North Vietnamese from upsetting his plan to withdraw U.S. forces and to leave behind a South Vietnamese government capable of defending its own territory. To him, it was a *vital* national interest for the United States to withdraw its forces from a very difficult and unpopular war—a strategic retreat of major proportions for a world power—in a way that would permit the nation to continue a leading role in the world and not be racked by internal cleavages that sapped the nation's strength.

The tragedy of Richard Nixon's policy in Cambodia is that he was probably correct that Cambodia could be the Achilles' heel of his grand strategy to extricate the United States from Vietnam with its honor intact. There is little doubt that Hanoi, with Peking's and Moscow's blessing, sought to oust the United States from the mainland of Southeast Asia in a humiliating manner; and preventing the buildup in the Cambodian sanctuaries and a North Vietnamese takeover of that country would go a long way in thwarting Hanoi's plan. But Nixon could not see that his gamble, although successful militarily in the short run, would begin his political downfall in the United States. His action in Cambodia inflamed public opinion and fueled the fires of a movement in Congress to restrict the power of the presidency. It also set the stage for a later effort to impeach Nixon when the Watergate scandals provided the spark his opposition needed to bring about his political downfall.[21]

This may seem a tenuous conclusion about the impact of the Cambodian affair on U.S. politics. But the hatred generated during May and June 1970 against the man in the White House should not be underestimated in calculating the reasons for his political demise in 1974. The Cambodian episode ignited, seventeen months after Nixon became president, all of the old fears and hatreds of him dating from the 1940s and 1950s, following more than a year of relative calm over his handling of presidential responsibilities. Whatever judgment historians make on this point, it will remain clear that Nixon, like Johnson before him, took a great risk in using U.S. forces in Southeast Asia. Had South Vietnam survived as an independent country after U.S. forces were finally withdrawn in 1973, history might well have recorded that Nixon's incursion into Cambodia in 1970 had succeeded in terms of its longer-term objective. But after the military debacle in South Vietnam in 1975 and the humiliating way in which Americans had to be evacuated from both Saigon and Phnom Penh, the Cambodian invasion in 1970 will probably appear in history to have been an unnecessary violation of a Southeast Asian country's neutrality and the beginning of a great confrontation between president and Congress over the commander in chief's constitutional authority to use U.S. forces outside the United States.[22]

7. The National Security Council and the War Powers Act

Thus far we have dealt with the substance of presidential decisions to use U.S. armed forces in support of national interests outside the Western Hemisphere. We have said little about the process by which their administrations helped them arrive at these decisions and the bureaucratic politics that may have been involved. In this chapter, we describe the mechanism that has been available to post–World War II presidents—the National Security Council, provided by legislation in 1947—and the ways in which postwar presidents have used it. Has the machinery adopted in the Nixon administration, and continued with some modifications in the Ford and Carter presidencies, now become so institutionalized that it can be called an "NSC system"? Moreover, does the War Powers Act of 1973, passed over the president's veto, significantly limit his constitutional authority and thereby pose serious questions about his ability to protect national interests in a crisis? The emphasis of this chapter, therefore, is on the decision-making process.

Before World War II, presidents generally relied on their cabinets as sounding boards for decisions about the use of force abroad. But some of them—particularly the strong presidents—tended to use individual advisers rather than the cabinet to help formulate their decisions. Wilson used Colonel House, and Franklin Roosevelt relied heavily on Harry Hopkins to help think through the difficult foreign policy issues of their administrations. The advice they got often ran counter to the proposals received from the State, War, and Navy departments, and it was the president's job to decide which advice to accept. There was little coordination among these three departments, even though they shared the same office building adjacent to the White House. Each group jealously guarded its bureaucratic purview, and, as a result, there was a serious lack of communication at the top echelons of government in 1940-1941, when the nation was drawn into war. The disaster at Pearl Harbor on December 7, 1941, so shocked the nation and Congress that it was inevitable this situation would be changed after the war was won.

The Senate made an extensive inquiry into the events leading up to Pearl Harbor and came to the conclusion that the nation could no longer afford the competition and lack of coordination that had existed in the executive branch before the war. The National Security Act of 1947 created a single Department of Defense, with three subordinate departments (Army, Navy, and Air Force) reporting to the president through a secretary of defense. It also created the Central Intelligence Agency to coordinate all "international" intelligence work for the military and civilian agencies, and it created a National Security Council (NSC) whose purpose was "to provide a comprehensive program for the future security of the United States" through the "establishment of integrated policies and procedures for the departments, agencies, and functions of the Government relating to the national security." A section of the act entitled "Coordination for National Security" specified that the NSC was "to advise the President with respect to the integration of domestic, foreign, and military policies relating to the national security so as to enable the military services and the other departments and agencies of government to cooperate more effectively in matters involving the national security."[1]

Membership on the NSC was altered somewhat after 1947, but its four principal members have remained the same: the president, designated as presiding officer; the vice-president; the secretary of state; and the secretary of defense. Subsequent legislation designated the chairman of the Joint Chiefs of Staff to serve as military adviser to the NSC and the director of the Central Intelligence Agency, in his capacity as coordinator of the intelligence community, to act as its intelligence adviser.

The president's assistant for national security affairs attends all meetings of the council.[2] The 1947 act also provided for an NSC staff, headed by a civilian executive secretary appointed by the president. During the Nixon, Ford, and Carter administrations, the post of executive secretary has not been filled because the president did not want a statutory officer reporting to the Congress. The assistant to the president for national security affairs has therefore assumed leadership of the NSC staff. The reporting functions required by law are now in the hands of a staff secretary, who is subordinate to the presidential assistant. Finally, the 1947 act listed these specific duties of the council, subject to the president's direction:

> (1) to assess and appraise the objectives, commitments, and risks of the United States in relation to our actual and potential military power, in the interest of national security, for the purpose of making recommendations to the President in connection therewith; and (2) to consider policies on matters of common interest to the departments and agencies of the Government concerned with the national security, and to make recommendations to the President in connection therewith.[3]

In sum, the president and Congress decided that the president should more effectively coordinate the activities and policies of the State Department, the Defense Department, and other agencies involved in protecting the security of the United States. *How* the president is to perform this function, however, has remained an ambiguous area. Each chief executive, beginning with Harry Truman, has used the NSC machinery in a manner that fitted his own management style.

Presidential Use of the National Security Council: 1948-1968

Truman was at first reluctant to use the NSC for decision-making purposes, preferring to bring together many advisers—both civilian and military—whenever a foreign policy crisis arose. He relied heavily on his secretaries of state—James F. Byrnes, George C. Marshall, and Dean Acheson. When the Korean war erupted, however, he decided to make greater use of the council as a deliberative body. He also gave considerable weight to the views of his field commanders—General Douglas MacArthur in the Pacific and General Dwight Eisenhower, NATO commander in Europe. In general, Truman preferred to let the State Department formulate broad national security policy, so the NSC staff remained small and primarily served to facilitate the flow of information from the departments to the president.

Dwight Eisenhower changed that. His long military career predisposed him to a strong staff system, and the NSC became a formal body with a large staff that carefully prepared papers and recommendations based on the concurrence of various departments and agencies. Eisenhower wanted "consensus" among his subordinates; as a result, many of the real issues were submerged in watered-down recommendations rather than being presented to the president as clear-cut choices. In addition to enlarging the NSC staff, the Eisenhower administration created a wholly new organization under the NSC—the Operations Coordinating Board (OCB)—whose function was to insure implementation of presidential decisions in national security affairs. In effect, the OCB took authority away from the State and Defense departments, and other agencies involved in the NSC process, to decide how best to carry out presidential decisions. Another special NSC body set up during this period was the Psychological Operations Board. This "layering" of organizations around the White House caused much frustration in the established bureaucracies of the departments and agencies, and resulted in a cumbersome method of decision making.

John Kennedy's operating style was almost the antithesis of Eisenhower's, and during his first months in office, the NSC machinery was reorganized and the OCB abolished. Kennedy all but ignored the formal NSC structure and dealt directly with individual officials he knew and trusted in the executive branch, without regard to rank or position. For example, he often bypassed the secretary of state and dealt directly with the under secretary and assistant secretaries, whom he liked personally. As a result, decision making became highly personalized in the Kennedy White House, and many ad hoc groups of advisers were called together to deal with specific problems of national security. During the Cuban missile crisis, for example, much of the planning was done by the Executive Committee of the National Security Council, which did not include the president. Robert Kennedy assumed leadership of the group, which included representatives from the departments of State, Defense, and Treasury; the Central Intelligence Agency; the Joint Chiefs of Staff; the U.S. representative to the United Nations; and at least three White House aides.

Lyndon Johnson revived the NSC during his five years in office, but after the United States intervened in the Vietnam war, the circle of people involved in decisions became ever smaller. The NSC meetings consisted of six persons who attended a regular Tuesday lunch at the White House: the president, Secretary of State Dean Rusk, Secretary of Defense Robert McNamara, CIA Director Richard Helms, Chairman of the Joint Chiefs of Staff Earle Wheeler, and Presidential Assistant for NSC Affairs, McGeorge Bundy (later Walt W. Rostow). Certainly Johnson consulted with people outside this small group on how to deal with the Vietnam war, arms limitation talks with the Soviet Union, and so forth. But within the executive branch, only a small circle of dedicated men advised him on the conduct of the major test of his presidency— the Vietnam war. This small group did not leave room for the president to hear dissenting points of view within his administration. In fact, because of the way Lyndon Johnson handled the NSC, policymaking became very fragmented, and the NSC staff became implementers of policy rather than formulators. The "can do" psychology permeated the system, and mistakes in judgment were therefore predictable.[4]

Nixon and Kissinger's National Security Council

When Richard Nixon entered the White House in 1969, his assistant for NSC affairs, Henry Kissinger, brought in a new concept of decision making. Although they discarded the idea of consensus, Kissinger and Nixon borrowed from the staffing procedures of the Eisenhower administration to set up a system of decision making designed "to make certain that clear policy choices reach the top, so that the various positions can be fully debated in the meeting of the Council." Nixon clearly stated his strong preference for hard choices: "I refuse to be confronted with a bureaucratic consensus that leaves me no options but acceptance or rejection, and that gives me no way of knowing what alternatives exist."[5] This required the president to stay out of day-to-day planning of foreign policy and permit the new process to work. This suited Richard Nixon, who preferred to work in relative seclusion, and it clearly suited the brilliant and controversial Harvard professor he had chosen as his national security adviser. In fact, it was a system of decision making that provided Henry Kissinger the opportunity to become the dominant figure in U.S. foreign policy for eight years.

The system Nixon and Kissinger instituted soon became firmly established in the foreign policy and defense community of the executive branch. It is useful, therefore, to look more closely at the structure Kissinger employed to carry out Nixon's wish to let the NSC deal with tough choices instead of bureaucratic compromises. The NSC itself met frequently in 1969 and 1970, but, in contrast to the Kennedy and Johnson administrations, the vice-president now joined the discussions. As in the Kennedy administration, however, the attorney general and the secretary of the treasury were given more voice in NSC deliberations. Under the NSC, three interagency groupings provided staff work from the bureaucracy for the policy formulation process: (1) interdepartmental groups, chaired by an appropriate assistant secretary of state,[6] (2) NSC policy planning committees, and (3) NSC crisis management committees.

The interdepartmental groups consisted of senior representatives, at the assistant secretary or deputy assistant secretary level, of the principal agencies involved in foreign policy planning: State Department (chairman), Defense Department, Joint Chiefs of Staff, Central Intelligence Agency, and the NSC staff. Depending on the issue under consideration, the Treasury Department, the Agency for International Development, the Arms Control and Disarmament Agency, the U.S. Information Agency, and others might have representatives at these meetings. The actual staff work was done by inter-departmental working groups, chaired by a country director or program director in the State Department. The six interdepartmental groups represented five geographical areas (Europe, East Asia, Latin America, Middle East/South Asia, and Africa) and one functional area (political-military affairs and arms control).

The NSC policy planning committees, all of them chaired by Kissinger, consisted of (1) the Senior Review Group, made up of under secretary–level officials in the aforementioned agencies, which reviewed the product of the Interdepartmental Groups "to insure that the issues, options, and views are presented fully and fairly" to the president and the NSC; (2) the Verification Panel, also made up of under secretary–level officials, whose function was "to gather the essential facts relating to a number of important issues of strategic arms limitation, such as Soviet strategic capabilities, and our potential means of verifying compliance with various possible agreements"; (3) the Vietnam Special Studies Group, which monitored the progress of Nixon's Vietnamization program; and (4) the Defense Program Review Committee, also at the under secretary–level, which studied "the major defense policy and program issues which have strategic, political, diplomatic, and economic implications in relation to overall national priorities."[7]

The crisis planning committees covered two key functions. First, the Washington Special Actions Group (WSAG), made up of Kissinger as chairman, the under secretary of state for political affairs, the deputy secretary of defense, the chairman of the Joint Chiefs of Staff, and the CIA director, was to integrate the political and military requirements of crisis action and help insure that "we have asked the right questions in advance and thought through the implications of various responses." This was the group that recommended what should be done during the 1973 Arab-Israeli war and in several other situations in which U.S. forces were moved in various parts of the world. Second, the Intelligence Committee, made up of the same people, was to oversee the covert operations that the NSC decided should be undertaken abroad without official

U.S. government support. Another intelligence committee decided policy and resource questions for the intelligence community.

The dramatic aspect of the elaborate NSC machinery set up in 1969 was the pervasive influence of Henry Kissinger, assistant for NSC affairs. Even the interdepartmental groups, headed by State Department officials, reported to NSC committees chaired by Kissinger. He initiated most of the National Security Study Memorandums, (NSSMs) that went from the president to the departments and agencies directing studies to be conducted on a wide range of foreign policy and military issues, and he briefed council members on the "options" when the NSC discussed the issues. After the president decided what course of action he wanted to follow, Kissinger drafted the National Security Decision Memorandum (NSDM) for his signature. Thus, he wielded enormous power over the foreign policy making machinery of the government with the support of President Nixon, who found in Kissinger the person he needed in the White House to retain control of foreign policy. The secretary of state, William Rogers, played a secondary role in the decision process, which adversely affected the morale of State Department officials. In 1973 he stepped down and was replaced by Kissinger, who many thought had been de facto secretary for five years. Kissinger did not relinquish his job as assistant to the president for national security affairs; he continued to chair committee meetings in that capacity, and when the National Security Council met, the deputy secretary of state represented the State Department. Kissinger attended these meetings as assistant to the president. This dual role continued in the Ford administration, until Kissinger came under strong congressional criticism in 1975 for keeping both jobs. He then relinquished his White House title to his deputy, Lieutenant General Brent Scowcroft, an air force officer who retired upon elevation to this position.

Despite the grumbling in the bureaucracy about Kissinger's pervasive domination of the NSC machinery and his "close-hold" style of operating, the NSC system that he and Nixon instituted in 1969 worked well in getting the various parts of the executive branch to produce courses of action likely to be effective in dealing with a broad range of foreign policy issues. Critics argued that the system worked only because of the driving energy of Kissinger; others believed that it would produce results regardless of who was in charge, because it engaged the energies of the whole bureaucracy and forced it to discard irrelevant considerations and focus instead on the real issues. The proof of the correct view would not emerge until Kissinger no longer dominated the machinery and a new president decided how he wanted the NSC to operate. In effect, the question was whether Kissinger had indeed created a *system* of foreign policy decision making or whether it was only a new process that had worked for but eight years.

Carter and Brzezinski's National Security Council

Jimmy Carter came to the White House in 1977 with a less formal style of operating than Nixon. But it soon became clear—as his assistant for national security affairs, Dr. Zbigniew Brzezinski, reorganized the NSC staff—that the previous structure would be changed only marginally to give more emphasis to functional areas. In the early months of the new administration, Brzezinski told the press that things would be much different than they had been under Kissinger, but the change was more involved with style and visibility than with the actual operating procedures. One major change, which the president himself insisted upon, was for the new secretary of state, Cyrus Vance, to assume a leading role in policy formulation. Despite press speculation that Brzezinski and Vance would become competitors in the foreign policy arena,[8] it seemed clear at the end of Carter's first year in office that these two highly competent men had achieved a good working relationship, and that Brzezinski was not following in Kissinger's footsteps by trying to overshadow the secretary of state. It was unlikely that Jimmy Carter would have tolerated the situation that Richard Nixon had allowed during his administration.

The Carter NSC abolished many of the committees established by Kissinger, but kept the general structure. The interdepartmental groups were retained with one change: the assistant secretary of defense for international security affairs chaired the group dealing with politico-military affairs. The other five, representing the geographical areas, continued to be chaired by State Department assistant secretaries. The president kept the option of establishing NSC ad hoc groups to handle special issues that do not fit into the six Interdepartmental Groups or are of sufficient importance to warrant a separate task force. He and Brzezinski would choose the chairman for any special group that is formed.

A Policy Review Committee (PRC) replaced the Senior Review Group to handle studies involving longer-range foreign policy issues such as the Panama Canal, the Middle East, or southern Africa. The major difference in this committee, compared to the Kissinger era, is that the chairman of the PRC is a full cabinet member (not a subcabinet official)—most often the secretary of state, although occasionally the secretary of defense or secretary of treasury might serve, depending on the subject under consideration. Brzezinski is a full member of the PRC, however, as are the director of the CIA and the chairman of the Joint Chiefs of Staff. The director of the Office of Management and Budget is frequently involved in PRC discussions, and Vice-President Mondale, whom the president asked to take a direct role in the policy formulation process, attends many PRC meetings.

The functions of the old WSAG, the Verification Panel, and the Intelligence Committee were subsumed in the Carter administration under a new body called the Special Coordination Committee (SCC), headed by Brzezinski. This group handles crisis planning, strategic arms limitation and arms control planning, and oversight of covert intelligence operations. The president and Brzezinski decide which of these two committees—Policy Review or Special Coordination—will be given action on a specific national security problem. It may be argued that Brzezinski thus exercises a strong influence in those areas of special interest to him, leaving other issues to the leadership of secretaries of departments. As of the beginning of 1978, however, no real problems of jurisdiction have come up.

As for the NSC papers prepared in the Carter NSC system, only the names have changed. The NSSM of the Kissinger era has become the Presidential Review Memorandum (PRM) of Brzezinski, and the NSDM has become the Presidential Directive (PD). The process of preparing and reviewing these PRMs is similar to the process under Kissinger, except that the secretary of state now has a larger role in bringing the studies to final form for the president's decision. This does not mean that the president usually accepts the recommendations.

The *style* of the NSC system is quite different under Carter, reflecting his personality and his way of conducting the business of the White House. Carter let it be known before he took office that he would try to appoint cabinet members who were compatible and would work together in relative harmony rather than in conflict, as had happened in so many previous administrations. In picking Cyrus Vance as secretary of state, Harold Brown as secretary of defense, Michael Blumenthal as secretary of treasury, and Brzezinski as national security adviser, Carter formed a national security team he thought would work well together. He also picked a vice-president he thought would work in harmony with this team and would take an active interest in national security problems. Vance and Brown had been colleagues in the Defense Department during the Johnson administration, and Blumenthal and Brzezinski had worked in the State Department during the 1960s. Vance, Blumenthal, and Brzezinski had also been involved in the Trilateral Commission, a private group sponsored by David Rockefeller in the early 1970s to look into political and economic relationships among the United States, Canada, Japan, and Western Europe. Members of this group had recruited Jimmy Carter while he was governor of Georgia and had worked with him during the 1976 election campaign.

Carter, unlike Nixon, is interested in personal contact with the NSC members and meets with them informally on regular occasions. In fact, formal NSC meetings are few, because Carter is in frequent direct touch with its key members and does not require as many formal meetings as Nixon did in his first term. Another factor that reduces the need for NSC meetings is cabinet members sitting on the Policy Review Committee, which produces the various options for presidential decision. Since the PRC's membership is basically the same as that of the

NSC, with the exception of the president, Carter apparently finds it easier to deal with recommendations from the PRC without a formal NSC meeting. The SCC, which has the same membership as the PRC, may be a different matter, because the president must be involved in decision making in crisis situations. There were few of these during Carter's first year in office, and it is not clear how much personal involvement the president will want in SCC discussions not related to crisis management.

The NSC staff, headed by Brzezinski, numbered ninety-six in August 1977, a drop of twenty-nine from what it had been in December 1976 under President Ford. Most of the professional staff (about thirty-nine people) were new, but others had previous experience on the NSC staff. Many of the new professionals were recruited from university faculties, and a high proportion of them had Ph.D. degrees. Although their numbers were fewer than during the Kissinger era, the work load, according to all reports, did not diminish—fourteen-hour work days six days a week are not uncommon. An NSC staff officer's job is to insure that policy recommendations coming to the president are fully developed and ready for Brzezinski's final stamp of approval before the president gets them. However, the NSC staff probably does not have as much "clout" with the other departments and agencies in the executive branch as in the Nixon years, because more of the responsibility for coordinating policy formulation and overseeing implementation of decisions now rests with the State Department. NSC staff members are always present at interdepartmental group meetings, but their role tends to be consultative rather than prescriptive.

Within the State Department, the Policy Planning Staff and the Politico-Military Affairs Staff are responsible for developing the responses to most of the PRMs sent from the White House. They assign studies to interagency working groups that coordinate their studies with those of other agencies doing similar projects in response to White House instructions. When the papers are finished at this level, the Policy Planning Staff or the Politico-Military Affairs Staff sends the study to the Policy Review Committee, where the final debate usually takes place and recommendations to the president are made. President Carter, like Nixon and Ford, desires clear-cut alternatives, and if the principal agencies disagree on the wisdom of recommendations, they are encouraged to make their dissenting views known to the president. During the first year of the Carter administration, about forty PRMs were prepared for his consideration and decision. Most of them dealt with important issues in U.S. foreign policy, and the president's decisions established guidelines for executive departments and agencies involved in national security affairs.

In a perceptive study of the Carter NSC system entitled "Brzezinski—Stepping out of His Backstage Role," Dom Bonafede wrote that "it appears that Carter has restored the prestige of the NSC staff following a brief eclipse during the Ford years and created a national security operation which, in effect, is an amalgamation selectively drawn from the experiences of his predecessors."[9] Carter, he asserts, wants a formally structured NSC staff to help him make decisions, but he also desires more flexible procedures like the regularly scheduled informal luncheon meetings with his top advisers. In effect, Carter has continued the systematic procedures of Nixon in getting the State Department, Defense Department, Central Intelligence Agency, and Treasury Department to produce the best thinking in the executive branch on specific national security and foreign policy problems, while adopting the informal style of Kennedy and Johnson in dealing with his principal subordinates. In addition, he has given the vice-president a role in these deliberations never before conferred on this statutory NSC member. And unlike any of his predecessors since Eisenhower, he has given a leading role to the secretary of state in the policy-planning process. This has given the Department of State a preeminence in foreign affairs that it has not enjoyed since Dean Acheson was secretary of state.[10]

Bonafede observes that "Carter has effectively split the roles played by Brzezinski and Vance, with the former managing day-to-day national security affairs for the president and directing policy studies, and the latter serving as Carter's personal envoy and negotiator and principal foreign policy adviser." It is also clear that Carter seeks advice from other key appointees, including his ambassador to the United Nations, Andrew Young, and his director for arms control, Paul Warnke. Thus Carter, unlike Nixon, apparently wants to be intimately involved in discussions with his key national security team of advisers and does not wish any of them to emerge as preeminent. Whether this style will produce better *decisions* is a question yet to be answered. What we know at present is that Jimmy Carter's style combines informal personal working relationships within the NSC system with a formal mechanism for obtaining the best possible staff work from the executive branch departments and agencies. Since that formal mechanism has endured for the tenure of three presidents, it is now generally referred to as the NSC system.

The President and the War Powers Act of 1973

During the early Nixon/Kissinger years, the media focused so much attention on Kissinger and his NSC staff that it often appeared that national security policy was made *only* in the White House. Clearly, Kissinger's secret negotiations to end the Vietnam war and open the way for Nixon's visit to China in 1971 lent credence to this mythology. Less attention was given to Congress's growing insistence that it be consulted before major decisions were made, particularly on arms limitation and economic agreements with the Soviet Union and on U.S. military and intelligence activities in various parts of the world. Two of Nixon's most dramatic foreign policy defeats were (1) Congress's enactment of the 1973 War Powers Resolution over Nixon's veto, prohibiting any president from using U.S. forces abroad for more than sixty days without the express approval of Congress; and (2) Congress's denial of any assistance—military, economic, or clandestine—to the anti-communist forces in Angola in 1975, despite the fervent urgings of Kissinger. Another defeat was the Senate's refusal to support Nixon's 1971 agreement with Brezhnev regarding "most favored nation" economic relations with the Soviet Union. These rebuffs, and others of lesser impact, made it clear to all who watched the Washington scene that Congress intend-ed to play an increasingly important role in foreign and national security policy, regardless of what Nixon, Ford, or Secretary of State Kissinger desired.

The War Powers Act of 1973 was the most dramatic demonstration of Congress's efforts to curtail presidential authority in national security affairs. It was the culmination of eight years' effort by congressional opponents of the Vietnam war to give Congress the authority to block unilateral decisions by the commander in chief for the use of U.S. forces outside the United States. Nixon's limited invasion of Cambodia in 1970 contributed greatly to the opposition, particularly in the Senate; and congressional testimony in July 1973 revealing that he had commenced secret bombing of Cambodia in 1969 without consulting or informing Congress further fueled their anger, which began to build as U.S. prisoners of war and U.S. forces were withdrawn from Vietnam early in 1973. In fact, the Senate had passed a war powers bill in 1972, but the House had refused to accept it. In July 1973, however, both houses took up the question again, and this time they approved somewhat similar bills by substantial margins.[11] The different versions were debated in conference committee for two months. On October 4, a compromise was reached, in which the Senate agreed to the less specific House language describing situations in which the president could engage in warfare without congressional authority. In the Senate version, the president was allowed to use U.S. troops overseas during emergency situations *only* (1) to repel, retaliate, or forestall an armed attack on the United States, its territories, and possessions; (2) to repel or forestall an attack on U.S. troops abroad; (3) to protect and evacuate U.S. citizens and nationals whose lives were under direct and imminent threat; (4) pursuant to specific statutory authority. In the House version, if there were no declaration of war or statutory authorization, the president could commit troops overseas only in response to "a national emergency created by an attack upon the United States, its territories or possessions, or its armed forces."[12]

The House passed the compromise version of the War Powers Resolution by a vote of 238 to 123 and the Senate, by a vote of 75 to 20. The resolution then went to President Nixon, who vetoed it on the grounds that it was dangerous as well as unconstitutional. In October 1973 the question was not whether Congress favored restricting the president's powers to engage in warfare without congressional approval, but whether it could muster a two-thirds majority to make it the law of the land. The vote in the Senate was never in doubt; an overwhelming majority in the upper chamber had long favored a curtailment of the president's authority. It is doubtful that House supporters of the measure could have mustered a two-thirds majority before October. In that month, two key events changed the political climate in Washington and made the override of the veto a good possibility: first, the Arab-Israeli war, during which Nixon alerted U.S. forces for possible use in the Middle East after Brezhnev apparently warned him that Soviet forces might intervene to save Egypt from defeat by the Israeli army; and second, Nixon's firing of Watergate special prosecutor, Archibald Cox. In the charged Washington atmosphere of November 7, the House voted to override the president's veto by 284 to 135, a four-vote margin in favor; the Senate voted 75 to 18, a thirteen-vote margin. Thus, Congress decisively agreed to restrict the president's powers to use military force abroad. But the measure did not have the president's concurrence. Was the act unconstitutional, as the president claimed? Could it be enforced without presidential concurrence? The legal question would be debated for years, or until the act was tested before the Supreme Court. But the *political* question was settled. Congress had declared overwhelmingly that it must have a role in any future decisions to use U.S. forces outside the United States—otherwise, it would make it impossible for a president to carry out his policies.

The War Powers Act states at the outset that its purpose is "to fulfill the intent of the framers of the Constitution of the United States and insure that the collective judgment of both the Congress and the President will apply to the introduction of United States Armed Forces into hostilities, or into situations where imminent involvement in hostilities is clearly indicated by the circumstances." The key section limiting the president's authority reads as follows:

The constitutional powers of the President as Commander-in-

Chief to introduce United States Armed Forces into hostilities, or into situations where imminent involvement in hostilities is clearly indicated by the circumstances, are exercised only pursuant to (1) a declaration of war, (2) specific statutory authorization, or (3) a national emergency created by attack upon the United States, its territories or possessions, or its armed forces.

The act instructs the president to consult with Congress "in every possible instance" before he sends U.S. forces into hostilities or into situations where hostilities might result. It requires him to send a written report to the speaker of the House of Representatives and the president pro tempore of the Senate within forty-eight hours, setting forth the circumstances necessitating the introduction of U.S. armed forces, the constitutional and legislative authority under which this introduction took place, and the estimated scope and duration of the hostilities. It requires the termination of the commitment of troops abroad within sixty days of the report, *unless* in the meantime Congress declares war, specifically authorizes continuation of the operation, or is physically unable to meet within a sixty-day period because of an attack on the United States. In the absence of any of these conditions, the president must withdraw the forces, although he may be given thirty additional days if he certifies to Congress that the safety of these forces requires the extension. Notwithstanding these provisions, however, the act gives Congress the right, by concurrent resolution, to force the president to terminate any such commitment of forces at any time after the introduction of the forces has taken place. Finally, anticipating that a constitutional challenge might prove successful at some future date, Congress specified that if any provision of the act should be declared invalid, the remainder of the provisions would "not be affected."[13]

The War Powers Act was so closely tied to the demise of Richard Nixon's presidency that some observers believed it would be repealed when another president occupied the White House and Congress was more willing to trust the chief executive. However, the opposite argument is also persuasive; namely, that a whole generation of Americans has become disillusioned with presidential power as a result of the Indochina involvement and their opposition to presidential authority to send Americans abroad to fight will remain strong for many years, or unless some other traumatic event shocks them into giving the president additional powers. The mood of Congress might also change when the senators and congress-men of the 1960s and early 1970s are replaced by younger legislators who were not in government when Lyndon Johnson sent half a million men to Vietnam on the basis of the Tonkin Gulf resolution of 1964.

After Jimmy Carter became president, he stated that he would have no difficulty working within the provisions of the War Powers Act. But after leaving the White House, Gerald Ford criticized the act and said it ought to be repealed. In a speech at the University of Kentucky in April 1977, Ford recalled the difficulty he had had getting in touch with members of Congress during the withdrawal of U.S. civilians from Da Nang when the final crisis occurred in South Vietnam in the spring of 1975:

> When the evacuation of Da Nang was forced upon us during the Congress's Easter Recess, not one of the key bipartisan leaders of the Congress was in Washington. Without mentioning names, here is where we found the leaders of Congress: two were in Mexico, three were in Greece, one was in the Middle East, one was in Europe, and two were in the People's Republic of China. The rest we found in twelve widely scattered states of the Union. This, one might say, is an unfair example, since the Congress was in recess. But it must be remembered that critical world events, especially military operations, seldom wait for the Congress to meet. In fact, most of what goes on in the world happens in the middle of the night, Washington time.[14]

Ford also stated flatly that "there is absolutely no way American foreign policy can be conducted or military operations commanded by 535 members of Congress on Capitol Hill, even if they all happen to be on Capitol Hill when they are needed."

But what roles should the president and Congress have in formulating foreign policy and in meeting foreign crises that may endanger the security of the United States? Ford had these words of advice for his audience and the nation:

> Where, then, does the balance of powers lie? It cannot lie in a constant rivalry for power. As Eugene Rostow has written, this "would tend to convert every crisis of foreign policy into a crisis of will, of pride and of precedence between Congress and the President." The balance must lie, instead, in a frank recognition of the basic strengths and weaknesses of both the executive and legislative branches of government, in the institutional capabilities and limitations imposed by the Constitution and by common sense. The bitter experiences of Vietnam and the national atmosphere in the last decade have encouraged, I believe, too much tampering with that basic machinery by which the United States government has run successfully for the past two hundred years. We must not abandon the wisdom of the ages in the passion of a moment. If we have disagreements of policy, let us resolve them as matters of policy, rather than escalating them into constitutional confrontations.[15]

Conclusion

The conclusion to be drawn from this discussion of the decision-making machinery of the executive branch, and Congress's successful effort to limit the president's war-making authority is that U.S. national security policy in the future will be more ambiguous. The country will not speak with one voice in international affairs as it did from about 1947 to 1973, and the president's judgment of what is in the U.S. national interest will not necessarily be accepted by the Congress. Perhaps this is wise in a democracy. But the nation's ability to deal effectively with the external environment may also be impaired by the growing conflict between the president and Congress over what kind of policies the nation should pursue to increase its security and economic well-being. It is the old argument debated by the framers of the Constitution: Is democracy threatened more by giving too much power to the executive or by giving him too little? In October 1977, one prominent American columnist came to the conclusion that it was time to call a halt to "Congressional Foreign Policy." As Joseph Kraft wrote:

"Congressional foreign policy—or more exactly, domination of foreign policy by the one-issue interests given so much prominence in the congressional process—is a recipe for paralysis, and ought to be ended. But President Carter has reaped the whirlwind of mistrust sown by the Johnson and Nixon administrations. He can rebuild trust of national security only by a long slow process of give and take with the Congress."[16]

8. The Panama Canal Issue

Few issues in U.S. foreign policy have so deeply divided the American people as the announcement in September 1977 that the United States would relinquish control over the Panama Canal at the end of this century. President Carter knew when he signed the two treaties with Panama that a majority of the American people opposed this action and that he would find it exceedingly difficult to obtain Senate ratification. Despite promises made in the 1976 presidential election campaign that he would never give up control of the canal, Jimmy Carter as president decided that it was in the national interest to grant Panama control over large parts of the Canal Zone immediately and full control over the canal by the end of 1999. Why did President Carter change the position of candidate Carter? Why are the American people dubious about the president's judgment in this matter, and why is a vociferous minority so determined to defeat ratification of the treaties in the Senate? What are the prospects for peace in Panama if and when the treaties are ratified?

Since 1903, when the United States acquired the rights to build a canal through the center of Panamanian territory, the construction of a waterway between the Atlantic and Pacific oceans has been an engineering achievement of profound national significance, inspiring national pride as few other achievements have in American history. The canal's completion in 1914 probably had a greater impact on the American people than Lindbergh's historic solo flight across the Atlantic and the astronauts' first landing on the moon. As David

McCullough wrote in his recent best-selling book on the building of the canal:

> The creation of the Panama Canal was far more than a vast, unprecedented feat of engineering. It was a profoundly important historic event and a sweeping drama not unlike that of war. Apart from wars, it represented the largest, most costly single effort ever before mounted anywhere on earth. It held the world's attention over a span of forty years. It affected the lives of tens of thousands of people at every level of society and of virtually every race and nationality. Great reputations were made and destroyed. For numbers of men and women, it was the adventure of a lifetime.[1]

Many of those who participated in this giant enterprise remained in the Canal Zone to help run the canal after 1914, and many of their children as well as other Americans have worked there for long periods of time, some continuously. Countless military men have passed through the canal on ships during wartime, and the waterway has been a great boon to international commerce from the day it began operations. Many Americans have had a large psychological investment in its efficient operation, and it was therefore understandable that most of them saw no reason why the existing legal arrangement between Panama and the United States should be altered in Panama's favor. In short, many Americans who have lived happily in the knowledge that "the canal is American" perceive no national interest that suggests changing the existing arrangements. Therein lies the dilemma for the U.S. government, specifically for the U.S. president: it has been clear to all of them—beginning with John Kennedy—that unless the United States changes the legal arrangements with Panama, U.S. national interests will suffer serious erosion in all of Latin America and in much of the world community. Furthermore, the security of the canal itself probably could not be insured, even with a great increase in the U.S. military presence in Panama. In 1977 President Carter decided that a new treaty arrangement could wait no longer, thereby insuring that the canal issue would become one of the most controversial matters he would face as president.

Historical Background

In January 1903, the United States and Colombia signed a treaty giving the United States the right to build a canal through the Isthmus of Panama, then a province of Colombia. This narrow strip of land between South and North America had provided a land route from the Atlantic to the Pacific oceans for several hundred years, even before the Spanish arrived in the new world. But it was only toward the end of the nineteenth century, following the success of a French effort to build the Suez Canal, that another French company decided to build a sea-level canal there. The French plan in Panama failed, however, and the U.S. government then began to study the feasibility of building a canal through either Nicaragua or Panama. When the choice was made for Panama in 1902, President Theodore Roosevelt used his enormous energy to conclude a treaty with Colombia and get on with the job of constructing the canal. For Roosevelt and other Americans who then felt the imperialist impulse, a canal was essential to move U.S. warships easily from one ocean to the other and to facilitate U.S. and world commerce. When a treaty was negotiated with Colombia early in 1903, therefore, it seemed only a formality to get the document ratified in Bogotá.

But the Colombian Senate unanimously rejected the treaty in August 1903, after months of debate and an effort to persuade Washington to amend its terms. Shock waves reverberated around the U.S. capital. President Roosevelt was angry. The day before the news reached Washington, Senator Cullom, chairman of the Senate Foreign Relations Committee, talked to the press about his luncheon conversation with the president. Roosevelt was prepared for bad news from Bogotá, Cullom said, but he still wanted a canal in Panama. When asked how a canal could be built without a treaty, he replied, "We might make another treaty, not with Colombia but with Panama." Asked whether the United States would foster a revolution in Panama, the senator replied, "No, I suppose not. But this country wants to build that canal and build it now."[2] And so it did. Within a few months, a U.S. cruiser was dispatched to Panamanian waters to show U.S. support for a revolutionary movement that declared Panama's independence from Colombia on November 6, 1903. The coup in Panama City, in which the Colombian garrison capitulated to the revolutionaries, was facilitated by a large sum of American dollars. Although no U.S. forces were involved in the uprising, few doubted there had been U.S. complicity. Washington recognized the new Panamanian government on the same day that it proclaimed its independence.

The way in which the U.S. government obtained a new treaty with the government of Panama to build the canal is not one of the nobler chapters in U.S. diplomacy. Negotiations were carried on in Washington with a Frenchman, Philippe Bunau-Varilla, who had been designated as Panama's negotiator until the new regime could select a permanent representative in Washington. Bunau had a financial interest in the bankrupt French company that had tried earlier to build a canal in Panama, and his negotiations were in part designed to obtain a payment from the United States for the French assets. Bunau hurriedly negotiated a treaty with U.S. Secretary of State John Hay, which proved to be very favorable to the United States. He then signed this treaty on behalf of the Panamanian government, knowing that a delegation from Panama was on its way to Washington for the express purpose of negotiating further with the United States, a fact known to the secretary of state. So the United States concluded a treaty on November 18, 1903, with a French national who did not have instructions to sign the document on behalf of Panama.[3] An immediate controversy ensued in the U.S. Senate and produced a heated debate over ratification of this treaty. The Panamanian government was persuaded, most reluctantly, to ratify the document only after Bunau-Varilla warned that Panama might meet the same fate that Colombia had if the treaty were not ratified quickly. It therefore did so early in 1904. Under terms of a separate agreement, the French company received $40,000,000 from the U.S. government for its property in Panama, the largest real estate transaction in history at that time. Bunau had indeed done his job! On May 4, 1904, the American flag was hoisted in place of the French tricolor at the headquarters of the new Panama Canal Company.

The way in which the 1903 treaty was negotiated and the pressure exerted on Panama to ratify it have rankled the sensibilities of Panamanians almost as much as the treaty's terms. In a report to the United Nations in 1971 concerning negotiations to scrap the 1903 treaty, the Panamanian foreign minister made the following points:

> Panamanian dissatisfaction dates from the very moment that a treaty was concluded which made construction of the canal possible. . . . Historically, this dissatisfaction is fully explained and justified by the circumstances in which the treaty was signed, for it was actually not negotiated with Panama but imposed upon that country and by its contents [sic], which impair national dignity and are the product of an era of rampant imperialism. It is a fact that there were two reasons why Panama wanted the Canal constructed through its territory: the first was that it should be an important factor in national development, and the second, that it should serve as a vital element in international communication. The United States, for its part, needed the Canal as a fundamental factor in building itself up as a world power and as a means of strengthening and expanding its industry and external trade. But Panama's legitimate aspirations were not taken into account in the 1903 Convention. Historically, this generated the evil myth that Panama is a compliant protectorate or abject colony of the United States, and is the reason why the rest of the world has failed to recognize my country's long and solitary struggle to reaffirm its independence and insist on its national dignity, a struggle which began the day after the signing of the 1903 Convention and has not yet been abandoned.[4]

Why did the treaty so arouse the nationalist sensitivities of the Panamanian leaders? The major points of the 1903 agreement were the following: (1) the United States had the right to construct a canal through a ten-mile-wide strip of Panamanian territory; (2) Panama granted the United States all the rights, power, and authority "which the United States would possess and exercise if it were the sovereign of the territory"; (3) the United States held this territory "in perpetuity" (unlike the proposed treaty with Colombia, which had specified a one-hundred-year lease); (4) Panama received ten million dollars upon ratification of the agreement and an annual payment of $250,000. As already noted, representatives of the new Panamanian government were not given an opportunity to see the text of the treaty before it was signed— even though they were on the train to Washington, D.C., before the signing took place at the home of Secretary of State Hay in the evening of November 18. It was not an auspicious beginning for relations between the United States and Panama.

The actual construction of the Panama Canal soon overshadowed the issue of how the treaty had been negotiated, and when the canal opened for traffic on August 15, 1914, it was hailed as the greatest engineering feat in history. The United States earned great prestige for this accomplishment, but the consciences of many Americans were still troubled about the treaty arrangement with Panama. In 1911 Theodore Roosevelt's statement before an audience at the University of California in Berkeley exacerbated this: "The Panama Canal I naturally take special interest in because I started it. There are plenty of other things I started merely because the time had come that whoever was in power would have started them. But the Panama Canal would not have been started if I had not taken hold of it. . . . Fortunately, the crisis came at a period when I could act unhampered [by Congress]. Accordingly, *I took the Isthmus,* started the canal and then left Congress not to debate the canal, but to debate me."[5]

In 1936 and again in 1955, the treaty was revised slightly, and the annual payment to Panama was increased. One of the most irksome aspects of the treaty was changed in 1936, when the United States abrogated its right to intervene in Panama to maintain public order. The nationalist sentiments of many Panamanians were not assuaged, however. After World War II pressure mounted in Panama to revise the treaty so that Panama would have residual sovereignty over the Canal Zone and also to modify the "in perpetuity" language of the treaty. In 1959, when the Panamanian government requested that its flag be flown in the Canal Zone along with the U.S. flag, riots broke out; U.S. military forces were used to prevent demonstrators from hoisting Panama's flag. In 1961, Panama formally asked the United States for negotiations on a new treaty, and in

1962 President Kennedy agreed to such talks. The negotiators announced agreement in 1963 that the Panamanian flag would be flown in the Canal Zone at all places where the U.S. flag was flown by civilian authorities. This action, in effect, signaled that the two governments agreed that Panama had sovereignty over the Canal Zone. On January 9, 1964, three days of rioting broke out after a group of Panamanians tried to hoist their flag in front of the American school in the Canal Zone and were routed by American students. In the ensuing mass violence in Panama City, twenty-one Panamanians were killed and hundreds wounded. Three Americans were also killed, and U.S. military forces were again used. For Lyndon Johnson, who had recently become president, it was a shocking reminder that a political volcano had become active in a neighboring country and that things would never be the same in Panama again. In fact, the riots of January 1964 set a new course in U.S.-Panama relations, one that led ultimately to agreement that Panama should be given control of the canal and all territory surrounding it in 1999.

As a result of the rioting, Panama broke diplomatic relations with the United States on January 10, 1964, and charged the United States with aggression before the UN Security Council. It also filed a complaint with the Inter-American Peace Commission of the Organization of American States and called on the Council of the OAS to take up its charges of aggression against the United States. The OAS then invoked provisions of the Rio Pact in the dispute and asked the parties to negotiate their differences. In April 1964, the governments of Panama and the United States agreed to restore diplomatic relations and appoint special ambassadors to seek solutions to the causes of the conflict between them. Negotiations for a new Panama Canal treaty commenced in January 1965, and later that year the presidents of the two countries agreed on principles to govern negotiations for three new treaties to replace the 1903 accord. In 1967 these negotiations were concluded, but the contents of the proposed agreement were leaked in Panama and the United States and created a furor in both countries. In 1968, a bloodless coup occurred in Panama, and General Omar Torrijos assumed leadership of his country. Two years later

Panama notified the United States that the 1967 draft treaties were unacceptable, and in 1971-1972 the Nixon administration tried unsuccessfully to reach an accord. In 1973 Panama again appealed to the UN Security Council for help, and the United States then vetoed a Security Council resolution calling for a new treaty in which "Panama's effective sovereignty over all of its territory" would be guaranteed. Later that year, Ambassador Ellsworth Bunker was designated as the new U.S. treaty negotiator, and the final phase in the long negotiations with Panama began.

The basis for a new treaty arrangement with Panama to cover jurisdiction in the Canal Zone and operation of the canal was set forth in a Statement of Principles signed in Panama City on February 7, 1974, by Secretary of State Henry Kissinger and Foreign Minister Juan Tack. These principles, which outraged conservative circles in the United States and produced a strong negative reaction among some senators and congressmen, pledged that the United States would turn over the Panama Canal to the Republic of Panama by a fixed date in return for Panamanian assurances that the United States could continue to defend the canal and insure its neutrality. The eight "principles" agreed to were the following: (1) the 1903 treaty would be abrogated and replaced by an entirely new treaty; (2) the concept of "perpetuity" would be eliminated, and the new treaty would have a fixed termination date; (3) U.S. legal jurisdiction over Panamanian territory would be terminated immediately in accordance with terms of the treaty; (4) the Canal Zone would be returned to Panama, with the United States retaining specified rights for its use for the duration of the treaty; (5) Panama would receive a "just and equitable" share of the benefits from canal operations; (6) Panama would participate in the administration of the canal and would assume full control of its operation upon termination of the treaty; (7) Panama and the United States would share in the protection and defense of the canal; and (8) the two countries would agree on any plans to enlarge the capacity of the canal.[6] The two treaties signed by President Carter and General Torrijos on September 7, 1977, embody these eight principles and set December 31, 1999, as the termination date of U.S. control of the Panama Canal.

The National Interests of Panama

Although Panamanian governments have generally been careful not to antagonize the powerful United States, the nationalistic sentiments of the Panamanians were never far beneath the surface. Even though the canal brought prosperity to the country and in the post-1945 period gave Panama the highest per capita income in Latin America, the 1.5 million Panamanians could see their country divided by a ten-mile-wide zone controlled exclusively by a foreign power. They resented this as much as any of the colonial territories of Britain, France, and Belgium had resented colonial rule. In 1946, the United States gave independence to its colonial ward, the Philippines; but there was no similar sentiment in the U.S. Congress, or in the Truman administration, to end a half-century of colonial rule in Panama—or at least to make a new agreement that would change the treaty provision by which the United States held the Canal Zone "in perpetuity." By the 1960s, after the European countries had given up most of their colonial territories in Asia and Africa, the Panamanian government decided that it was time for a confrontation with the United States. The 1964 riots in the Canal Zone and in Panama City provided the pretext. What is remarkable, in retrospect, is that the Panamanian government showed so much restraint between 1964 and 1977—thirteen years—in pressing its case. At no time did it adopt violent tactics against the United States. Perhaps the Panamanians believed that time was on their side and that patience would win out.

The letter of Foreign Minister Juan Tack in 1971 to the UN secretary general clearly shows how Panama viewed its national interests (the following statements are listed according to the four basic national interests described in Chapter 1):

Defense of homeland: Foreign Minister Tack quoted from a United Nations report: "On 10 January 1964, Panama requested the Security Council to consider a grave situation which had arisen between Panama and the United States in connection with the Panama Canal. Panama charged that the situation had been brought about by the repeated threats and acts of aggression of the United States which infringed on the territorial sovereignty of Panama and constituted a serious danger to international peace and security." Panama therefore maintained that the continued division of its country and the use of U.S. troops to prevent it from exercising sovereignty in the Canal Zone constituted a vital threat to its defense interest.

Economic well-being: "The existence of the Canal Zone has deprived Panama since 1903 of its only international harbours and has imposed upon it a condition of servitude which is permanently impoverishing its trade. Thus, we are confronted with an inconceivable phenomenon: a country with two coastlines where, because of its position on an isthmus, the oceans almost meet, has had its maritime development—which would have helped to consolidate not only Panama's territorial unity but also the unity of other huge areas of Latin America— effectively and ineluctably blocked (*sic*)." The economic interest therefore was also at the vital level.

World order: Panama emphasized this as a national interest only to the extent that the Canal Zone represented an in- justice. All Latin American states could sympathize with Panama's plight, as its appeal to the OAS in 1964 had under- scored. Panama's world order interest was evidently major.

Ideological: Panama made its strongest case here: "Gen- eral Panamanian policy toward the Canal Zone is not based on passing incidents. It is rooted in a historic cause: the need to uphold rights which were violated at the very beginning of Panama's existence as an independent nation." At another point, Foreign Minister Tack states: "The fundamental issue, in the view of my Government, is the need to terminate the Convention of 1903, which has been and still is the permanent cause of conflict between our two countries. It prevents the free exercise by Panama of its sovereignty over the whole of its territory, it makes our political independence no more than nominal and deprives us of our economic independence. The existence of this alien authority, which has entrenched itself in the middle of our territory, disrupts our integrity and impedes our efforts to achieve optimum development."[7] For Panama, this, too, was a vital interest.

The Interests of Latin American States

For all Latin American countries, the Panama Canal has become a test case of the United States' willingness to embark on a new relationship in the Caribbean area, a relationship based on justice and mutual respect for national interests. Most Latin American governments see the Canal Zone as a legacy of the past, when U.S. power dominated the political and economic life of the continent and when the United States used military forces to intervene in the Caribbean area whenever it suited its purposes. Although relations have improved since the 1930s, when Franklin Roosevelt inaugurated his "good neighbor" policy, there remains widespread suspicion that different presidents have different views on Latin America. The U.S. support for an insurrection in Guatemala in 1954 and for the Bay of Pigs operation in Cuba in 1961 were reminders of how the U.S. attitude changes. Panama, therefore, has become the key to U.S. relations with the rest of Latin America, and the outcome of the debate within the United States will decide in large measure whether future relationships will be increasingly friendly or increasingly strained. Although it is risky to generalize about Latin America, most of the Latin governments view their interests vis-à-vis the Panama Canal issue roughly as follows:

Defense of homeland: The continuing presence of U.S. forces in the Panama Canal Zone is a reminder of both the military protection the United States provides in this area and the potential threat of U.S. intervention in the political affairs of these states. President Johnson's use of U.S. forces in the Dominican Republic in 1965 increased the awareness of this threat. Therefore, the defense interest of these states is probably at the major level insofar as a U.S. military presence in Panama is concerned.

Economic well-being: Many Latin American leaders privately look upon U.S. control of the Panama Canal as insurance against some radical government's coming into power in Panama and either using the canal for political purposes in relations with certain Latin American countries or raising tolls to the point where they hurt other states' economies. However, Latin American leaders are satisfied that the new treaties provide for continued U.S. control of the canal until the year 2000 and that Panama should by then become a politically and economically stable country. The economic interest is therefore major.

World order: Latin American countries gave full support to Panama in 1964 and again in 1973 when it appealed to the United Nations for help in obtaining a new treaty with the United States to replace the hated 1903 treaty. Whatever doubts may exist about Panama's ability to run the canal and to protect its own territory, there is no question among Latin American states today that Panama has the right to full sovereignty over its territory and that the United States should grant it. Moderate Latin American governments are also concerned that failure to solve the Panama problem peacefully might increase Castro's influence there and cause political instability elsewhere. The world order interest is therefore also major.

Ideological: This is the most important interest for Latin American nations insofar as the Panama Canal issue is concerned. It touches the deep national sentiments of all Latin Americans who want to preserve their independence and sovereignty in international relations. The ten-mile strip of U.S.-owned territory running through Panama is nearly as frustrating, and causes nearly as much resentment, as if the strip ran through their own countries. There is an identity of ideological interests between Panama and the other Latin American countries, all of which have a continuing fear of being manipulated by the great powers. The Panama Canal issue is a litmus test of the United States' intention to pursue justice and human rights in Latin America rather than its own political and economic advantage. In ideological terms, Panama is a *vital* issue for most Latin American countries; therefore, they solidly support Panama.

Sol Linowitz, senior U.S. adviser to the Panama treaty negotiations, put the Latin American case in clear terms to the

American Legion convention in August 1977:

> The Panama Canal issue involves far more than the relation-
> ship between the United States and Panama. It is an issue which
> affects all U.S.–Latin American relations, for all the countries of
> Latin America have joined with Panama in urging a new treaty
> with the United States. In their eyes, the canal runs not just
> through the center of Panama, but through the center of the
> Western Hemisphere. Indeed, the problem significantly affects
> the relationship between this country and the entire Third
> World, since the nations of the Third World have made
> common cause on this issue—looking upon our position in the
> canal as the last vestige of a colonial past which evokes bitter
> memories and deep animosities.[8]

United States Interests in Panama

Panama is an excellent example of how a nation's interests
change over time, in this instance the United States' interests.
In 1903 President Theodore Roosevelt and his administration
unquestionably believed that a canal in Panama, or in
Nicaragua, was *vital* for the United States' new role as a world
power (world order interest) and for its growing world
commerce (economic interest). From a defense and ideological
standpoint, the canal was a *major* interest because it
underscored the United States' military role in the Caribbean
and signalled a renewed interest in "manifest destiny," an
ideological concept that appealed to many Americans and
swelled their national pride. During World War II, the canal
became a vital defense interest because it was essential for
moving troops and supplies expeditiously from one ocean to
another. After World War II, however, the canal declined as a
defense interest and a world order interest. The United States
maintained a two-ocean navy and the new aircraft carriers were
too large to transit the canal. During the Vietnam war, for
example, the carrier U.S.S. Independence, based at Norfolk,
Virginia, sailed to the Far East by way of Africa because the
Panama Canal could not accommodate it for the shorter Pacific
route. In economic terms, too, the canal is no longer of such
interest as in earlier periods. Because of improved technology,
large container ships and supertankers are more efficient in

transporting the world's goods and its oil, but they are too large to use the Panama Canal. Finally, from an ideological standpoint, the United States has been on the defensive in the United Nations and in the Organization of American States for fifteen years because of the archaic relationship it maintains with a tiny Latin American state—Panama—in an age when colonialism is dead. Thus, what was a legitimate vital interest in Panama seventy-five years ago is no longer so in 1978. And the problem of redefining U.S. national interests in the Panama Canal has occupied the attention of the last four U.S. presidents. By 1977, when President Carter signed the two new treaties and sent them to the Senate for ratification, the U.S. interest in the Panama Canal could be assessed as follows:

Defense of homeland: In 1977, neither the Joint Chiefs of Staff nor the secretary of defense argued that the Panama Canal was a vital interest of the United States. General George Brown, chairman of the Joint Chiefs, stated before the Senate Foreign Relations Committee in September 1977 that "the Joint Chiefs of Staff recognize the Panama Canal as a major defense asset, the use of which enhances U.S. capability for timely reinforcement of U.S. Forces." He went on to argue that "U.S. military interests in the Panama Canal are in its use, not its ownership. Therefore, any new treaty must assure that access to and security of the Panama Canal are protected in times of war and peace. This assurance is provided by a permanent regime of neutrality to be maintained by the United States and Panama."[9] Secretary of Defense Harold Brown, addressing the committee the same day, pointed out another aspect of the canal's defense, namely, the United States' "ability to defend the canal from hostile acts—which cannot be ignored. Such hostile acts might not be external. If Panama and other Latin American countries, or major elements of the Panamanian population, became hostile to the United States, then protecting the canal against internal threats, terrorism, and guerrilla actions would become much more difficult. Such occurrences are far less likely under the new treaty than they would be if the long unsettled status quo were to continue."[10] The defense interest is therefore at the *major* level.

Economic well-being: The U.S. economic interest is based on the continued efficient operation of the canal on a non-discriminatory basis, and today this is a *major* rather than a vital interest. The case for the new treaties in this regard was put before the House International Relations Committee in September 1977 by chief U.S. treaty negotiator, Ambassador Ellsworth Bunker: "Two U.S. foreign policy interests are involved in the new canal treaties. The first is our interest—for reasons of both trade and defense—in assured use of an efficiently operated and secure Panama Canal. The second is our interest in cooperative and productive relations with Latin America. The nations to the south of us are important not only as neighbors sharing the same hemisphere, but also as partners in trade and investment, as sources of important raw materials, and as collaborators in building a secure, peaceful, and prosperous world community."[11] Ambassador Bunker's point could be applied as well to the world order interest.

World order: Secretary of State Cyrus Vance made a clear case for the U.S. world order interest before the Senate Foreign Relations Committee on September 26, 1977: "These treaties, in my judgment, will gain us respect among other nations of the world—both large and small—because of the responsible way they resolve complex and emotional issues which have been with us for most of this century. The treaties are the culmination of 13 years' work by four American Presidents of both major political parties and their Secretaries of State. . . . They are, above all, a triumph for the principle of the peaceful and constructive settlement of disputes between nations." At another point the secretary stated: "I believe the ratification and implementation of these treaties will be the single most positive action to be undertaken in recent years in our relations with Latin America."[12] These and other statements of U.S. leaders made it clear that getting ratification of the new canal treaties was a *vital* U.S. world order interest, because the alternative would be a serious blow to U.S. relations with Latin America and with much of the rest of the world. Vance addressed this point when he stated: "It would be all too easy for me to emphasize today that if 13 years of effort were lost, and these treaties were rejected, our relations with Panama would be shattered; our standing in Latin America damaged immeasurably; and the security of the canal itself placed in jeopardy. Indeed, all of these things could and might happen if these treaties were not ratified. But that is not the major reason for supporting them. They deserve support because they are in our interest, as well as the interest of Panama."[13]

Ideological: Finally, it was clear from the debate in the United States that there was a *major* ideological reason for having a new treaty relationship with Panama. Secretary Vance put the case forcefully by arguing that the United States must get rid of its bad image: "The treaties, as negotiated, represent a fair and balanced reconciliation of the interests of the United States and Panama. . . . They symbolize our intentions toward the hemisphere. And they prove, once and for all, the falsity of the tired charges that we are imperialistic exploiters bent only on extracting Latin American raw materials and using the continent for our own economic interests."[14] And Ambassador Bunker put it even more bluntly in a speech in Pittsburgh: "The problem is that we cannot stop the clock of history. We have to cope with reality; we must look to the future; and we must understand that the conditions which created Panama and shaped the world in 1903 do not prevail today." Further on he asserted: "These two treaties protect, in my judgment, our interests in every important respect. They adjust our profile in Panama to a level commensurate with our interests. They eliminate the vestiges of an era which has long since taken its proper place in the history books."[15]

The Debate in the United States

The Panama Canal issue was raised to national attention in the United States in February 1974, when Secretary Kissinger and Foreign Minister Tack signed the Statement of Principles in Panama City. Strong opposition was heard in both houses of Congress and continued for the next three years. On October 7, 1975, a conference report approved in the House by a vote of 212-201 expressed the sense of Congress "that any new Panama Canal treaty or agreement must protect the vital interests of the United States in the Canal Zone and in the operation, maintenance, property and defense of the Panama Canal." In the Senate, a resolution introduced on March 4, 1975, by Senator Strom Thurmond and cosponsored by slightly more than one-third of its members, read in part as follows: "The Government of the United States should maintain and protect its sovereign rights and jurisdiction over the canal and zone, and should in no way cede, dilute, forfeit, negotiate, or transfer any of these sovereign rights, power, authority, jurisdiction, territory, or property that are indispensably necessary for the protection and security of the United States and the entire Western Hemisphere."[16]

The Panama Canal issue also received attention in the presidential election campaign of 1976, when Jimmy Carter was asked in the second televised debate with President Ford, on October 6 in San Francisco: "Would you, as President, be prepared to sign a treaty which at a fixed date yielded administrative and economic control of the Canal Zone and shared defense which, as I understand it, is the position the United States took in 1974?" Carter replied in part, as follows: "I would never give up complete control or practical control of the Panama Canal Zone, but I would continue to negotiate with the Panamanians. When the original treaty was signed back in the early 1900s, when Theodore Roosevelt was President, Panama retained sovereignty over the Panama Canal Zone. We retained control as though we had sovereignty. Now I would be willing to go ahead with negotiations. I believe that we could share more fully responsibilities for the Panama Canal Zone with Panama. . . . But I would not relinquish practical control of the Panama Canal Zone any time in the foreseeable future." In response, President Ford said: "The United States must and will maintain complete access to the Panama Canal. The United States must maintain a defense capability of the Panama Canal, and the United States will maintain our national security interests in the Panama Canal."[17] (Republican candidate Ronald Reagan categorically pledged never to negotiate a new treaty with Panama and referred to its leader as a "tinhorn dictator.")

The significance of Jimmy Carter's statement is that although he appeared to take a hard line against giving up

control of the canal, he recognized Panama's sovereignty over
the Canal Zone and left open the possibility of negotiating a
new treaty that would relinquish control sometime beyond the
"foreseeable future." The new treaties his administration
finally worked out with Panama in the summer of 1977 called
for the United States to turn over control of the canal and all
remaining territory on December 31, 1999, but they also gave
the United States the right to defend the canal beyond the year
1999, if necessary. The president could therefore argue that he
was not giving up "practical control" in the zone so long as the
United States retained the right to return in case of an external
threat. This point was clarified by President Carter and
General Torrijos in Washington in October 1977, when they
agreed to an additional statement about the right of defense:
"The correct interpretation of this principle is that each of the
two countries shall, in accordance with their respective
constitutional processes, defend the canal against any threat to
the regime of neutrality, and consequently shall have the right
to act against any aggression or threat directed against the
Canal or against the peaceful transit of vessels through the
Canal." To protect Torrijos against charges in Panama that
this statement gives the United States the right to intervene in
Panama's internal affairs, the statement further stipulates:
"This does not mean, nor shall it be interpreted as a right of
intervention of the United States in the internal affairs of
Panama. Any United States action will be directed at ensuring
that the Canal will remain open, secure and accessible, and it
shall never be directed against the territorial integrity or
political independence of Panama."[18]

But the real question in the United States was not what *kind*
of treaty there should be with Panama, but *whether* there
should be a new treaty at all. In his address to the American
Legion convention cited earlier, Sol Linowitz made a forceful
case for the treaties:

> Our primary interest in the canal is to assure its free, open, and
> neutral operation on a non-discriminatory basis. I am
> convinced that the greatest threat to the operation and security
> of the canal would be to try to insist upon retention of the

present outmoded treaty and its anachronistic provisions—
provisions which have in the past and can so easily again—
trigger hostility and violence. If we do not approve a mutually
agreeable basis for a new treaty, we may find ourselves in the
position of having to defend the canal by force against a hostile
population and in the face of widespread, if not universal,
condemnation.[19]

But the opposition to the treaties argued that Panama could
not be trusted to keep the canal open to all shipping if it got
control of the waterway. Retired chairman of the Joint Chiefs
of Staff, Thomas Moorer, told the Senate Foreign Relations
Committee that the Panamanian leader, General Omar
Torrijos, was openly leftist in his political sympathies and
would seek closer relations with Cuba. He was quoted by the
Washington Post as saying: "Do not be surprised, if the treaty
is ratified in its present form, to see a Soviet and/or a Cuban
presence quickly established in the country of Panama."[20] This
type of argument, and the public support it drew, caused many
members of the Senate to remain undecided on whether to vote
for ratification of the treaties when they were presented to the
Senate early in 1978. The main reason was that American
public opinion was still very skeptical of the new treaties
despite the Carter administration's best efforts to educate it. A
Gallup poll conducted in October 1977 showed that 46 percent
of the public opposed the treaties, 39 percent favored them, and
15 percent were undecided.[21] Other polls showed an even larger
proportion opposing the treaties. The tough political question
for President Carter was whether an educational program for
the American public would increase the number of those
favoring the treaties and whether two-thirds of the Senate could
be mustered to vote for them early in 1978.

The national interests of the United States, Panama, and the
Latin American countries in obtaining a new canal treaty
arrangement may be summarized on a national interest matrix
(Chart 8.1). That is, Panama has a vital interest in getting a new
treaty insuring its control over all its territory and eventual
control of the canal itself. The United States has a major
interest at stake in the Panama Canal, but a vital interest in
seeing that the canal issue is resolved peacefully.

CHART 8.1

```
        Issue:  New treaties between US and Panama


Basic interest at stake                  Intensity of interest
                          Survival   Vital     Major        Peripheral

   Defense of homeland               Panama    US
                                               Latin America

   Economic well-being              Panama    US
                                               Latin America

   Favorable world order                       US        Latin America
                                                          Panama

   Ideological                       Panama    US
                                     Latin
                                     America
```

Scenarios for U.S.-Panamanian Relations

Given the high stakes involved in Senate ratification of the new Panama Canal treaties, what are the likely scenarios that could emerge in this situation? The obvious one that loomed at the end of 1977 was that the U.S. Senate might not ratify the new treaties early in 1978, as the Carter administration hoped. This was a real possibility: a UPI poll of senators during November 1977 showed that twenty-nine opposed the treaties, only thirty-nine were in favor, and thirty-seven were uncommitted. Since treaties require a two-thirds majority for approval, opponents needed only five more votes, or thirty-four if all others voted affirmatively, to prevent ratification—a not inconceivable possibility in view of the large number of uncommitted senators.[22] The Senate majority leader, Robert Byrd, subsequently stated that he planned to bring the treaties up for debate and approval in the Senate early in 1978 but that he would do so only if he could be sure of a two-thirds vote for ratification. The prospects for an early favorable vote in the Senate were not at all clear, therefore, and this sets the stage for the first scenario.

Scenario 1: The U.S. Senate rejects ratification of the Panama Canal treaties by a vote of sixty-two in favor, thirty-five against, and three absences. In this situation, the national interests of the three principal parties to the canal controversy will change from what they had been in September 1977, when the treaties were signed. Chart 8.2 illustrates this:

CHART 8.2

Issue: Senate rejects Panama Canal treaties				
Basic interest at stake		Intensity of interest		
	Survival	Vital	Major	Peripheral
Defense of homeland		Panama US	Latin America	
Economic well-being		Panama	US Latin America	
Favorable world order		Panama US	Latin America	
Ideological	Panama	Latin America	US	

The significant changes are that the ideological interest of Panama now becomes *survival,* and the defense interest of the United States moves up to *vital.* Why? Because rejection of the treaties after thirteen years of waiting will be a crushing blow to Panama and will generate deep emotional reactions. Getting the Americans out of the Canal Zone will then become almost a holy war against a colonialist power, and mass violence will almost inevitably ensue. The U.S. defense interest in the Panama Canal will become vital, because it will then be necessary to defend the Canal Zone and the Americans living there against terrorist attacks and violent demonstrations by Panamanians.

The likely results of this scenario would be the following: General Torrijos resigns as head of the Panamanian govern-ment and turns over leadership to a nationalistic group pledged to take the canal issue to the United Nations and have the United States branded as an unlawful occupier of Panamanian territory. President Carter asks for calm and tells Panama he will resubmit the treaties to the Senate in 1979 with a view to including several amendments designed to produce a two-thirds majority in favor of ratification. Treaty opponents in the United States are elated and double their efforts to elect senators and congressmen in 1978 who share their conservative views. A wave of anti-Americanism engulfs Latin America, and demonstrations against U.S. embassies and U.S. business interests are widespread.

Scenario 2: A preliminary vote in the Senate on ratification of the Panama Canal treaties indicates that a majority of senators (fifty-seven) are in favor of the treaties, thirty-two are opposed, and eleven others either did not vote or remained uncommitted. Senator Byrd, the majority leader, announces that the Senate will put off further discussion until June 1978. In this situation, there is no rejection of the treaties, but the negative vote is so close to thirty-four that President Carter is unwilling to risk an immediate and final vote on the issue. The implication is that ratification might be put off until after the November 1978 congressional elections. The likely repercussions of this turn of events would be as follows:

In the United States, opponents of the treaties claim a victory and try to make ratification a key issue in the 1978 elections in order to delay final action until 1979 and use the treaties issue to elect senators and congressmen who share their antitreaty viewpoint. The Carter administration redoubles its efforts to obtain a favorable vote in June 1978, or sooner, and pleads with uncommitted senators to "help the president" in this crucial foreign policy crisis.

In Panama, General Torrijos's government tries to put the best face on the situation and cautions Panamanians not to judge too quickly President Carter's ability to bring the reluctant Senate to his viewpoint. Panamanian students become more difficult to control, however, and demonstrations urging Torrijos to take the issue to the United Nations increase. There are minor incidents in the Canal Zone, precipitated by Americans, over various provisions of the treaties pertaining to Panamanian rights in the zone. General Torrijos is able to contain mass demonstrations in Panama but warns that he is powerless to prevent incidents from occurring in the zone and spilling over into Panama—as occurred in 1964. General Torrijos begins privately to explore his options in anticipation that the U.S. Senate will not ratify the treaties.

In Latin America, press comment asks whether the United States is capable of wise leadership in the Western Hemisphere and whether the Carter administration can deliver on foreign policy commitments in Panama or anywhere else in Latin America. Leftist groups become more vocally anti-American, and their leaders suggest that Castro was right: only strong action against the United States ever gets results.

Scenario 3: The Senate ratifies the Panama Canal treaties, with two amendments previously approved by President Carter and General Torrijos. Great satisfaction is expressed in Washington, Panama, and Latin American capitals about the favorable outcome of thirteen years of negotiations. Within a year, however, Panamanian nationalists begin to press for a faster transfer of zone territory to Panamanian control and for complete control of the canal by 1985. General Torrijos asks for negotiations with the United States to revise the treaties following student demonstrations in Panama City.

In this situation, the national interests of Panama, the United States, and Latin America will be similar to those shown in Chart 8.3. The significance here is that although Panama perceives its economic and ideological interests to be vital, the United States has vital defense and economic interests. Washington has deep concerns about whether Panama could run the canal efficiently by 1985 and about whether U.S.

CHART 8.3

Issue: Panama requests turnover of Canal in 1985				
Basic interest at stake		Intensity of interest		
	Survival	Vital	Major	Peripheral
Defense of homeland		US	Panama	Latin America
Economic well-being		US Panama	Latin America	
Favorable world order			Panama Latin America US	
Ideological		Panama	US Latin America	

defense capabilities in the Caribbean could be protected in the 1980s if Canal Zone installations were denied. Latin American countries would have a major interest in the issue, particularly from an economic standpoint.

The policy implications of this scenario could be ominous for U.S.-Panamanian relations if not handled with great care. There is almost no likelihood, particularly before the 1980 U.S. presidential elections, that President Carter would agree to new negotiations to turn the canal over to Panama sooner. Even a request from Panama for negotiations would prove highly embarrassing to the administration, which staked so much of its prestige on getting the treaties ratified by a reluctant Senate. Looking at the issue from General Torrijos's standpoint, however, he might conclude that Panama had given up too much by agreeing to the treaty amendments—giving the United States the unilateral right to protect the canal after the year 2000—and he might be persuaded by poor economic conditions in Panama to seek greater financial benefits from the canal. Although it is unlikely that Torrijos could be ousted as Panamanian leader if he refused to accept the demands of Panamanian nationalists for treaty changes, he might decide to shift the onus onto Washington for a refusal to discuss these questions, rather than take a hard line himself against reopening the treaty question. The most likely outcome of this scenario is that General Torrijos will wait until 1981 to ask the United States for negotiations. Washington will probably refuse to turn the canal over at an earlier date, but it might be willing to negotiate some of the less crucial provisions of the 1977 treaties.

The Outlook

As of the end of 1977, the third scenario was the most likely outcome of the political situation.[23] It is almost inconceivable that a large majority of the U.S. Senate would permit a minority to strike a disastrous blow to U.S. foreign policy, as would surely be done if the treaties were rejected by thirty-four senators who care nothing about Latin American and world opinion and refuse to make changes in the U.S. relationship with Panama. It is more likely that the ratified treaties will become a rallying point for conservative U.S. politicians who wish to unseat moderate and liberal candidates in senatorial and congressional elections in 1978 and 1980. Depending on the political mood of the U.S. electorate in the next few years, the slogan "Remember the Canal Sellout" might be heard in certain districts where elections are won and lost by a few thousand votes. Whether the Republican Party will accept this line is problematical; much depends on how the battle for control of that party looks when the nominating convention meets in 1980 to choose its presidential candidate. If conservative political forces led by Senator Helms of North Carolina and former Governor Reagan of California are in the ascendancy in the party leadership by 1980, then the Panama treaties could be an important rallying point in the election campaign. If the Republicans nominate a moderate such as Senator Baker of Tennessee or Governor Thompson of Illinois, the Panama issue will not be important in the 1980 elections.

In Panama, General Torrijos will probably become a national hero and be elected president of his own country. Forty-eight years old in 1977, he will set his eye on remaining the country's leader until the canal is turned over to Panama on December 31, 1999, or earlier. Torrijos will have much prestige in Panama and in Latin America, and he will become one of the United States' leading friends in Latin America. He may even help the United States to improve relations with other states in the Caribbean area, including Cuba. Senate ratification of the treaties will usher in a whole new era in Western Hemisphere relations, and Jimmy Carter will become the most respected U.S. president (among Latin Americans) in this century.

In the final analysis, the Panama issue turns on whether the U.S. public is prepared in 1978 to let reason prevail over emotion in resolving this crucial matter. Unlike most foreign policy issues, which result from the United States' expanded world role since 1945, this one predates both world wars and is deeply tied up with another period in U.S. history— one that stirs the longings of many Americans for a simpler era in U.S. relations with Latin America. President Carter risked much on the need for a new relationship with Panama and Latin America. The maturity of the United States as a nation will be tested in the way the Congress responds to his leadership on this key issue in the next several years as the Canal Zone is gradually returned to Panama.

9. The Prospect of Quebec's Separation from Canada

On November 15, 1976, the viability of the Canadian Confederation was placed sharply in question: the voters of Quebec Province gave a majority of seats in the provincial assembly to the Parti Québécois, whose avowed objective is the independence of Quebec. This unexpected event sent shock waves throughout Canada, but particularly to the federal government in Ottawa headed by Prime Minister Pierre Elliott Trudeau, himself from Quebec. The election also brought into the open an intense discussion that has dominated Canadian politics for the past decade: can Quebec be persuaded to remain in the confederation, and if not, can Canada survive as a nation? For Prime Minister Trudeau, the separation of Quebec would be a political calamity, because it would mark the failure of more than a decade of intense effort by his government to persuade Quebecers to remain in Canada; and it would cause his ruling Liberal Party to lose its majority status in Canadian politics. For René Lévesque, premier of Quebec, independence would mark the culmination of a dream that French Canadians have kept alive for more than two hundred years—to be free of English domination and to have the fruits of sovereignty. The outcome of the emerging struggle between Ottawa and Quebec would have a profound effect not only on the future of Canada, but it would also deeply affect the interests of its southern neighbor, the United States.

Claude Morin, one of the new Quebec government leaders, stated a few weeks after the election that "what we shall propose to the rest of the nation of Canada when the time has come is a new type of association which shall take into account requirements of economic independence as well as the historical and natural aspirations of Quebecers to be the masters of their own national destiny."[1] Prime Minister Trudeau expressed his deep concern in a year-end television interview: "I'm letting people know that they shouldn't count on me to keep Quebec in by force of arms if Quebec overwhelmingly decides that it doesn't want to be a country in Canada." Trudeau said he did not believe that more concessions to Quebec, at the expense of federal authority, would dissuade the Parti Québécois from pushing its program of separation. He conceded that violence could erupt over this issue: "We have all kinds of contemporary examples of the absurdity of trying to solve the differences of ethnic or religious principles by arms. You start shooting and you don't easily stop."[2]

Most Canadians are keenly aware of the historical background of the Quebec problem, but most people in the United States are not. In 1775, for example, the American Continental Congress sent Benjamin Franklin to Montreal in an effort to persuade Quebec's leaders to join the thirteen colonies in their struggle against British domination. But this effort foundered because the Americans would not give Quebecers assurances of cultural autonomy if they joined in forming the United States. Having lost its freedom when France was defeated by Britain in 1759 and then withdrew from North America, Quebec decided to insulate itself and jealously guarded its language and culture from English influence for over two hundred years. Indeed, French Canadians refused to be drafted for overseas duty in both world wars and have kept their national aspirations alive for two centuries, even though they had little chance of success until the 1970s.

Following the U.S. Civil War, Britain decided for political and security reasons to merge its two largest North American colonies—Quebec and Ontario—into a confederation and give it a large degree of self-government. The British North America Act of 1867 was seen as the basis on which Britain could carve out a continental nation in North America that would remain within the British Empire (later Commonwealth) and be able to resist the expansionist tendencies of the United States, tendencies that gained momentum after its civil war. The North America Act guaranteed Quebec cultural and, to a large degree, social autonomy within the new confederation; and on this basis of partnership between English-speaking and French-speaking provinces, the new nation of Canada was formed. Britain continued to provide for Canada's defense and conducted its foreign relations. Quebec's political leaders followed traditional ways of running the province for nearly a century, and the price they paid was economic stagnation, social immobility, and the undereducation of several generations of Quebec citizens. The cultural insularity of the French-speaking Quebecers caused most of them to become second-class citizens in their own country while English-speaking residents dominated trade and commerce and the financial institutions of Quebec. English-speaking Canadians made little effort to learn French or to deal with French Canadians as fellow citizens. In good British tradition, they assumed that if one did not speak English and adopt English manners, one simply did not count.[3]

Things began to change rapidly in Quebec in 1960 with the beginning of the "Quiet Revolution," initiated by a new provincial premier, Jean Lesage. The power of the church over the educational system and political life was broken, and the new government instituted a modernization program for Quebec's backward economy. Lesage attracted to his cause a group of brilliant young leaders to help lift Quebec out of its backwardness and assert a new role in Canadian and world affairs. Two of these bright young men were Pierre Elliott Trudeau and René Lévesque—currently the prime minister of Canada and the premier of Quebec, respectively. Both were members of the provincial Liberal Party of Quebec during the early 1960s and were associated with the national Liberal Party led by Lester Pearson, prime minister of Canada from 1963 to 1968. Lévesque broke with the Liberals, however, and in 1967 helped form the new Parti Québécois, which was dedicated to the eventual separation of Quebec from Canada. Trudeau, on the other hand, remained with the Liberals and in 1965 was appointed a cabinet minister in Ottawa. After the 1968 national elections, he became prime minister and has remained so since then. Personal rivalry between these two highly talented French Canadian political leaders has had some influence on their relationships since 1968, but their differences are centered on the issue of whether Canada or Quebec should come first in their loyalties.

When Trudeau formed his government in Ottawa in 1968, it was clear to him and to other Liberal Party leaders that time was beginning to run out in Quebec and that significant measures would have to be taken by the federal government to accommodate the national aspirations of the six million French-speaking Quebecers. The Liberal Party thought that Trudeau, a well-known French-Canadian professor of law, would be a good choice as prime minister because they felt he could undercut the appeal of Quebec nationalists who demanded independence. The Liberals also knew they could not remain a major national party without Quebec, where they drew much of their support in national elections.[4]

One of Trudeau's first efforts to bridge the gulf between Quebec and the rest of Canada was to push through legislation declaring that both French and English were official languages of Canada. This was designed to placate those French Canadians who chafed under the necessity of speaking English whenever they traveled outside their province as well as those who lived in other provinces but were not able to carry on official business in their native tongue. Instead of satisfying the Quebecers, however, the official languages act only whetted the appetite of those who wanted to make French the *only* official language in Quebec. As a result of this sentiment, the Quebec provincial assembly adopted legislation in 1975 making French the official language, much to the chagrin of the English-speaking minority. The irony is that this act was pushed through by the ruling Liberal Party government of Robert Bourassa in the hope that it would satisfy moderate nationalist sentiment in Quebec and undercut the separatist appeal of the opposition Parti Québécois. The effort failed to prevent the Parti Québécois from winning the election, but it indicated that the language issue could unite Quebecers of nearly all political persuasions, especially the 80 percent who spoke only French or used it as their first language. Thus, when Lévesque's government came to power, one of its first objectives was to carry the language issue a step further by requiring all children in Quebec to attend French-speaking public schools unless one of the parents had attended an English primary school. This requirement was waived for those who had lived in Quebec for less than three years, and the act clearly did not prevent parents from sending their children to private English-speaking schools if they wished. The law was resented particularly by immigrant families in Quebec whose children could not obtain a public education in the English language.

A powerful impetus to Quebec nationalism was provided by French president Charles de Gaulle, who visited Montreal in July 1967 and addressed a large crowd with the words: "Long Live Free Quebec." It might well be said that independence sentiment caught fire in Quebec that day and that many of Prime Minister Trudeau's policies since then have been a valiant effort to douse the fire before it burns down the house of Canadian confederation. The Ottawa government was so outraged at de Gaulle's behavior that it refused to allow him to continue his trip to the Canadian capital, and he was obliged to return to France. But his objective had been served—to renew the struggle that was halted on the Plains of Abraham at Quebec City in 1759, when General Montcalm was defeated by General Wolfe and France abandoned North America to the Anglo-Saxons. Ten years later, in November 1977, René Lévesque, the potential premier of an independent French-speaking state in North America, was received in Paris by the French government with a welcome usually accorded only to heads of state. The president of France, Valery Giscard d'Estaing, was quoted as saying that Quebec had a right to self-determination and that Premier Lévesque could count on France's support for whatever course of action his government chose to take.[5] The French government thus appeared to lend its support to the Quebec independence movement in the forthcoming debate within Canada.

The National Interests of Canada

To understand the future of Quebec and its impact on the rest of Canada and the United States, let us first examine how Canada sees its overall national interests and the policies it has pursued to defend and enhance them. Shortly after coming to power in 1968, the Trudeau government initiated a study of Canada's objectives in foreign policy. The result was a series of pamphlets published by the Department of External Affairs in 1970 entitled *Foreign Policy for Canadians*. The first of these was a lucid statement of Canada's objectives in the world, and it placed considerable emphasis on defining Canada's national interests in a rapidly changing international environment.[6] At the outset, the Ottawa government stated that Canadian foreign policy must reflect the domestic needs of the Canadian people: "Canada, like other states, must act according to how it perceives its aims and interest. External activities should be directly related to national policies pursued within Canada, and serve the same objectives. . . . In essence, foreign policy is the product of the government's progressive definition and pursuit of national aims and interests in the international environment. It is the extension abroad of national policies."[7] In a section entitled "Basic National Aims," this document states: "In developing policies to serve the national interests, the Government has set for itself basic national aims," which embrace three essential ideas: (1) that "Canada will continue secure as an independent political entity." (This aim corresponds to the aforementioned "defense interest" of a sovereign state.) (2) that "Canada and all Canadians will enjoy enlarging prosperity in the widest possible sense" ("economic well-being" interest.) (3) that "all Canadians will see in the life they have and the contribution they make to humanity something worthwhile preserving in identity and purpose." (This aim corresponds to an "ideological interest" because it reflects what Canadians believe they stand for as a people.) The Canadian document has no category relating specifically to "world order interest." But this objective is addressed in another section: "Canada has less reason than most countries to anticipate conflicts between its national aims and those of the international community as a whole. . . . Peace in all its manifestations, economic and social progress, environmental control, the development of international law and institutions—these are international goals which fall squarely into that category."[8]

This statement of the Canadian government's foreign policy priorities was based on "two inescapable realities, both crucial to Canada's continuing existence" (survival interests): (1) "Internally, there is the multi-faceted problem of maintaining national unity. It is political, economic and social in nature; it is not confined to any one province, region or group of citizens"; (2) "Externally, there is the complex problem of living distinct from but in harmony with the world's most powerful and dynamic nation, the United States."[9] These and other pronouncements by the Trudeau government early in its tenure in Ottawa showed that it feared two principal threats to Canada's status as a fully independent country: first, the separation of Quebec, which would deprive Canada of nearly 30 percent of its population and isolate the four Atlantic provinces from the rest of the country; and second, the danger to Canada of an overwhelming dependence on the United States for economic well-being and the danger of the cultural impact of 220 million Americans on 22 million Canadians. The Trudeau government concluded that these issues were closely linked in securing the political viability of Canada because, in order to improve the prospects for keeping Quebec in the confederation, Canada must become a multicultural society not tied inextricably to the English-speaking colossus to the south. Trudeau thus sought to prevent Quebec from moving away from Canada and at the same time, to prevent Canada from moving toward the United States. In a word, the survival of the Canadian state was in jeopardy if the federal government was unable to build a strong national unity around a distinctly Canadian cultural identity. For Trudeau and the Liberal Party, it became a race against time: they believed there could be no separate Canadian identity without the participation of Quebec. Yet, Quebecers were told by the Parti Québécois that they could not retain their French-based cultural identity unless they formed a political state of their own. According to Dale Thompson, René Lévesque regularly told his fellow Quebecers that if independence were not achieved within ten years, "no one will have the right to speak French in Quebec."[10]

In the fall of 1972, Canadian Secretary of State for External Affairs, Mitchell Sharp, wrote a long article for the official journal *International Perspectives* entitled: "Canada-U.S. Relations: Options for the Future." In it, Sharp clearly laid out the dilemma in Canadian foreign policy posed by the overwhelming influence of the United States and outlined the policies the Trudeau government would follow to cope with this apparent threat to Canada's national interests. In the introduction, Sharp stated:

> The Canada-U.S. relationship, as it has evolved since the end of the Second World War, is in many respects a unique phenomenon. It is by far our most important external relationship, but it is more than an external relationship. It impinges on virtually every aspect of the Canadian national interest, and thus of Canadian domestic concerns. Because of the vast disparity in power and population, it is also inevitably a relationship of profoundly unequal dependence; the impact of the United States on Canada is far greater than Canada's impact on the United States.[11]

Sharp's concern was that Canada's strategic dependence on the United States, which had grown out of World War II, had caused the country to become economically dependent as well and that cultural pressures were also growing at an alarming rate. The thrust of his argument was that Canada would lose its independence if it continued along the road of "continentalism" and that the trend must be reversed. He cited three options for Canadian policy in relation to the United States: "a) we can seek to maintain more or less our present relationship with the United States with a minimum of policy adjustments; b) we can move deliberately toward closer integration with the United States; c) we can pursue a comprehensive long-term strategy to develop and strengthen the Canadian economy and other aspects of our national life and in the process to reduce the present Canadian vulnerability."[12] Sharp gave several reasons why the first two options were unacceptable to

Canadians and then argued strongly for option three:

> The basic aim of the third option would be, over time, to lessen
> the vulnerability of the Canadian economy to external factors,
> including, in particular, the impact of the United States and, in
> the process, to strengthen our capacity to advance basic
> Canadian goals and develop a more confident sense of national
> identity. . . . The accent of the option is on Canada. It tries to
> come to grips with one of the unanswered questions that runs
> through so much of the Canada-U.S. relationship, which is
> what kind of Canada it is that Canadians actually want. It is in
> no sense an anti-American option. On the contrary, it is the one
> option of all those presented that recognizes that, in the final
> analysis, it may be for the Canadian physician to heal himself.[13]

Since Canada's new policy toward the United States was
enunciated in 1972, the Ottawa government has enacted an
investment review law that now screens all new foreign
investment to insure that Canada's economic interests are
protected; it has placed restrictions on Canadian advertising on
U.S. television programs watched by Canadians; and it has
given support to Canadian writers, artists, musicians, and
other cultural activities in order to create a greater Canadian
awareness of a distinct national identity. It has also tried to
promote an appreciation of French language and culture in the
English-speaking parts of the country. All senior Canadian
officials were obliged to learn French and English. These
programs generated some criticism because many English-
speaking Canadians saw them as an effort to "buy off"
Quebecers, to persuade them to vote against the Parti
Québécois. Insofar as U.S.-Canadian relations are concerned,
the implementation of option three has not had a serious effect
on U.S. economic interests in Canada; but official relations
between representatives of the two countries became less
cordial. By 1976, relations improved again as Canada
experienced economic difficulties at home.[14]

In sum, Canada's national interests in the 1970s might be
stated as follows:

Defense interest: Canada's contribution to continental

defense is small but significant and must be closely integrated with that of the United States. There is little reason to change that relationship.

Economic interest: With two-thirds of its imports and two-thirds of its exports being with the United States, Canada feels it must diversify its trade and other economic relationships if it desires to escape creeping integration into the U.S. economy— with the implications of political dependency.

World order interest: Canada needs to demonstrate an independent policy in the world in order to avoid being seen as an American satellite by other nations; and it should build closer relations with Francophone nations in order to make French Canadians feel more comfortable within the Canadian confederation.

Ideological interest: Canada must instill a deeper appreciation of its own cultural identity in order to avoid being absorbed into the U.S. cultural orbit. If it cannot solve the cultural identity problem, it will find it difficult to remain separate from U.S. culture. Some observers have called this the new Canadian nationalism. It might also be termed Canada's struggle for survival.

The National Aims of Quebec Separatists

Although the Parti Québécois campaigned primarily on a reform platform in the provincial election of November 1976, it has never left a doubt about its ultimate goal: independence and sovereignty in economic association with the rest of Canada, particularly Ontario. The party's program was outlined in a 1975 pamphlet published in several languages and entitled "Summary of the Programme and the Statutes of the Parti Québécois." In a section entitled "The Political Life in a Sovereign Quebec," the party manifesto states:

> Now, four centuries of a common history have made Quebecers a *nation*. Quebecers have an indisputable desire to live together and to preserve their own culture as it has been enriched by the contributions of each ethnic group which has chosen to live with us. . . . Meanwhile, Quebec does not yet have the political

levers which will give it the means to guarantee its cultural and economic existence. In effect, the power is exercised at the federal parliament by a foreign majority, and with one government of eleven in the federal-provincial conferences. Quebec is always a minority in Canada. No people can run the risk of entrusting its destiny to others.[15]

The party promised to gain independence for Quebec by democratic means once it was voted into power. Its plan was first, to ask Ottawa to give it the powers of sovereignty, except those the two governments would agree upon "to develop an economic association" between them; second, if Ottawa does not accept this proposal, to hold a referendum in Quebec to obtain the consent of the citizens to proceed with independence; third, to give Quebec a new constitution; and fourth, to ask for admission to the United Nations and seek the recognition of other countries. In 1977 the Lévesque government reversed the order of the first two steps—the referendum is to be scheduled first.

Once independence is achieved, according to the party document, Quebec's foreign policy would be guided by two basic goals: (1) to "safeguard the interests of the Quebec people, peace, security, and the necessity of interdependence and economic and socio-cultural contributions of other states"; (2) solidarity of the Quebec people with "the people on the road to development," presumably with the Third World nations. Quebec would follow policies that promote freedom for people desiring independence, oppose all forms of colonialism, refuse to be a party to any guarantee of regimes that do not accept the UN Charter on Human Rights, seek "good relations with the international community," and create a "research unit" that would "oversee the elimination of political intervention" by multinational companies operating in Quebec. "As long as Quebec is a part of the Canadian federation," the document asserts, "it will be impossible to be recognized as a member of the international community and to participate in the cooperation and exchanges which are becoming stronger and stronger among nations. In the past, we have been isolated from the world in many respects."[16]

After coming to power in November 1976, the Parti Québécois began implementing its domestic program, most notably a new language law that requires most children to attend French-speaking public schools. It promised to hold a referendum in Quebec within two or three years, and it has begun drafting the rules that will govern the referendum. An opinion poll conducted in October 1977 showed that fewer than one-fifth of the eligible voters favor outright independence for Quebec and that only 45 percent favor it if it could be accomplished in economic association with Canada, particularly with Ontario.[17] René Lévesque, however, believes that when Quebec declares its independence, other provinces will inevitably agree to economic association, because it will be in their interest as well as Quebec's. In an article he wrote for *Foreign Affairs* before becoming premier, Lévesque stated: "Such a scenario would call, as a decisive first step, for a customs union, as full-fledged as both countries consider to be mutually advantageous. . . . For indisputably such a partnership, carefully negotiated on the basis of equality, is bound to be in the cards." He envisaged that Quebec would develop along social democratic lines "rather comparable to the Scandinavian models"; and in foreign policy, he thought "Quebec's most privileged links, aside from its most essential relationship with the Canadian partner, would be first with the United States—where there is no imaginable reason to frown on such a tardy but natural and healthy development." Thereafter Quebec would look to other Francophone or "Latin" countries and to France itself—"who would certainly not be indifferent to the fact that this new nation would constitute the second most important French-speaking country in the world."[18] Judging by the warm reception Lévesque received in Paris in November 1977, he can count on diplomatic support from at least one European power. The major question remained, however: what would U.S. policy be if and when Quebec declared its independence from Canada?

United States Interests in Canada

Much has been written about the "special relationship"

between the United States and Canada in the past twenty years; and indeed, there was a special way in which Washington and Ottawa conducted their business—more informal, more diversified among various government departments and agencies, and more frequent interchanges at many levels of government. The special relationship was most notable in the defense field, where the two countries formed the North American Air Defense Command in 1958 and entered into several other agreements whereby their armed forces worked in close harmony. It was also notable in the economic field, where Canada's economic needs were usually given special consideration because of the enormous trade between the two countries—the largest of any two states in the world. To a lesser extent, it was notable in the way in which the two countries looked at the rest of the world, especially toward Europe and the need to support NATO against the Soviet threat.

However, this special relationship began to show strains during the 1960s, particularly in the way the two countries viewed their world order interests. The Vietnam war had much to do with the growing disenchantment in Canada with Washington's judgment in foreign policy, and Canada did not follow the U.S. lead in trying to isolate China from the world community. Moreover, Canada did not break relations with Castro's Cuba and continued to trade in nonstrategic goods. Washington was displeased when Canada decided in May 1970 to float the Canadian dollar without consultation. Then, in August 1971, the special relationship between the two countries came to an end: the United States imposed a 10 percent surcharge on all imports into the country—in order to force a devaluation of the U.S. dollar—and refused to give special consideration to Canada. By 1972, a new relationship had developed between Ottawa and Washington in which neither could afford to take anything for granted.

As the Parti Québécois rose to power in Quebec in November 1976, Ottawa and Washington had once again to take a close look at their relationships. Shortly after Jimmy Carter entered the White House in January 1977, Prime Minister Trudeau made an official visit to Washington, D.C., and conferred with the president about many topics of mutual concern. Trudeau was invited to address a joint session of Congress on February 22, and he reaffirmed the close ties Canadians have with Americans: "The friendship between our two countries is so basic that it has long since been regarded by others as the standard for enlightened international relations. No Canadian leader would be permitted by his electorate consciously to weaken it. Indeed, no Canadian leader would wish to, and certainly not this one." But it was clear from the direction of his address that Trudeau wanted to talk about Quebec and wanted to reassure his U.S. audience that Canada would solve this problem in due course: "I say to you with all the certainty I can command that Canada's unity will not be fractured. Revisions will take place; accommodations will be made. We shall succeed. . . . We may have to revise some aspects of our constitution so that the Canadian federation can be seen by six and a half million French-speaking Canadians to be the strongest bulwark against submission by some two hundred twenty million English-speaking North Americans." Then, taking account of a possible less favorable outcome, Trudeau declared: "The sudden departure of Quebec would signify the tragic failure of our pluralist dream, the fracturing of our cultural mosaic, and would likely remove much of the determination of Canadians to protect their cultural minorities."[19]

At his news conference on February 23, following the prime minister's visit, President Carter was asked whether he thought there was much concern in the United States over the future unity of Canada. Carter made the most specific comment about the Quebec question that any U.S. president has so far given:

There's a great deal of concern in this country about the future of Canada and I have complete confidence, as I said in an interview with the Canadian news media, in the sound judgment of the Canadian people. I'm familiar—even more familiar today than I was two days ago after Prime Minister Trudeau's visit—with the problems in Quebec and the inclination of some of the French Canadians to have an independent status from the rest of the Canadian Provinces. I don't know what's going to be the ultimate outcome. But I believe that we are so closely tied together with Canada on a mutually beneficial basis, sharing problems, sharing opportunities, sharing trade, sharing manufacturing companies that have joint ownership, our exchange of energy sources, our sharing of the St. Lawrence Seaway, the Great Lakes as far as water pollution is concerned, the bringing of Alaskan oil and natural gas down to us that we have got to have a continuing relationship with Canada. *My own personal preference would be that the commonwealth stay as it is and that there not be a separate Quebec province.* But that's a decision for the Canadians to make and I would certainly make no private or public move to try to determine the outcome of that great debate.[20]

The president seemed to be saying that Canadian unity was a very important interest of the United States, that he personally hoped Quebec would not secede from the confederation, but that U.S. policy would be to let Canadians work out the problem themselves. To which the *Washington Post* commented:

Astonishingly, President Carter chose to take a public position on Canada's national unity and the Quebec separatists' challenge to it. So far, he's done no great harm. But he's set a highly dubious precedent for himself. It's one thing to comment on civil liberties, and the lack of them, in the Soviet Union or other closed and oppressive societies. . . . Separatism, on the other hand, is largely a *political* issue in Canada; to the extent that this issue turns on a fundamental principle, it is the principle of "self-determination," which happens to be another of those human rights that Americans hold dear.[21]

Americans have taken Canada for granted so long that it comes as a surprise to be asked, "How important is Canada to the United States?" Canadians have long fretted about the United States' "being more interested in Cambodia than in Canada," as one Canadian official put it, because for them their southern neighbor is an overwhelming interest. But how does one describe the U.S. interest in Canada? Using the four basic interests described in Chapter 1, these interests might be stated as follows:

Defense of homeland: Canadian territory and airspace

probably constitute a *survival* interest of the United States insofar as any warfare involving the Soviet Union is concerned. In strategic terms, Canadian territory and airspace cannot be separated from U.S. territory and defense planning.

Economic well-being: Canada is by far the largest trading partner of the United States. In 1975, 21 percent of all U.S. exports went to Canada, almost twice the amount exported to Japan; and 23 percent of all U.S. imports came from Canada. The book value of U.S. investment in Canada is $34 billion, and U.S. companies have a controlling interest in many of Canada's largest industries. There is an enormous amount of tourism—about 70 million people annually cross the long border in both directions. The U.S. economic stake in Canada is therefore *vital.*

World order: Canada wants to be seen in the international community as a small developed country having a deep interest in the Third World, and the United States no longer expects to have Canadian support in many of its dealings with the rest of the world. Nevertheless, the two nations share a strong interest in defending Europe and maintaining strong Western econo-mies, as well as in the Middle East and Africa. Therefore, the United States probably has a *major* world order interest in having an outward looking, internationalist neighbor.

Ideological: Here the two countries share a great deal: in their belief in human dignity, in the rule of law and justice, in representative government, in a free-market economy, in social mobility, and in giving economic and technical assistance to less developed countries. The United States probably has a *vital* interest in the continuation of a democratic, progressive, and friendly Canadian confederation as a neighbor.

In a word, the U.S. interest in Canada is deep. Therefore, it comes as a shock to Americans that Canada might break up; and if Canada does so, it could be the most important foreign policy problem to face the United States since World War II. Therefore, it is imperative to assess correctly what the U.S. interest should be in the contingencies that might occur in the next few years.

Crisis in Canada: Three Scenarios

Given what we know at the end of 1977, what are the most likely ways in which the Quebec issue could unfold in the next two or three years? What are the likely responses of the principal players in the drama: Ottawa, Washington, and Quebec? What national interests are involved, and what will the parties probably do to defend those interests if Quebec moves toward independence? If Prime Minister Trudeau's prediction proves to be correct and if the voters of Quebec do not give the Parti Québécois a majority to proceed with separation, then presumably there will be no crisis. But what if the vote in a referendum is close and if Premier Lévesque decides that he has a mandate to proceed with negotiations with Ottawa for separation? Or what if the referendum fails to produce a majority and violence breaks out in Quebec—and Lévesque is unable to contain it? Finally, what if the referendum produces a majority in favor of separation, but only in "association" with Canada: if Ottawa turns down association, what then?

Before looking at various scenarios, it is desirable first to assess how the leaders of Canada, the United States, and Quebec will probably view their national interests in three different situations: (1) in the period before a referendum on Quebec independence is held; (2) after the referendum, assuming the Quebec government then approaches Ottawa regarding separation in "association"; and (3) failure of negotiations between Ottawa and Quebec and the Quebec government's declaration of independence. Let us assess these scenarios on the national interest matrix.

First, as Chart 9.1 suggests, none of the three parties perceives a physical threat to its homeland. Second, both Canada and Quebec believe there are vital economic issues at stake, but this factor is of only major interest to the United States. Third, Canada and the United States both feel a vital stake in how a vote on independence for Quebec will be perceived by the rest of Canada and by the outside world; for Quebec, this is of lesser importance. Fourth, from an ideological standpoint, Canada

CHART 9.1

Issue: Referendum on Quebec Independence				
Basic interest at stake		Intensity of interest		
	Survival	Vital	Major	Peripheral
Defense of homeland			Canada US Quebec	
Economic well-being		Canada Quebec	US	
Favorable world order		US Canada	Quebec	
Ideological	Canada	Quebec	US	

has a survival interest at stake in the vote on separation; Quebec has a vital interest in obtaining independence, but not a survival interest; the United States has a major, but not vital, interest because Quebec presumably would remain liberal and democratic regardless of the referendum's outcome. In short, Canada has the largest stake in the outcome of the referendum; Quebec is a close second.

Chart 9.2 suggests the following: First, none of the three parties would fear for the physical security of its homeland if

CHART 9.2

Issue: Quebec asks Canada for independence and economic association				
Basic interest at stake		Intensity of interest		
	Survival	Vital	Major	Peripheral
Defense of homeland			Canada US Quebec	
Economic well-being		Quebec	Canada US	
Favorable world order		Quebec US Canada		
Ideological	Canada	Quebec	US	

Quebec seeks independence and economic association with Canada. Second, Quebec would have a *vital* economic interest in working out an arrangement with Canada to protect its own economy, but Canada would not have as high an interest in accommodating the economic needs of an *independent* Quebec, especially if this required significant concessions by other provinces. In Ontario, however, the large trade with Quebec might raise its interest to vital.[22] Third, Quebec would have a *vital* interest in how the world viewed negotiations between Ottawa and Quebec because it would need economic help elsewhere if it could not trade on a favorable basis with other parts of Canada, particularly Ontario. The United States would also have a vital world order interest because the outcome of these negotiations could have a deep effect on the future of other provinces, with some possibly asking for association with the United States. For Canada, these negotiations are *vital* for its standing with the rest of the world and its position vis-à-vis the United States. Fourth, Quebec would have a vital ideological interest in obtaining independence in "association" with Canada; but for Ottawa, the interest may be *survival*—i.e., to prevent the disintegration of the country. On the other hand, there would be a limit beyond which Ottawa could not go to accommodate Quebec; it *cannot* agree that Quebec should be fully independent; the United States interest would remain at the major level as far as ideological factors are concerned. As this assessment implies, all three parties would be very interested in working out a mutual accommodation between Quebec and Canada—but not if the other provinces have to make large economic concessions to Quebec or if Quebec insists on gaining full independence and adopting an independent foreign policy.

Chart 9.3 suggests the following. First, an independent Quebec not in association with Canada would have great fears for its security, i.e., a vital interest, particularly if violence occurs in Quebec between pro-separationists and anti-separationists. Both the U.S. and Canada's defense interests would also rise to the vital level. Second, for Quebec, working out economic arrangements with other countries would become a survival interest and could produce severe internal problems. The U.S. economic interest would be major, and

CHART 9.3

```
┌─────────────────────────────────────────────────────────────────────────┐
│                                                                           │
│        Issue:  Independent Quebec fully detached from Canada              │
│                                                                           │
│   Basic interest at stake                    Intensity of interest        │
│                                 Survival   Vital      Major      Peripheral│
│                                                                           │
│      Defense of homeland                   Quebec                          │
│                                            US                             │
│                                            Canada                         │
│                                                                           │
│      Economic well-being        Quebec                Canada              │
│                                                       US                  │
│                                                                           │
│      Favorable world order                 Quebec     Canada              │
│                                            US                             │
│                                                                           │
│      Ideological                Quebec     US         Canada              │
│                                                                           │
└─────────────────────────────────────────────────────────────────────────┘
```

Basic interest at stake	Intensity of interest			
	Survival	Vital	Major	Peripheral
Defense of homeland		Quebec US Canada		
Economic well-being	Quebec		Canada US	
Favorable world order		Quebec US	Canada	
Ideological	Quebec	US	Canada	

Canada would have only a major interest in helping Quebec deal with its economic situation. Third, Quebec would have a vital world order interest in getting diplomatic recognition from Europe and the United States in order to protect its independence. The United States would face a serious dilemma because its attitude would be strongly influenced by Ottawa's view. Nevertheless, it probably will have a vital world order interest. Fourth, Quebec would also have a survival ideological interest in asserting its newly won independence and in charting its own future independently of Ottawa. The United States would probably have a vital interest in supporting Quebec's independence if Canada does not object strongly to it. The conclusion is clear: if Quebec cannot work out a satisfactory arrangement with Canada to protect its economic interests, it will have to turn to the United States for help; and such help would probably be given if Washington was convinced that Ottawa will make no further effort to prevent separation.

In light of the national interests involved, what policies are the principal parties likely to follow in the three scenarios described above? In my view, Quebec, Canada, and the United States will probably take the following courses of action.

Scenario 1: The government of Quebec sets a date, probably in 1979, for a referendum on whether Quebec should become an independent state with special economic ties to Canada. The rules governing the referendum and the campaign preceding the voting are weighted in favor of those favoring "sovereignty in association" with Canada and negotiations to work out this relationship. The campaign by the Parti Québécois is strongly nationalistic, appealing to French-speaking residents to terminate two hundred years of English dominance and protect the language and culture of six million Quebecers against further encroachments by English-speaking Canadians. It assures Quebecers that a satisfactory economic arrangement with Canada will be negotiated. The Canadian government and other provinces seek to influence the decision of Quebec voters by (1) calling for a referendum of *all* Canadians to decide whether Quebec should be given independence, citing the constitutional questions involved; (2) taking strong issue with the assertions of the Parti Québécois that it will be able to work out an economic arrangement with the rest of Canada; and (3) emphasizing the advantages to Quebecers of remaining in the Canadian Confederation, especially with new federal concessions to permit greater autonomy for Quebec as well as other provinces. The U.S. position will be that of an interested, friendly neighbor who is not willing to take sides in a family quarrel. The U.S. press and some political leaders will take sides, however, some supporting the idea of self-determination as a basic American ideal, and others fearing an independent and nationalistic new nation on the approaches to the St. Lawrence Seaway. The debate in Canada will become bitter at times, and acts of violence could occur in Montreal and elsewhere, as they did in 1970, when extremists assassinated a provincial government minister.

If the results of the referendum show clearly that there is *not* majority support in Quebec for independence, the government of René Lévesque might resign and call for elections in order to obtain a new mandate to continue in power. However, if the referendum is near fifty percent, or more, in favor of independence with economic ties to Canada, the Quebec government could then announce plans to begin negotiations with Ottawa and the other nine provinces to arrange for a customs union between an independent Quebec and Canada. The second scenario would then come into focus.

Scenario 2: The Quebec government calls for negotiations

with other provinces with a view to finding a suitable arrangement for Quebec to be independent but in association with Canada economically. Negotiators will seek to persuade the rest of Canada that such an arrangement would be in its best interests because it would keep open the provincial market while satisfying the needs of Quebecers for nationhood. Quebec will warn of the serious consequences to Canada if no agreement is reached and will try to convince Quebecers that any breakdown in negotiations would be due to English Canada's continuing disdain for the French-speaking population. Canada's position in these negotiations will be reasonable yet firm on the point that Quebec cannot have it both ways: secession from the confederation and the continuing benefits flowing from membership in the greater Canada. The views of other provincial leaders, particularly those of Ontario and Alberta, will be given prominence in these negotiations, and Prime Minister Trudeau would stand aloof from them. The U.S. official position will remain one of a friendly bystander, but it might work behind the scenes to see whether there is room for compromise between the Quebec and Canadian positions, a compromise that could persuade Quebec to remain in some kind of loose political as well as economic relationship with the other provinces, thus avoiding a splitting of the confederation. The United States will be concerned about Quebec separation encouraging further disintegration of Canada, and the problems this would create for the United States and the international community. The potential for limited violence during these negotiations is substantial, especially in Montreal.

If negotiations between Quebec and the rest of Canada do not produce agreement—either on separation "in association" or on continued Quebec membership in Canada with greater autonomy—the situation in Quebec could become tense, and serious violence could flare up. Ottawa would do everything reasonably possible to prevent this from occurring, but it may not be able to do so.

Scenario 3: Negotiations with Ottawa and the other provinces have reached an impasse, and the Lévesque government decides to hold elections in Quebec in order to obtain a mandate for independence without an economic arrangement with Canada. The Parti Québécois is returned to power with a majority of seats in the assembly, but without a majority of the popular vote. Lévesque thereupon declares Quebec's independence and asks for international recognition and admission to the United Nations. In this situation, the Canadian government has two alternatives: (1) it can denounce Quebec's declaration of independence as illegal—as Britain did in Rhodesia in 1965—and ask the international community not to grant recognition; or (2) it can wash its hands of Quebec and try to build greater unity among the remaining nine provinces. The second course seems unlikely, however, if Trudeau remains prime minister during the next few years. In a year-end TV interview that was broadcast nationally on January 1, 1978, Trudeau said he was prepared to use force to counter any "illegal" actions taken by the Quebec government to gain independence from Canada: "I'm not going to be shy about using the sword if something illegal is attempted in the Province of Quebec," he said to his interviewer, Bruce Phillips of the CTV network. Trudeau recalled that in 1970 he had used force against a terrorist group in Montreal that sought Quebec independence by violent actions. If the Quebec authorities acted illegally, he declared, "obviously we will have to take the kind of action that we took in 1970 when the law was broken."[23] Lévesque's problem, in this scenario, will be to try to gain international recognition and economic assistance. France might give recognition, as would some Francophone states. Some Latin American states might also do so. The major question, however, is what the United States' position will be.

If it came to this, U.S. policy would change, because U.S. interests toward Canada would escalate, as noted above. So long as the issue of separation has not yet been decided, the U.S. interest favors a united Canada. But once Ottawa decides that it cannot prevent Quebec from declaring its independence, then the U.S. interest will be to reach an understanding with the new state and encourage Quebec to cooperate with Canada and the United States, much as Canada and the United States now conduct their relations. In a word, it would be in the U.S. interest to adopt a friendly and accommodating attitude toward an independent Quebec so long as Quebec reciprocates this attitude and seeks good economic and defense relationships with the United States and Canada. However, if the new Quebec government's policies move toward neutralism in foreign policy and nationalization of private business at home, the U.S. attitude will undoubtedly be very different. This is because the United States cannot afford to see an unfriendly state on its northern border any more than Moscow can afford to have an unfriendly Poland or Finland on its western border. The real problem will then be whether Lévesque as premier of an independent Quebec can control both the extremist elements within the Parti Québécois and the radical conservative elements strongly opposed to separation from Canada.

All of the above assumes that the citizens of Quebec and the rest of Canada will be rational and peaceful while the country decides whether it will be one sovereign state, or two, or more. But is a peaceful transition from confederation to independence for Quebec really the most likely way in which the change will take place? One writer, Wayne Reilly, maintains that "during the past several years a number of events suggest that some form of internal war is a distinct possibility in regard to Quebec's political future" and that history shows that most separations of political entities from larger states usually are accompanied by violence.[24] In 1977 a group of Canadian scholars published a volume entitled *Must Canada Fail;* one of them, Richard Simeon, suggested that if current efforts fail to prevent disintegration of the confederation, "we will be forced, and perhaps in the near future, to face some frightening and unpleasant possibilities. The civility and tolerance on which we pride ourselves will be severely tested. We will face a situation which, when faced by other countries, has frequently led to civil war."[25] So violence is a possibility in Canada. But what circumstances could produce it? And could it be contained?

Two situations that could develop in Quebec in the next few years might lead to violence. First, if the referendum on Quebec independence fails and the radical wing of the Parti Québécois concludes that Lévesque's peaceful, constitutional method of bringing about independence for Quebec will not achieve the results it desires—then or in the future—the party could split up. The extremists might form their own party and adopt violent tactics in spite of Lévesque's caution.[26] Second, if Quebec fails to reach a negotiated settlement in association with the rest of Canada and if the English-speaking minority in Quebec feels so threatened that it adopts violent tactics to prevent Lévesque from declaring full Quebec independence and asking for international recognition, confrontations between English-speakers and radical Quebecers could trigger violence, which federal forces would in all likelihood deal with as severely as they did the 1970 violence in Montreal. Only this time, federal intervention might spark civil war if Lévesque hesitates or opposes the introduction of federal forces into Quebec.

Violence, or the prospect of violence, can change the national interest of countries most affected by the issues involved in a tense political situation—and Quebec would be no exception. The rational appraisal of interests made by the governments of Canada, the United States, and Quebec, as outlined above, probably would escalate sharply if serious trouble erupted in Montreal, which holds both the largest concentration of English-speakers and the most radical elements of the Parti Québécois. Should there be serious violence there, either after a referendum or if negotiations between Ottawa and Quebec break down over the issue of separation, Canadian troops may well be used to restore order—whether the Quebec government asks for them or not. If armed insurgency resulted and Quebec became a battleground between federal forces and the terrorist organization, the U.S. defense interest in this situation would certainly be raised to the vital level, and U.S. policy would be directed toward preventing foreign interference in the internal Canadian struggle and encouraging negotiations to end the strife. Although such violence in Quebec would probably be short-lived, as it was in 1970, Quebecers could well be radicalized by resentment against federal military intervention and thus give the insurgency wide public support. In that case, the United States and Canada would have a very different situation to deal with, one that is beyond the scope of this discussion.

The Outlook

1980 is likely to be a critical year for Canada, for Quebec, and for the United States. Prime Minister Trudeau's government must hold general elections before the summer of 1979, and 1980 is a presidential election year in the United States. If Premier Lévesque holds a referendum in 1979 and a majority of Quebec voters support his proposal to start negotiations with Ottawa to obtain independence, such negotiations will very likely be conducted (if Ottawa is willing to discuss the question at all) in the early months of 1980. This might suit the prime minister, because he is expected to hold federal elections in 1978 or early 1979, and the separation issue would probably be the key point on which the balloting would turn. Knowing this, Lévesque might propose negotiations sooner, but he must calculate whether Quebec opinion is sufficiently mobilized behind separation to hold a referendum in 1979. In the United States, President Carter's efforts to keep the Quebec issue out of U.S. politics might be no more successful than were his and President Ford's efforts to keep Panama out of the election campaign in 1976. Indeed, Quebec will probably become a key political issue in the United States and thus make it more difficult for Washington to remain a friendly bystander as scenarios 1 and 2 are played out.

Many Canadian political observers believe that Prime Minister Trudeau is too shrewd a politician to allow his country to split up and that, in the end, a bargain will be struck between Ottawa and the provinces to give them all more autonomy within the confederation—and that Quebec will accept such an arrangement. This is the view of a highly respected Canadian journalist, Bruce Hutchison, who stated in an article entitled "Canada's Time of Troubles": "To Mr. Trudeau pragmatism is the essence and natural operating method of democracy."[27] Those Canadians who share this view believe it may be necessary for Canada to offer Quebec the right to have diplomatic representatives in some countries, either within or separate from Canadian embassies. But Ottawa would insist on the right to conduct economic planning for the whole of the country and on the right to control defense relations for the whole country. Quebec would still be part of

Canada for security and economic planning purposes. The question is whether, in the final analysis, Quebecers will reject independence in favor of economic and political realities; and here the optimists may underestimate the nationalist sentiments of Quebecers and may miscalculate the effects of violence in persuading Lévesque to push for full independence in the belief that the outcome is inevitable. And such action could trigger a counteraction by extremists on the right. No one knows what Lévesque's policy will be if and when terrorists repeat the tactics they adopted in 1970, when both federal and provincial police dealt with the situation in a great show of strength, including the imposition of martial law. Lévesque deplored the massive use of force in 1970. But if violence occurs again while he is premier, how forcefully would he deal with the groups responsible?

The United States, as suggested above, could be accommodating toward Quebec nationalist leaders so long as things are peaceful in Canada and so long as the Ottawa government has decided that it cannot keep Quebec in the confederation unless it is willing to use force—and that it will *not* use force. But if serious violence breaks out in Quebec and it appears that Lévesque will either be ousted by more radical forces or be persuaded to join them, the United States could confront a crisis more serious than those that occurred in Cuba or in Chile. One hopes that the Quebec issue will never come to that and a compromise will be found between Ottawa and Quebec. But it would be foolish to assume that something worse cannot happen.

10. The Threat of Race War in South Africa

Unlike Canada or Panama, South Africa is to most Americans a far distant country; and until the Carter administration made an issue of its racial policies, it was not believed that U.S. interests were deeply involved in South Africa. Although the U.S. Navy has long considered South Africa of great strategic importance and although U.S. multinational corporations have invested more than a billion dollars there, the U.S. government has not acted as if it needed to concern itself about this far-off country. A few officers in the State Department and in the intelligence agencies warned their superiors for some years that the ending of Portuguese rule in Angola and Mozambique would focus black African attention on the white minority regimes in Rhodesia and South Africa, but their warnings were largely ignored until 1974, when a coup occurred in Portugal. The reasons for this neglect were that the Nixon administration did not foresee that Portugal would decide so soon to give up its colonial empire in Africa, nor did it want to jeopardize U.S. military bases in the Azores by pressing Portugal to give independence to its colonies. Furthermore, the United States was deeply absorbed during the 1960s and early 1970s in the Far East, the Middle East, and Europe. In short, southern Africa in general, and South Africa in particular, did not receive much attention from Secretary of State Kissinger until the Portuguese government was overthrown in April 1974.

When the Carter administration came to power in 1977, it significantly changed U.S. policy toward the government of

South Africa; from what it had been since 1948, when the Afrikaner-dominated National Party won the general elections in South Africa and formed a government that has remained in power every since. In effect, the Carter administration has taken a strong ideological line against the South African regime and has pressured it to relax the thirty-year-old policy of racial repression of the nonwhite majority. That posture fitted well the president's announced policy of using human rights as a test of other countries' values to the United States as friends and allies. Were South Africa simply another small underdeveloped country in need of U.S. economic and military assistance— such as Korea or the Philippines, where political repression of another kind exists—there probably would not be such a fuss made. But South Africa is different from most other noncommunist regimes: it has the capability of engulfing its neighbors and perhaps the great powers in a large war in Africa. And that poses a more difficult dilemma for U.S. policymakers because the assessment of U.S. national interests becomes more complicated than simply admonishing a government about its poor record on the human rights question. It could become a matter of pushing South Africa into war.

South Africa represents an excellent example of how U.S. national interests are constrained by domestic political considerations in the United States. One of the key *value* factors that helps to determine how important an interest is, is "sentimental attachment" (see Chapter 2). This has to do with the way various ethnic groups of Americans view other countries and how their opinions affect the president's and his advisors' perceptions of U.S. interests abroad. For many years American Jews have had great influence on U.S. national policies in the Middle East, and Greek Americans had an enormous influence on U.S. policy toward Turkey following the Turkish occupation of a part of Cyprus in 1974. But only recently has the U.S. black community come to assert itself in political terms vis-à-vis U.S. interests and policies in southern Africa. In 1976, U.S. blacks voted almost nine to one for Jimmy Carter and then demanded that their views on foreign as well as domestic affairs be heard and acted upon. It was probably natural that President Carter should urge, and finally persuade, his fellow Georgia Democrat, Andrew Young, to give up a seat in the U.S. House of Representatives to become his chief representative at the United Nations, the first black to fill that position. During his first year in that role, Young had a profound impact on U.S. relations with black African nations, particularly in Nigeria, where the government of that key African state had only a year before refused a visit by Secretary of State Kissinger. Being black and having credentials as a civil rights militant in the 1960s were clearly advantages to Young; but more important for U.S. relations with black African states, his appointment was seen as a clear signal that the new U.S. president was redefining U.S. national interests in Africa and that those interests would henceforth give more attention to black African views and aspirations and less attention to what European powers with interests in Africa wanted. Above all, the new policy would take a strong line against the racial policies practiced in Rhodesia and South Africa. To many black African leaders, 1977 seemed to indicate that the United States had finally turned a corner and that black views would be given preference over white views in determining U.S. policies in Africa.

But there was a more crucial reason for the shift in U.S. policy toward southern Africa in 1977: namely, the world order interests of the United States changed sharply after some 15,000 Cuban troops went into Angola in 1975 and turned the tide of a civil war there in favor of Marxist MPLA forces led by Agostino Neto. The Cubans, of course, could not have gotten to Angola without Soviet transport, and they could not have turned the tide of battle without large amounts of Soviet equipment. Thus, the balance of power in southern Africa was in danger of being upset: Cuban mercenaries were fighting a proxy war for the Soviet Union and thus threatening the West's political and economic position in southern Africa. When the U.S. Congress cut off all U.S. aid to the noncommunist forces in December 1975—over the strong protests of President Ford and Secretary Kissinger—the outcome of the civil war in Angola was predictable. Cuban troops are still in Angola and have been reinforced during the latter part of 1977—despite predictions that Castro would withdraw most of them after the world recognized the Neto government as the legitimate government in Angola. Despite hopes in the Carter administration that Castro might reduce his forces in Africa in return for normal diplomatic and trade relations with the United States, he told a group of U.S. Congressmen on December 5, 1977, that the presence of Cuban troops in Africa was not negotiable. According to the *New York Times,* he asserted: "If the issue of Cuban-American relations is placed in the context of Africa, the restoration of relations will not advance. We are not willing to enter into any kind of compromise on that."[1] In effect, Castro told the U.S. government that he intended to continue promoting Marxist revolutions in Africa. What he did not say was that his troops could not possibly remain in Africa without full Soviet support. Therefore, was the issue with Cuba or with Moscow? Or was the key the way black African states perceived their own interests vis-à-vis the United States, South Africa, and the Soviet Union?

South Africa's National Interests

South Africa is governed today, as it has been since 1948, by descendants of the Dutch, Germans, and French Huguenots who came to the area three hundred years ago (as the French settlers had gone to Quebec) and who have long since severed their attachments to Europe. The National Party, headed today by Prime Minister John Vorster, is rural-based, Calvinist by religion, and fiercely dedicated to the idea that South Africa is God's gift to the white man. The Afrikaners, as they are known, make up about 60 percent of the total white population of 4.3 million and speak their own language. The remaining 40 percent of the whites are English-speaking and have their cultural roots in the British Isles. Most of them came to Africa following Great Britain's ouster of the Dutch as the colonial power in 1806. English-speaking whites dominated the political life of South Africa from 1910, when it was given dominion status, until 1948, when the Afrikaners obtained a parliamentary majority. Since that time, the government has pursued a repressive apartheid policy not only against the 18.6

million black Africans in the country, but also against 2.4 million coloureds and 750,000 Asians, to whom the British and the English-speaking population had accorded a special status before 1948. As more and more black Africans were encouraged to come to South Africa to work in the mines and do the manual labor in the cities, they were strictly segregated and repressed whenever they violated any of the extremely elaborate race laws imposed by the Afrikaner-dominated government. Despite the efforts of the opposition parties to get the government to liberalize some of its apartheid policies, successive National Party governments have stubbornly refused to do so.

The tough mentality of the Afrikaners is an important aspect of how South Africa sees its national interests today. Those observers who know the country well are not confident that any significant changes will occur in the near future. John de St. Jarre, writing recently in *Foreign Affairs*, describes the Afrikaner this way:

> Afrikaners retain a revolutionary image of themselves. Unlike the English, French or Portuguese in Africa, they turned their backs on their European origins. In search of land and solitude they swept north in successive migratory waves and clashed with black tribes pushing south. They were not innovators but a practical people who had a talent for modification. . . . The Church and Africaans remain as pivotal to Afrikaner nationalism today as Judaism and Hebrew do to Zionism, although their racial ideologies are entirely different. They regard themselves in all seriousness as Africa's first freedom fighters—against British imperialism—and although they lost the war they finally won the peace.[2]

The national interests of South Africa are determined today solely by Afrikaners, and to a very large degree by their political leader and prime minister, John Vorster. He became prime minister in 1966 and in the general elections of 1977 led his party to a smashing victory by capturing 134 seats out of 165 in parliament—an increase of 18 over the previous total. At the age of sixty-one, he is clearly in control of the politics of his country, and his view of what South Africa must do to defend its national interests will be followed by most of the white population, even though liberals fought his racial policies in the election campaign. After Portugal decided in 1975 to grant independence to Angola and Mozambique, Vorster adopted a détente policy toward his black neighbors immediately to the north in the hope of working out an accommodation with the new regimes there that would not put South Africa's racial policies on the line.

John Barratt, director of the South African Institute of International Affairs, states that during this period Vorster apparently had hopes of forging new links with African nations that would lead to peace rather than war on the continent: "The basis of the South African détente policy was indicated in Prime Minister John Vorster's speech of October 23, 1974, in which he said *inter alia* that Southern Africa had come to a crossroads, where it had to make a choice between peace and the escalation of strife. Zambia's response came in a speech by President Kenneth Kaunda a few days later, in which he referred to Mr. Vorster's 'crossroads' speech as 'the voice of reason' which Africa had been waiting a long time to hear."[3] Unfortunately for peace in southern Africa, these beginnings of an accommodation between South Africa and its neighbors came to a halt in 1975, when an African solution to internal strife in Angola faltered. Both South Africa and Cuba intervened in Angola to tip the scales in the civil war. And once the outcome was clear there, Rhodesia became a burning issue, because the illegal government of Ian Smith refused to negotiate for majority rule despite strong British and U.S. pressure. Another issue that surfaced at this time was the future of Southwest Africa, or Namibia, which South Africa had administered as a League of Nations mandate since 1920, but which the United Nations declared illegal in 1966 because South Africa refused to grant independence for the area.

With the Portuguese buffer zone in Angola and Mozambique gone, Vorster then had to decide whether to bow to international pressure on both Rhodesia and Namibia, in hopes of salvaging some international support for a slower evolution in his own country, or to stand fast in the face of mounting pressure at home and abroad. Being a conservative pragmatist rather than an ideologue, Vorster wished to trade cooperation with the United States (in the person of Secretary of State Kissinger) in return for tacit U.S. support for South Africa in the United Nations and with moderate black African leaders, who ultimately would decide whether there could be a détente with South Africa or whether there would be protracted warfare. In the summer and fall of 1976, Vorster tried to strike a bargain with Kissinger: give help on majority rule in Rhodesia and independence for Namibia in return for U.S. diplomatic support for South Africa and for the muting of criticism of Pretoria's apartheid policies. This deal would serve South Africa's short-term interests and buy time for its government to find ways to build new bridges to black Africa.

The Carter administration's emphasis on human rights made it impossible for Vorster's plan to work. One of the first indications of a change in U.S. policy was the testimony by Philip Habib, under secretary of state, before the Subcommittee on Africa of the House Committee on International Relations on March 3, 1977—six weeks after the Carter administration took office. Speaking of the importance of South Africa's role in achieving peaceful settlements of the political problems in Rhodesia and Namibia, Habib made the new policy clear:

So long as we are assured of the South African willingness to be helpful, the United States will be prepared to continue its consultations with South Africa's leaders on these issues. It should be made clear to all, however, that the United States has no interest in any proposed solution that would compromise the legitimate interests of the people involved and their desires for majority rule with full sovereignty and independence. Moreover, our willingness should in no way be construed as an acceptance of that country's domestic policies. The violence in Soweto and elsewhere bears grim testimony to a society that must change, and change radically, or face the sure calamity of racial violence and chaos.

Habib concluded by stating that the United States would continue to speak out publicly on events in South Africa and make known its views on how peaceful change could come to that racially divided country. He foresaw that the reaction of the white South Africans might have the opposite effect: "We must remain sensitive to the danger that the attitudes and reactions of the outside world to events in South Africa could have the unfortunate effect of engendering greater isolation and resistance to change. We must take care that our own actions nurture, rather than inhibit, the changes that we believe can and must be made."[4]

Seymour Topping, managing editor of the *New York Times*, interviewed Prime Minister Vorster during an extensive visit to southern Africa in the fall of 1977 and reported: "Vorster was clearly jolted by the shift in United States policy from the Kissinger acceptance of a durable Afrikanerdom, with some mellowing, to the Carter alignment with black nationalism. Yet he exuded a sense of confidence and of quiet pride in his place in history. 'I have always seen my role as one of trying to bring peace to my part of the world. But then, I think I have nothing to prove in this regard. The record is there for each and everyone to make his own assessment.' " Vorster said he had tried in recent years to foster accommodation with the black African states and had been rebuffed. His efforts to hold out economic inducements to his neighbors had failed because of the rush to a showdown on the racial issue. Vorster therefore was prepared for a much tougher internal situation within South Africa in the coming years, Topping reported.[5]

The increased repression of the nonwhite majority in South Africa in the autumn of 1977 and the government's handling of the inquiry into the prison death of black leader Stephen Biko were clear evidence that it had adopted a "siege mentality" similar to the one that had enabled the Afrikaners in the nineteenth century to defeat the massive attacks of the Zulu tribes in the great Battle of the Blood River, an event that is part of the folklore of every Afrikaner. Indeed, the huge election victory of Vorster's government in November 1977 showed that even English-speaking South Africans were moving to his political side as time seemed to be running out on the policy of accommodation with black Africa.

Any doubt that may have remained in Vorster's mind about the Carter administration's attitude toward his regime was dispelled when he met Vice-President Walter Mondale in Vienna in mid-May and found the vice-president very tough on the human rights question. In fact, in a press interview after their meetings, Mondale made what *Time* magazine called a "misstep that Washington has been gently attempting to correct ever since."[6]

The exact wording of the question and the vice-president's reply was:

> *Question:* Mr. Vice President, could you possibly go into slightly more detail on your concept of full participation as opposed to one-man one-vote? Do you see some kind of a compromise?"
> *Answer:* "No, no. It's the same thing. Every citizen should have the right to vote and every vote should be equally weighted."[7]

South Africa was outraged at Mondale's public statements, and several of its leaders said his prescription was tantamount to suicide for their society. Even some liberal democratic observers in the United States and elsewhere were surprised because in the United States the votes of citizens are not equally weighted in elections for president and the Senate due to the electoral college system and the equal number of senators for states. More important, however, the vice-president seemed to be prescribing a new constitutional system for South Africa, a system it could under no circumstances accept without giving up its whole way of life—unpalatable as that way of life was to most Americans. In effect, the vice-president had touched on a *survival* ideological interest of the South African government.

Prime Minister Vorster's reaction to U.S. pressure was defiant and self-righteous. In an important speech on August 5 celebrating the fiftieth anniversary of the Department of Foreign Affairs, he strongly criticized the Carter administration for bowing to domestic pressures and shifting its diplomatic support to black Africa at the expense of South Africa. He also appealed to the African nations to be reasonable toward their southern neighbor and to see the larger danger that threatened all of them, the movement of Marxism into the continent. Part of his remarks are quoted here to reveal his thinking about South Africa's national interests:

I have told you that the United States of America would like to win the favor of Africa at all costs. At present there is more conflict and violence in Africa than ever before. General hatred for South Africa and general contempt against colonialism has been the binding factor in the past to preserve the unity of the African states. On this 50th anniversary of your department, I would like to make use of this platform to say to the rest of Africa: It is time that you come to your senses, otherwise you will destroy yourself in the process. Contempt for colonialism and hatred for South Africa is not enough, and will become increasingly so, to keep the rest of the African states together. Present happenings in Africa are proof enough. Africa must take note that the militants amongst them have jeopardized the future and prosperity of the people and have done them an injustice. The present deteriorating condition of many African states today has brought about an awakening in many African states. The time has come for Africa to take stock of itself and in doing so it will notice that those states that have made genuine progress are the states that have deemed the interest of their own welfare and prosperity higher than the vendetta against South Africa. And I do not doubt that the voices of those moderate states will in the long run become louder and clearer and finally become the voice of the whole of Africa. I believe that South Africa, the gateway to Africa, has an obligation to fulfill. And I believe that each one of us here tonight is willing and eager to assist, each in his own way, to fulfill that obligation. And I believe that in this process, South Africa is indispensable to the free world. The same free world that, because of its own actions, is busy blocking its own way. I would like to say to the leader of the Western World: "Do not make it impossible for South Africa to play its role in the free world. If, as a result of your actions, South Africa is destroyed, what will take its place? What can take its place?" The message of my country and my people to the free world is this: "Why make an enemy of the one country in Africa on which you can finally, when crisis arrives, depend?"[8]

The South African government's crackdown on opposition groups in October 1977 set off a worldwide reaction, which ultimately led to a UN Security Council Resolution banning the sale of all arms to that country. Reports from South Africa indicated that the government there anticipated this action and even economic sanctions, but was determined to guarantee internal security in the face of what it perceived to be the growing hostility of the United States. In fact, Foreign Minister R. F. Botha was quoted as telling his countrymen that the United States was now a greater threat to South Africa than the Soviet Union: "The Carter Administration has decided that the white people of South Africa have to be ploughed under." Botha said U.S. pressure on South Africa was "encouraging radical militants in southern Africa," with the danger that U.S. policy would "cost the lives of many thousands of non-Americans, both black and white alike."[9] By the end of 1977, therefore, it seemed clear that South Africa had decided not to cooperate with the Carter administration in trying to find a peaceful solution to the problems of southern Africa. However, there was no evidence that the Vorster government would actively try to block a peaceful resolution of the Rhodesian and Namibian issues, which it could do if mass violence occurred, especially if mass violence were supported by Cuban troops.

A summary of South Africa's national interests would be the following:

Defense of homeland: Until Portugal decided to grant independence to Angola and Mozambique in 1975, South Africa experienced no real threat to its homeland from abroad. With both Angola and Mozambique now governed by Marxist governments and Rhodesia under strong pressure to grant majority rule, it may be concluded that defense of South African territory against foreign forces has reached at least the vital level. The Vorster government's strong measures against dissidents in October 1977 were inspired by a need to improve internal security at a time when external pressures were mounting. In terms of ability to defend its territory, South Africa believes it has the necessary arms to repel any attack from African territory.

Economic well-being: The high standard of living among South Africa's white population would not be possible without the presence of millions of nonwhite workers in all walks of life. It is probably a *vital* interest of the government to maintain the apartheid policy with its low wages for blacks and other nonwhites. In his election campaign during November 1977, Vorster asserted to his party supporters that majority rule "will affect your standard of living" and admonished them to vote for the party that "will guarantee your security." In the same speech he scoffed at the UN arms embargo against South Africa and reassured his audience that the government could handle its own defense problems: "We can deal with anything that comes out of Africa before breakfast," he boasted.[10]

World order: Vorster's plea to southern Africa in his August 5, 1977, speech showed a deep concern about the growing isolation of South Africa and his concern that the United States had abandoned his country. South Africa's world order interests were therefore vitally affected by events of 1977, although these events seemed to harden the government's resolve to defend itself in the face of growing isolation in the world.

Ideological: Reading the campaign rhetoric of South African leaders at the end of 1977, one might conclude that preserving rigid apartheid in South Africa was tantamount to survival of the white minority government. But if it were at the survival level, this would imply little if any flexibility in the apartheid policy and in the way of life in South Africa. Several observers have speculated that Vorster, after obtaining a huge election mandate, would find ways to ameliorate some of the worst features of that system. Vorster told Seymour Topping that certain constitutional reforms could give coloureds—those of mixed blood—and the Asians a limited role in the political life of the country. But he was unwilling to consider this for the black population. He felt that improved living conditions for blacks and a degree of self-government would come gradually. His view was that South African blacks are far better off economically than those of any other country in Africa.[11] South Africa's ideological interest in preserving its way of life is clearly at the *vital* level; whether it goes to survival depends on events in 1978 and later.

United States Interests in Southern Africa

During most of the period after 1945, the United States

attitude toward southern Africa was one of "benign neglect." Except for a flurry of excitement in the early 1960s, when Belgium relinquished colonial control over the Congo and that country was torn by civil war, U.S. policy has permitted the European powers and the new African states to work out relations that are amenable to U.S. investments. When Rhodesia declared its independence from Britain in 1965, the United States went along with Britain and other countries in refusing diplomatic recognition to the white minority government there; but it resumed buying Rhodesian chrome in 1970 despite a UN sanction against such trade. Portugal retained an iron grip on Angola and Mozambique during the 1960s and 1970s; and U.S. policy did nothing to upset the Portuguese rule, because its key Azores possessions in the Atlantic were thought to be of vital strategic importance to NATO. Until 1974, therefore, southern Africa seemed like one part of the world where U.S. interests could afford to be peripheral in most instances, and certainly no higher than major in a few cases, such as South Africa.

All this changed suddenly when the Portuguese dictatorship was overthrown in April 1974. Within a year a civil war had started in Angola to determine the political orientation of that key African territory. For Secretary of State Henry Kissinger and President Gerald Ford, Africa was now a new dimension in U.S. foreign policy, and the key question was: just how great is the U.S. national interest in southern Africa? On August 31, 1976, in a speech in Philadelphia, Kissinger stated the basis for the U.S. ideological interest: "The relationship between the United States and Africa is unique. We were never a colonial power, but America's character and destiny have been permanently shaped by our involvement in a tragic aspect of Africa's past. Twenty-three million black citizens testify to this heritage and all the American people have been profoundly affected by it. In this generation the affirmation of equality and black dignity in America has coincided with assertions of black nationhood in Africa. Both represent a great human struggle for freedom; both compel our support if America's principles are to have meaning."[12] Although Kissinger's critics have accused him of ignoring Africa during his eight years as

director of U.S. foreign policy, once he grasped the implications of the Portuguese withdrawal and the Soviet intervention,
he threw himself wholeheartedly into the task of fashioning a
new foreign policy for Africa during his last year as secretary of
state. His critics also accuse him of tacitly agreeing *not* to put
pressure on South Africa to change its rigid apartheid policy in
return for Prime Minister Vorster's support in pressuring
Rhodesia's white minority government. But Kissinger's public
criticism of the Vorster regime's racist policies belies this
charge. For example, Kissinger stated in a speech in Boston on
August 2, 1976: "South Africa's internal structure is explosive
and incompatible with any concept of human dignity. Racial
discrimination is a blight which afflicts many nations of the
world. But South Africa is unique in institutionalizing
discrimination in an all-pervasive, enforced separation of the
races which mocks any definition of human equality."
Kissinger then appealed to Vorster's government: "The
United States appeals to South Africa to heed these warning
signals. The United States, true to its own beliefs, will use all its
influence to encourage peaceful change, an end to institutionalized inequality, and equality of opportunity and basic
human rights in South Africa."[13] These are not the words of a
man who has made a deal to soft-pedal white racism in South
Africa in exchange for cooperation in Rhodesia and Namibia.

If Prime Minister Vorster had doubts on this score, however,
the Carter administration dispelled them in dramatic fashion
during its first year in office. Vice-President Mondale's Vienna
meeting with Vorster in May was designed to convey high
administration views on South Africa and to make clear that
there would be no compromise with South Africa's internal
policies toward nonwhites. Unfortunately, Mondale got into
the semantic argument over "one man, one vote" when he
talked to the press after the meetings. But his message to Vorster
was clear: South Africa could not count on U.S. diplomatic
support anywhere unless it began to change its rigid apartheid
system and work toward "full participation" by all South
Africans in South Africa's political life. In an interview with a
South African journalist in October 1977, the vice-president
recalled the Vienna meeting with Vorster and reiterated for

South African readers what he had said earlier:

> In my discussion with Mr. Vorster, I set forth what I thought
> were the three fundamental elements [of peace in southern
> Africa]—one, that in Rhodesia we want to see the present
> negotiations successfully concluded, leading to majority rule
> and the independence of Zimbabwe during 1978; in Namibia,
> we want to see a transition to independence within the
> framework of the Security Council Resolution 385, achieved by
> the end of next year; and in South Africa, we look for steps now
> to begin a progressive transformation away from apartheid and
> toward full political participation for all South Africans. I
> might point out that as to South Africa, we have no blueprint.
> We have no road map for South Africa. It would be
> presumptuous of us to have one. We understand the complexi-
> ties and the long history of interracial relations in South Africa.
> I said as much to Prime Minister Vorster when we met in
> Vienna. I also told him it was important to begin soon the
> process of transforming South Africa into a society in which
> there could be full rights, justice and political participation for
> all of her people. It was our judgment that this tide of human
> history could not be stopped and should not be stopped. I made
> clear that while we were not trying to tell South Africa what it
> should do, we were determined for our own part that if such
> changes did not take place, it would be increasingly difficult for
> the United States to maintain the good relations with South
> Africa that had been enjoyed in the past and which we would
> very much like to continue. We want a good relationship with
> South Africa.[14]

The vice-president's words do not seem much stronger than
those Dr. Kissinger had used a year earlier. But President Carter
apparently concluded that they needed to be orchestrated by his
whole administration. And indeed they were. Not only the vice-
president, but also the secretary of state, the U.S. representative
to the United Nations, the assistant secretary of state for African
affairs, and many other officials made similar points in
speeches and testimony before Congress. All of it was not
required to convince Mr. Vorster of the Carter administration's
policy; but it was important for Mr. Carter's new emphasis on
U.S. *ideological* interests around the world, i.e., his human

rights campaign. And here is the nub of the U.S. dilemma in southern Africa: how to make U.S. interests in that area compatible with the interests of black Africa without at the same time triggering a racial war in South Africa.

This dilemma was sharply articulated by former Under Secretary of State George Ball in an article in *The Atlantic Monthly* entitled "Asking for Trouble in South Africa." Ball took sharp issue with the idea of "one man, one vote" in South Africa because it raised expectations among black South Africans that he did not believe the United States was prepared to fulfill:

> No special prescience is required to foresee that our continued harping on the principle of "one man, one vote" is bound to encourage the hopes and ambitions of non-whites and increase their discontent with their current state. Yet, if our economic, social and political sanctions do not produce the majority rule we have promised, and South Africa is caught up in a desperately unequal guerrilla struggle, what help will we provide? Will we furnish the insurgents with the weapons to use in killing the white population? . . . Finally, will we intervene militarily to overthrow the current repressive South African government? Against the background of our Vietnam disillusionment, what could be more unlikely? Yet if, having encouraged insurrection by talk of "one man, one vote," we then refuse assistance, how will we justify that to American blacks? *Will not the implication of hypocrisy make us an easy target for the demagogues of the Third World and the propagandists of the Kremlin?*[15]

Ball especially feared a repetition of the backlash to U.S. rhetoric in 1956, when, after hearing Secretary of State Dulles proclaim for three years the U.S. government's intention to "roll back the Iron Curtain," the Hungarian Freedom Fighters staged their revolution only to find the United States unwilling to come to their rescue when Soviet tanks rumbled into Budapest. Would the United States be willing to send forces to help nonwhite South Africans achieve political "justice" if they staged a mass revolution and then faced annihilation at the hands of the South African military? Ball believes the

United States would not intervene; but what about the Soviets? "The Soviet Union (directly or through surrogates such as the Cubans) or even China, could greatly enhance its standing throughout the Third World by helping the embattled blacks—which would enormously intensify the Cold War condiment in the already overspiced South African stew." Ball concluded that U.S. diplomacy should strive for achievable ends rather than "stirring the blacks to insurrection while driving the Afrikaners into fierce resistance to any change whatever," which he charged is a prescription for unleashing "a resistible force against an immovable body—and the breakage could be frightful."[16]

How, then, do we assess United States interests vis-à-vis South Africa in the late 1970s? Judging by the many statements that U.S. officials have made in 1977 and the degree of U.S. economic involvement in South Africa, U.S. interests at this time appear to be as follows:

Defense interest: In terms of proximity to North America, South Africa cannot qualify as more than a peripheral interest of the United States. However, its strategic location between the South Atlantic and Indian oceans and its excellent port at Cape Town make it a major defense interest in terms of deployment of the U.S. Navy. Nevertheless, South Africa poses no direct threat to the United States nor its citizens and must therefore be considered only a peripheral defense interest.

Economic interest: U.S. private investment in South Africa amounts to about $1.5 billion, and approximately 350 U.S. firms have direct investments there. This represents about 17 percent of the total foreign investment in South Africa, running substantially behind that of Great Britain. South Africa has abundant supplies of many important minerals of value to U.S industry, and in 1975 it exported $0.8 billion to the United States while importing $1.3 billion in U.S. goods. Because of its strong economy and the large U.S. investment there, South Africa must be considered a *major* economic interest of the United States.

World order: Because it has the most dynamic economy in Africa and possesses the best military force in southern Africa,

South Africa must be counted as a *major* world order interest of the United States. However, it is clearly not a *vital* world order interest, no matter how hard Prime Minister Vorster argues that his country is the best hope against communist penetration of the whole continent. In truth, South Africa today is a growing danger to U.S. world order interests *because* of its unwillingness to shed apartheid and begin bringing nonwhites into its political life. If serious violence should occur in South Africa in the next few years, it could become a *vital* world order interest of the United States to prevent a full-scale race war, which could bring Soviet troops into Africa and threaten a great power confrontation there.

Ideological interest: Here the U.S. interest has clearly risen from the peripheral level, where it had been for much of the postwar period, to the *major* level in 1975, when South Africa's internal racial policies made it impossible for the United States to cooperate with it in the Angolan situation. The Carter administration's rhetoric in 1977 might lead one to conclude that the U.S. ideological interest has risen to the vital level; but for the reasons given by George Ball, the United States would probably not be willing to use force to support an ideological interest there. In sum, the overall U.S. interest in South Africa is at the *major* level, primarily for economic and ideological reasons; it is therefore unlikely that the U.S. government would be willing to support or defend the current government there if it got into serious difficulty, either with its own population or with its neighbors.

Interests of Black African States

As in the Panama case, the South African problem must also be seen in the context of its continental environment. But unlike Panama, which has the solid support of its Latin American neighbors, South Africa has had no political support among southern African states since Portugal left the scene. The collective interests of South Africa's northern neighbors seem to be as follows:

Defense interest: Since international pressure forced South

Africa to withdraw from Angola in 1976, the black African states are not concerned at this time about attacks from South Africa on their soil. The potential remains, however, and this interest must therefore be put at the *major* level.

Economic interest: Various reports indicate that there is a considerable clandestine trade between South Africa and the southern African states, which find it useful to continue this trade with South Africa despite the racial issue. In most cases, however, this is not a large economic factor, and this interest must therefore be seen by most states as being *peripheral.*

World order: It is more difficult to generalize here. Some black African states are willing to cooperate with South Africa if it begins to change its racial policies, but others seem determined to promote revolution in South Africa. In general, however, South Africa is a *major* world order interest of most black African states because it could engulf the region in warfare if its internal situation reaches the breaking point.

Ideological: Here there is no question of the intensity of interest—South Africa is a *vital* ideological interest of black African states because its apartheid policies are so reprehensible to their sense of justice. It is here that the breaking point could be reached in their relations with the Vorster regime, for these states could be radicalized quickly if a race war flared in South Africa.

Future Scenarios

What, then, are the most likely situations that could arise in South Africa in the next few years? How could they affect the security of the region and, perhaps, force the United States to become involved with more than words of advice? Here are three situations which could occur, along with an assessment of the interests of South Africa, the United States, and black Africa. Predictions as to what policies the three parties are likely to adopt to deal with the situations are also made.

Scenario 1: Prime Minister Vorster announces a partial loosening of the apartheid policy and a willingness to give coloureds and Asians a special status in South African society by establishing separate parliaments for them and modifying the apartheid laws. Vorster also agrees to discuss with black African leaders ways in which parts of the black population may be brought into the South African political framework.

In this scenario, Vorster decides to accept the counsel of the United States and other friendly states and moves toward accommodation with South Africa's nonwhite population. He does not contemplate full participation for the black majority, something Vice-President Mondale urged upon him at Vienna; however, he does plan to bring the coloureds and Asians into the political picture, giving them representation in separate parliaments and providing them civil liberties not greatly different from those accorded whites. Vorster feels strong enough politically following the national elections of November 1977 to deal with the extreme elements of the Nationalist Party, and he is willing to concede the United States' view that continuation of the current inflexible internal repression is a road to disaster for his country. In these circumstances, the interests of the three parties most directly involved would be those shown in Chart 10.1.

CHART 10.1

Issue: South Africa modifies apartheid policies			
Basic interest at stake	Intensity of interest		
	Survival	Vital	Major	Peripheral
Defense of homeland		South Africa	Black Africa	US
Economic well-being		South Africa	US Black Africa	
Favorable world order		South Africa Black Africa	US	
Ideological		South Africa Black Africa	US	

This chart suggests several points. First, with regard to *defense of homeland,* South Africa has a vital interest in preserving its territory and institutions against internal and external threats, but the United States has only a limited defense interest in southern Africa. Black Africa's fears of attack from South Africa in this situation are at the *major*, not the vital, level. Second, with regard to *economic well-being*, South Africa has a vital interest in maintaining its flourishing economy, which is heavily dependent on continued foreign investment. The United States and black Africa have a major interest in this factor because of the benefits of South Africa's trade with them. Third, with regard to the *world order*, South Africa and black Africa both have a vital interest, in this scenario, in resolving the internal conflicts of South Africa without resort to war or mass violence. The United States' interest here is at the major level. Fourth, with regard to *ideology*, both South Africa and black Africa have a vital interest in preserving their value systems in South Africa; and it is here, because of deep-seated emotional differences over what constitutes a "just" South African society, that their interests are most likely to conflict. The United States' ideological interest is *major;* it sides with the black African viewpoint but not to the extent of seeking to unseat the Vorster regime.

The policy implications of the national interests outlined in this scenario are the following: The U.S. government will applaud Prime Minister Vorster's initiative and encourage concessions to all elements of South African society. The United States will urge black African states to refrain from criticizing Vorster's efforts and to encourage him to do more by offering inducements through trade and goodwill missions, and soft words in the United Nations.

Black African states will be divided over Vorster's initiatives, but the moderate governments will go along with the U.S. lead so long as there is no new outbreak of repression in South Africa. The Soviet Union and Cuba may encourage leftist African regimes to denounce Vorster's program, but the latter will probably be in the minority. The success or failure of Vorster's policies in this scenario depends primarily on whether nonwhite South Africans see them as a genuine beginning of a process to abandon apartheid and to lay the foundation for a new and more equitable society.

Scenario 2: Prime Minister Vorster decides to stand firm

against all pressures to modify South African political life and warns both the United States and black Africa that they will be responsible for massive bloodshed if they encourage nonwhites in his country to employ violence against the regime. Vorster proceeds with plans to establish autonomous homelands for most South African blacks and maintains a strict ban on public opposition to government policies.

In this scenario, it is clear that following the November 1977 elections, Vorster feels strong enough politically to maintain the apartheid policies indefinitely and that this is a lesser evil than moving toward majority black rule—which he considers to be the outcome of Vice-President Mondale's prescription of "one man, one vote." In this scenario (Chart 10.2), the national interests of the three parties would be somewhat different from those in Scenario 1:

CHART 10.2

Issue:	South Africa reinforces apartheid policies			
Basic interest at stake		Intensity of interest		
	Survival	Vital	Major	Peripheral
Defense of homeland	South Africa	Black Africa	US	
Economic well-being			South Africa	Black Africa
Favorable world order		Black Africa	South Africa US	
Ideological	South Africa	Black Africa	US	

Chart 10.2 suggests several points. First, with regard to *defense of its homeland,* South Africa has a *survival* interest in preserving its territory and institutions in the face of growing conflict. The U.S. interest is still major. Black Africa's interest moves up to *vital,* because the prospects for war have increased considerably in these circumstances. Second, with regard to *economic well-being,* South Africa has clearly subordinated its economic interests, because it is willing to pay a large economic price—trade embargoes and the like—to maintain the rigid apartheid policies. Black Africa's economic interest drops also

in these circumstances. The U.S. interest remains at the major level because of heavy U.S. investments and trade. Third, with regard to the *world order,* South Africa also subordinates its interest in the attitude of the rest of the world—including the United States—to a major role. Black Africa increases its interest because of fear that war will result from the South African policies and that they will become involved whether they wish to or not. Fourth, with regard to *ideology,* the South African interest rises to the survival level, because it is unwilling to make any concessions and in effect rejects pressures from both the United States and Western Europe. A siege mentality has set in. Black Africa's ideological interest rises to the *vital* level, because its views will be polarized at the opposite extreme as South Africa hardens its view at the other. The United States, despite the outrage felt by large segments of its society, will continue to have a *major,* not a vital, interest at the ideological level—one precluding the use of force to change the situation within South Africa.

Several policy conclusions can be drawn from this analysis of Scenario 2. The United States will conduct a "damage limiting" policy in southern Africa, seeking to restrain the radical elements in black Africa who wish to start a holy war against South Africa. At the same time, it will begin to exert political and economic pressure on South Africa to get it to change its policies. It might also begin supporting a rival white political faction in South Africa in the hope of providing a rival voice to Vorster's government, a voice around which dissident white groups can rally. However, the United States would not seek the overthrow of the Vorster government by force because the resulting chaos might play into the hands of the Soviet Union. In effect, this scenario implies a growing confrontation between South Africa and the rest of Africa, with the prospect that the Soviet Union and Cuba might try to take advantage of the situation in order to radicalize the politics of southern Africa to their own advantage. Insurgency will grow in South Africa, and bloodshed will increase.

Scenario 3: The South African government announces that it will partition the country into two sectors, with the western and far northern areas becoming the homeland of the black population and the rest being the homeland of the whites, coloureds, and Asians who wish to remain. The Vorster government offers citizenship in the new South Africa to coloureds and Asians who pass a qualifying test, with a target of about one million nonwhites to be given full voting rights in the South African political system.

In this scenario, the Vorster government partially accepts U.S. proposals for full political participation by nonwhites. However, blacks will not be given the citizenship and equality in South Africa but will be offered full participation in the political life of a new homeland, or several homelands as they may choose, where South Africa would be willing to relinquish sovereignty and insist only that the new territory be demilitarized. In effect, South Africa would create a new buffer zone made up of black South Africans to replace the buffers of Namibia and Rhodesia. Blacks in this new territory would be able to work in South Africa for specified periods of time, but they would not be given citizenship nor would their families be allowed to accompany them. The new country would have its own government and could declare its full independence if desired. But it would have to renounce its right to establish an armed force and also declare its intention not to become hostile toward South Africa. The coloureds and Asians will be gradually integrated into South African society on the model of the U.S. experience. Whites would still outnumber nonwhites, and in a restricted franchise would hold a three-to-one majority at the polls. Given this scenario, what would be the national interests of the parties involved (Chart 10.3)?

Chart 10.3 suggests several points. First, with regard to the *defense of homeland,* South Africa's interest is again at the vital level. Black Africa's drops back to the major level, because the risk of a race war in South Africa is probably diminished if South Africa turns over a substantial part of its territory to a new black homeland, or homelands, in which blacks will have sovereignty. Second, with regard to *economic well-being,* Scenario 3 returns to the pattern in Scenario 1, because it suggests that South Africa is sufficiently concerned about its economic well-being to make significant changes in its

CHART 10.3

Issue: South Africa decides on partition			
Basic interest at stake	Intensity of interest		
	Survival	Vital	Major	Peripheral
Defense of homeland		South Africa	Black Africa	US
Economic well-being		South Africa	Black Africa US	
Favorable world order		South Africa Black Africa	US	
Ideological		South Africa	US Black Africa	

political structure. And the black African states as well as the United States would see possibilities for continuing trade with this new South Africa, even if it refused to give citizenship to blacks but instead provided them with a real homeland. Third, with regard to the *world order,* South Africa and black Africa would have a vital interest in seeing whether this significant change in South Africa could work before either abandoned the idea. Much would depend on how sincere the Vorster government was in giving adequate land and resources to the new black nation, and how faithfully it integrated the coloureds and Asians into its white society. The United States would support this program if it could be sold to a majority of black African states. Fourth, with regard to *ideology,* South Africa's interest would still be at the vital level, but this implies some flexibility. The black African ideological interest would be mixed—some states would view it as *vital* to prevent a partition of South Africa, but most would view it as worth a try, particularly if the United States and Western Europe urged that it be given a fair chance.

The policy implications of Scenario 3 are these: the United States would not reject the partition plan, but neither would it lend support until it had firm assurances from Vorster that partition would be fair to blacks as well as to the coloureds and

Asians. This would mean South Africa would have to give up not only much good land, but some important mining areas as well. A phony partition in which the blacks get only marginal land would not satisfy the requirement that the territory of South Africa be divided equitably.

And here is where the whole scenario would probably falter. Is it reasonable to believe that South African whites would be willing to give up large and profitable areas of their country for the purpose of getting peace on their borders and within their homeland? The history of South Africa since 1948 does not provide much optimism. On the other hand, Prime Minister Vorster might be enough of a realist to see that considerable sacrifices will have to be made if whites in South Africa hope to retain majority rule for themselves and peace with their neighbors.

The Outlook

In his article on South Africa, Seymour Topping cites the editor of a South African newspaper who predicts that South Africa will have black majority rule within four years. "The National Party, he predicted, would cave in under the pressure of internal violence, guerrilla infiltration from Black Africa and international economic sanctions."[17] This seems too simple an outcome for the struggle looming in South Africa. The Vorster government will more likely be able to withstand the internal pressures for a long time, with various degrees of repression against its opposition. Indeed, South Africa's position vis-à-vis its neighbors is not unlike that of Israel surrounded by Arab countries: both have the military power and the will to defend their homelands and their way of life, and they will make great sacrifices to do so—including ignoring the advice of the United States. The greatest difference in the two situations is that Israel probably can count on U.S. support if the Soviets or any combination of Arab states should pose a real threat to the existence of Israel; but this could not be said for South Africa if it is faced with a force of Cuban-backed guerrillas overrunning large portions of its territory. The reasons are not hard to find, for they lie in the ethnic background of the two segments of American society most directly affected by events in these two parts of the world. Regarding the Middle East, the powerful Jewish community in the United States considers Israel to be a vital interest of the United States. But in the South African case, the large black community in the United States is strongly opposed to the racist South African regime and has brought great pressure to bear on U.S. policy to abandon its "benign neglect" stance and get on the side of the black African states. Both the Ford and Carter administrations have now done so. But South Africa's determination to stand firm has not been shaken. On the contrary, no one familiar with the history of the Dutch settlers in South Africa and their tenacity over three hundred years believes they will be swayed by sentiments or the so-called logic of the situation when they feel their survival is at stake. That is why it would be foolish to assume that Prime Minister Vorster will acquiesce in having his country accept majority black rule. He will probably never permit it. This leaves two alternatives: either a massive and prolonged race war in southern Africa in which the most advanced weapons will be used by the Pretoria government, or some kind of partition that permits the whites to remain the majority in the new political system. The world will have the answer in the next few years.

11. Epilogue:
The Challenge to Carter

Most observers of the U.S. political scene agree that U.S. foreign policy has been in transition during the 1970s. But they disagree about the future: will it bring a new consensus at home and a more peaceful world abroad? Or will the 1980s bring greater divisions at home and a less stable world order? Henry Kissinger probably represents a pessimistic view and Zbigniew Brzezinski a more optimistic view. Whatever answers the 1980s may bring, however, there will be three fundamental changes in the way the United States views its national interests and formulates its foreign policy.

The first change is the way we look at the use of conventional military force as a tool of foreign policy. The Vietnam experience and the new balance of nuclear terror between the United States and the Soviet Union have taught us that military intervention outside North America can be costly and dangerous and must be undertaken only for national interests that are truly *vital* to the well-being of the country.

The second change is our new awareness, since the 1973 Arab oil embargo, that the United States is vulnerable to manipulation by foreign countries—both in key natural resources such as oil and in the financial stability of its economy. The huge U.S. balance of trade deficits at the end of 1977 and the sharp decline in the value of the dollar were signals of a potential economic crisis that could have vast repercussions for both the domestic economy and the world economic order.

The third fundamental change is that the United States no longer has a consensus on foreign policy goals and may not achieve this goal in the near future. This results only in part from the Vietnam experience. More important, it is bound up in the generational mood that surfaced in the mid-1960s, when children born after 1945 were coming to maturity and challenging the assumptions held by earlier generations about America's place in the world. It is not yet clear whether this new generation, and the one following it in the 1980s, will be equally, or less, prepared than the 1945 generation to make sacrifices to enhance U.S. security and economic well-being. At the beginning of 1978, the trend was not at all clear, and the lack of consensus persists.

What these changes require, it seems to me, is a far more rigorous effort by the U.S. government—both executive and legislative branches—to define U.S. national interests for the 1980s and 1990s so that the choices are clear and the costs are carefully calculated. The record of Congress and the American people in 1977 in facing up to the implications of the huge increase in oil imports raises questions about whether this country will look realistically at its interests in the 1980s, when world oil production will begin to decline and energy costs will rise shockingly. The human rights campaign by the Carter administration may be admirable in reemphasizing the basic ideological interests of the American people; but if it does little to protect U.S. economic well-being and to increase international security in the face of growing Soviet ambitions and international terrorism, then what is its real value?

If war can be averted in the Middle East and if Israel and its neighbors can begin to establish a peaceful relationship in the next few years, the most important national interest of the United States will be its own economic well-being and that of the noncommunist world. The real danger is that if the standard of living of Americans goes down as a result of increasing energy costs, protectionism will become a real threat in the 1980s and cause deep problems for the Western alliance. The political impact on Europe of the 1973 oil embargo is a foretaste of what democratic governments are capable of doing when national economies are threatened. It may be concluded, therefore, that U.S. policymakers must have a clear idea of what tools of policy should be employed to deal with threats to the economic well-being of the United States and the Western world. Some have argued that force may have to be employed if there is another oil embargo. But the current mood of the American public casts doubt that force would be approved to resolve *any* economic issue. And force may not work.

In the final analysis, correctly defining national interests and properly selecting policy tools to support them will count for little if the American internal consensus on foreign policy is not rebuilt. It is a cliché to say that Congress reflects the mood of the American people and that Congress is now divided because the country is divided. But there was a time in the early post-1945 period when statesmen appeared in the Congress, men such as Senator Arthur Vandenberg and Speaker Sam Rayburn, who took the leadership in molding a consensus in foreign policy. Is it impossible for this to happen again, at a time when a new president, Jimmy Carter, needs help from Congress in fashioning a realistic foreign policy for the 1980s?

Former President Gerald Ford, in his speech at the University of Kentucky (see Chapter 7), summed it up as well as anyone when he said:

We need to seek once again a common ground on which the President, the Congress and the American people can proudly and firmly stand through crisis and calm. We must decide again, as a nation, what is important to us, what goals we will set, what dangers we will risk, what burdens we will bear, in our dealings with the wider world. The Congress has the responsibility to do now what it does best—debate these great issues, openly, freely and thoroughly—and help us find a new path on which we all may travel together. The new administration—free of the burden of war, unfettered by mistakes of the past—has an historic opportunity to lead America to a new age in foreign policy: an age in which the goals and commitments we hold precious as a nation may be fulfilled through the quiet, beneficient strength that commands respect and invites cooperation.[1]

Several major events occurred during the early months of 1978 that provided hope that the U.S. government was beginning to pull itself together on foreign policy and to deal effectively with a series of international issues that had been left in abeyance for several years. The most notable example was Senate ratification of the Panama Canal treaties after three months of debate. The Carter administration staked its credibility on getting the Senate to approve the treaties, a feat which the Johnson, Nixon, and Ford administrations had not been able to accomplish during the previous decade. Although the president's view of the national interest prevailed by the thinnest of margins on both votes (68 for and 32 against), it was nevertheless a clear victory for Jimmy Carter on a crucial issue in American foreign policy.

Following this victory, the president decided to do battle on another critical issue: whether to meet the defense needs of Egypt and Saudi Arabia, as well as those of Israel, in the search for a lasting Middle East peace. The stakes were nearly as high as in the Senate's Panama Canal debate, with pro-Israeli forces determined to block the president's plan to sell F-15 fighters to Saudi Arabia. The administration decided to treat the Saudi Arabian sale and the sale of F-5 aircraft to Egypt as a "package"—meaning that Israel would get additional fighter planes only if the other sales were also affirmed by Congress. The president's view of U.S. interests in the Middle East prevailed on this issue, and the Senate voted 54-44 to support the administration's policy. The vote affirmed Senate support of the president's backing of President Sadat of Egypt in his search for a Middle East peace settlement based on United Nations Resolution 242, which calls for Israeli withdrawal from Arab territories occupied during the 1967 Middle East war. It also provided tacit congressional support for Carter's tougher policy toward Prime Minister Begin's government in Israel, which continued to insist that the occupied Arab territory on the West Bank of the Jordan River was part of the historic Israeli homeland and could not be relinquished. The vote represented a significant victory for Carter's efforts to reassert presidential authority in matters of U.S. national interest.

Turkish aid was another issue. In 1974, after Turkey invaded Cyprus to prevent the Greek Cypriot majority from uniting the island with Greece, Congress cut off the sale of military equipment to Turkey. In retaliation, Turkey denied the United States use of vitally important military facilities on Turkish soil and talked about withdrawing from the military organization of NATO unless the United States lifted its embargo on arms sales. Turkey also claimed that no progress could be made in negotiations with Greek Cypriots as long as the United States refused to sell Turkey spare parts for equipment previously purchased. In 1978, President Carter decided that U.S. interests involved in the continuing use of Turkish bases were of much greater importance than the question of Turkish forces in northern Cyprus, and he chose to do battle with pro-Greek elements in Congress over the issue. The outcome of this battle was indicative of his determination to assert presidential prerogative in defining U.S. national interests.

Neither of the cases cited above compares in importance, however, with the battle in the Senate over ratification of a new strategic arms agreement with the Soviet Union. President Carter knew from the time he took office in January 1977 that there would be strong Senate opposition to a new SALT accord, and his delay in submitting a treaty to the Senate resulted in part from the realization that he needed to regain enough authority in foreign policy to enable his administration to overcome congressional opposition. As with the Panama Canal issue, the president must win over a *two-thirds* majority of the Senate in order to approve the agreement. It seems unlikely that 67 senators will vote in favor of a SALT agreement in 1978. Therefore, the president will probably submit a new SALT agreement to the Senate in 1979, in hopes that a campaign of public education will eventually win grass-roots support for the treaty and persuade undecided senators to accept his view of the national interests involved.

In all of these cases, the fundamental question is not the specific foreign policy issue involved, but rather the authority of the president to be the *primary* influence in defining national interests. Obviously, Congress will play a far more important role in foreign policy than it has in the recent past; but some members of Congress, and some important pressure groups in the United States, are convinced that *Congress* should play the primary role in deciding national interests—

just as it has the primary role in declaring war. In the wake of presidential abuse of power during the 1960s and early 1970s, it is as difficult for President Carter as it was for President Ford to assert presidential authority in foreign policy; but Carter realized early in 1978 that he had to make an effort or resign himself to having little credibility with allied governments. He feared that adversaries might be misled into believing the American president powerless to defend U.S. interests. As we learned from President Kennedy's dealings with Nikita Khrushchev, the president must be able to convince Kremlin leaders that he *does* speak for the United States and that he will *not* be undercut by a Congress which cannot itself agree on many issues of foreign policy. In sum, the real issue in American foreign policy in 1978 remains the authority of the president to decide U.S. national interests in consultation with Congress without being hamstrung by the legislative branch.

The struggle for control will continue as Carter deals with current problems. For example, the early months of 1978 brought the conflicts within black African states before the American public in a manner reminiscent of the way Southeast Asia burst upon the American scene in the early 1960s. Indeed, many of the statements made by politicians, journalists, and some government officials in early 1978 caused those with keen memories to recall similar sentiments expressed during the Kennedy administration regarding Laos, Cambodia, and Vietnam. Hints of a new domino theory being applied to Africa were heard, and critics asked when President Jimmy Carter "would draw the line" on Soviet and Cuban penetration of Africa.

Every new American president is obliged to face such Soviet challenges and to decide how the United States should respond to them, but the crucial question is whether the new chief executive will resist the temptation to conclude that the United States can and should intervene with large amounts of money and arms anywhere in the world simply because the Soviet Union supports a leftist government or an insurgency. Cuban and Soviet armed intervention in several African countries does not automatically mean that a *vital* U.S. interest is at stake. However, some of the rhetoric heard in the United States during the early months of 1978 suggests that many Americans believe this to be true. Vietnam should have taught us that the role of world policeman is not one the American people will accept. In light of this fact, the task of an American president is to correctly define U.S. interests in various areas of the world and take a strong stand *only* in those places where the stakes are indeed vital. In my view, no part of Africa today fits that category. I therefore hope that the Carter administration will refrain from becoming deeply involved in Africa, because to do so would court another tragedy in American foreign policy.

Notes

Chapter 1

1. This definition and its elaboration is contained in the author's article "National Interests and Foreign Policy: A Conceptual Framework for Analysis and Decision-Making," *British Journal of International Studies,* October 1976, p. 247.

2. This in no way denies the importance of bureaucratic and interest group influence in deciding what is in the national interest. The point here is that eventually a cabinet secretary, or in serious situations, the president, must determine how deeply the national interest is affected by an external event, or threat, and what policies are required to deal with it. In the United States, the president's perception of the national interest is the one that will be debated by Congress and the public—particularly when he decides that a vital interest is at stake and that military action may be required. (See Chapters 3 and 4 for illustrations of how four U.S. presidents dealt with this question.)

3. These value factors and cost factors are described in some detail in Chapter 2.

4. These terms were first used in Nuechterlein, "National Interests and Foreign Policy," pp. 149-150.

5. There have been several authoritative studies on this crisis as well as a well-documented film entitled "Missiles of October," produced for television in 1974. Robert Devine, ed., *The Cuban Missile Crisis* (Chicago, 1971) contains the texts of important statements made during the crisis as well as critical analyses by a number of writers on President Kennedy's handling of this crisis.

6. This analysis does not take account of the Soviet Union's

subsequent threat to President Nixon that it might intervene if the United States did not restrain Israeli armies after they took the offensive against Egyptian forces. That threat, if carried out, would have changed the whole complexion of the war and clearly would have involved a vital world order interest of the United States.

Chapter 2

1. This discussion will focus on U.S. criteria, in order to illustrate the ingredients that should be taken into consideration under each of the sixteen factors. However, it is my view that most of these factors are also applicable to other major powers if the wording of the factors is altered to meet the political situation in a specific country. For example, "risk of public opposition" might be changed to "risk of *party* opposition" for the Soviet Union; or, "sentimental attachment" might be changed to "*cultural* attachment" for France; or, "risk of congressional opposition" might be changed to "risk of *adverse vote in parliament*" for Britain.

2. Spain lost its great power status when the United States defeated it in the Spanish-American War and forced it to give up Cuba, the Philippines, and Guam. The United States then became the first non-European country to become a great power. Japan followed a few years later when it defeated the Russian navy and went on to extend its influence in Northeast Asia.

3. The War Powers Act, passed by Congress in 1973 over the veto of the president, limits his use of the armed forces to deal with threats other than a direct threat to the United States (defense interests). This legislation was a sharp break with historical precedent and was enacted in the wake of congressional displeasure over the way President Nixon used the armed forces to bring about a peace treaty in Vietnam. It is unlikely that such legislation would have passed had a Democratic president been in the White House. (See Chapter 7.)

Chapter 3

1. Patrick Devlin, *Too Proud To Fight: Woodrow Wilson's Neutrality* (New York, 1975), p. 686.

2. Newton D. Baker, *Why We Went To War* (New York, 1936), pp. 138-139.

3. Arthur S. Link, *Wilson: Campaigns for Progressivism and Peace* (Princeton, N.J., 1965), p. 411.

4. Ibid., p. 414.

5. Gilbert C. Fite and Norman A. Graebner, *Recent United States History* (New York, 1972), p. 103.

6. Woodrow Wilson, *The Public Papers of Woodrow Wilson*, ed. Ray Stannard Baker and William E. Dodd (New York, 1925-1927), vol. 2, *The New Democracy* (1925), pp. 407-414.

7. Ibid., pp. 422-426.

8. Ibid., pp. 428-435.

9. Wilson, *Public Papers*, vol. 1, *War and Peace*, (1925), pp. 6-16.

10. Link, *Wilson: Campaigns for Progressivism and Peace*, p. 410. In a footnote, Link quotes J. Howard Whitehouse as saying, after a meeting with Wilson on April 12: "He said the position of Russia was very uncertain. It might be that in setting up their new form of Government and working out domestic reforms they would find the war an intolerable evil and would desire to get to an end of it on any reasonable terms. It would be a serious blow to the Allies if that took place."

11. Ross Gregory, *The Origins of American Intervention in the First World War* (New York, 1971), p. 123.

12. It was not lost on Roosevelt that British forces occupied Iceland, a crucial stepping stone from Europe to North America, only a week before the Germans had planned to do so.

13. Franklin D. Roosevelt, *The Public Papers and Addresses of Franklin D. Roosevelt* (New York, 1938-1950), vol. 9, *War and Aid to Democracies, 1940*, pp. 260-261.

14. Ibid., p. 391.

15. Ibid., pp. 494-495.

16. William Stevenson, *A Man Called Intrepid: The Secret War* (New York, 1976), claims that Roosevelt's secret correspondence with Churchill during this period showed that the president was not entirely truthful with the American people, that he was working clandestinely to provide the British with as much war material as the United States was able to give.

17. See Robert E. Sherwood, *The White House Papers of Harry L. Hopkins* (New York, 1948), pp. 222-223.

18. Roosevelt, *Public Papers*, 9:606-607.

19. These and the following quotations are excerpted from Roosevelt's "Fireside Chat on National Security," ibid., pp. 633-644.

20. Ibid., p. 640.

21. Ibid., p. 669.

22. See Henry L. Stimson and McGeorge Bundy, *On Active Service*

in Peace and War (New York, 1947), Chapter 15.

23. James McGregor Burns, *Roosevelt: The Soldier of Freedom, 1940-1945* (New York, 1971), Chapter 1.

24. *Documents on American Foreign Relations*, vol. 4, World Peace Foundation (Boston, 1942), p. 21.

25. Ibid., p. 39.

Chapter 4

1. Some may argue that China was a major land power when it intervened in Korea in 1950 and that North Korea could not have launched its attack without large military support from the Soviet Union. Nevertheless, Soviet troops were not involved, and Chinese forces entered the war only after U.S. forces moved into North Korea and threatened to go to the Chinese border.

2. Harry S. Truman, *Memoirs* (New York, 1955-1956), vol. 2, *Years of Trial and Hope*, p. 351.

3. Dean Acheson, *Present at the Creation* (New York, 1969), p. 405. Emphasis added.

4. Acheson, *Present at the Creation*, pp. 414-415.

5. Harry S. Truman, *Public Papers of the Presidents of the United States, Harry S. Truman, 1950* (Washington, D.C., 1965), pp. 528, 531, 536.

6. Ibid., p. 541.

7. Ibid., pp. 741-742.

8. Eric F. Goldman, *The Tragedy of Lyndon Johnson* (New York, 1969), p. 380.

9. *The Pentagon Papers, New York Times* ed. (New York, 1971), document 21, pp. 133, 135.

10. Ibid., p. 133.

11. Lyndon B. Johnson, *The Vantage Point* (New York, 1971), p. 115.

12. Lyndon B. Johnson, *Public Papers of the Presidents, Lyndon B. Johnson, 1963-1964* (Washington, D.C.: 1965), pp. 931-932.

13. Congressional Quarterly Service, *Congress and the Nation*, vol. 2, 1965-68, "Tonkin Gulf Resolution Text," p. 636. Emphasis added.

14. Johnson, *The Vantage Point*, pp. 118-119.

15. Ibid., p. 145.

16. Ibid., p. 149.

17. Ibid., pp. 151-153.

18. Johnson, *Public Papers 1965*, p. 794.

Chapter 5

1. Possible exceptions were Roosevelt's statements during the election campaign of 1940 and his arguments for Lend-Lease early in 1941, in which he continued to assure the country that he did not believe U.S. forces would have to fight in Europe. Later in 1941, he stopped making these assertions, knowing that it was only a matter of time before the United States would be in the war.

2. Senator Joseph McCarthy of Wisconsin had become a national figure by this time, as a result of his campaign to show that the U.S. government harbored communist subversives. He and other Republicans sought to convince the country that the communists had come to power in China because of Truman's inept policies.

3. These kinds of questions are usually analyzed in considerable detail by the State Department's Policy Planning Staff, the Office of Plans and Policy in the Joint Chiefs of Staff, the secretary of defense's Planning Staff, and the National Security Council Staff. Although there is no claim here that the planning staffs address all these factors in this fashion, it is certain that they assess many of them and provide their best judgment to the president and the National Security Council before the decisions are made at that level.

4. North Korea and the Soviet Union, which supported the invasion, may well have concluded that the U.S. withdrawal of its occupation troops from Korea meant that the United States did not consider this to be a vital interest and would not fight there. Secretary of State Acheson's speech at the National Press Club in February 1950 to the effect that the U.S. defense line in the Pacific included Japan and the Philippines also implied to the world that Korea was not part of that defense perimeter.

5. It is noteworthy that a Vietnam-frustrated Congress voted this legislation over a presidential veto in 1973 and that its constitutionality has been questioned by some legal experts. President Ford continued to argue that the legislation was not binding on the president. For a more detailed discussion of the war powers legislation, see Chapter 7.

6. This "Vietnamization" of the war finally became U.S. policy in the Nixon administration, after Johnson decided in 1968 to deescalate the war and seek a negotiated settlement with the North.

Chapter 6

1. Sihanouk had long charged that the SEATO agreement, which gave protection to Thailand—Cambodia's historic enemy—was a

threat to his country and that the United States would not stand in the way if Thailand and South Vietnam decided to crush his kingdom between them.

2. *Foreign Affairs*, October 1967, pp. 113-114.

3. Ibid., p. 111.

4. Ibid., p. 121.

5. Richard M. Nixon, *U.S. Foreign Policy for the 1970's: A New Structure for Peace*, Report to the Congress by the President, February 18, 1970, pp. 63, 64.

6. Ibid., p. 71. Emphasis added.

7. In a deposition given by former President Nixon in 1976 concerning the wiretaps of White House aide, Morton Halperin, the *New York Times* reported on March 11, 1976 that Nixon had stated for the first time that the Cambodian incursion was endorsed by his national security adviser, Dr. Kissinger, and that his secretary of state, William Rogers, and his secretary of defense, Melvin Laird, were opposed to the operation.

8. The secret bombing of Cambodia had first been reported by William Beecher in a *New York Times* article on May 9, 1969. This leak caused a furor in the White House and led to the installation of wiretaps on prominent journalists and administration officials in an effort to determine the source of this breakdown in security.

9. *Department of State Bulletin*, May 11, 1970, p. 602.

10. *Department of State Bulletin*, May 18, 1970, p. 617.

11. *Department of State Bulletin*, May 18, 1970, p. 618.

12. *Department of State Bulletin*, May 18, 1970, p. 619, 620.

13. *Department of State Bulletin*, May 18, 1970, p. 620. Emphasis added.

14. This view of Nixon was supported in his TV interview with David Frost on ABC television May 19, 1977, when the former president asserted that his only regret was that he had not acted earlier and more strongly to deal with the North Vietnamese sanctuaries.

15. *Congressional Quarterly*, May 15, 1970, p. 1315.

16. *Congressional Quarterly*, May 15, 1970, p. 1316.

17. *Congressional Quarterly*, May 15, 1970, p. 1317.

18. *Department of State Bulletin*, June 22, 1970, pp. 763-764.

19. *Department of State Bulletin*, July 20, 1970, pp. 67, 72.

20. The so-called Cooper-Church amendment to the Foreign Military Sales Bill before the Senate would have forced the president to obtain specific authorization from Congress to continue military operations or grant military aid of any kind to Cambodia.

21. When the House Judiciary Committee discussed impeachment

charges against Nixon in the summer of 1974, one of the articles of impeachment dealt with the secret bombing of Cambodia, ordered by the president in March 1969, and subsequent administration efforts to keep this action secret from Congress. The article was debated in committee and finally voted down with twelve members favoring and twenty-six opposing its being forwarded to the House. The debate showed, however, how deeply the Cambodia issue in general had affected the attitude of many members toward the president and his foreign policy. (U.S., Congress, House, Committee on Judiciary, *Debate on Articles of Impeachment*, 93rd Cong., 2d sess., 1974, pp. 490-517.)

22. It is of some note here that the area known as the Parrot's Beak in Cambodia, where Nixon sent U.S. troops in 1970, again received world attention at the beginning of 1978, when Cambodian and Vietnamese troops clashed there in fierce fighting. The communist government in Phnom Penh apparently tried to oust the Vietnamese from this and other areas they occupied in eastern Cambodia, just as U.S. and South Vietnamese troops had done in 1970. Now a unified communist Vietnam resisted this attempt, and there appeared little chance that Cambodia would be more successful in removing Vietnamese forces from its territory than it had been when Sihanouk and Lon Nol were in charge of the country. (*New York Times*, January 1, 1978, p. 1.)

Chapter 7

1. Title I, Sec. 101(a), Public Law 253, 80th Cong., 1st sess.

2. In 1977, President Carter considered the desirability of making the secretary of the treasury a statutory member of the NSC, but made no decision. Nevertheless, Secretary Blumenthal plays a key part in the NSC decision-making system.

3. Title I, Sec. 101(b), Public Law 253.

4. Only a few officials were willing to take issue with administration policy on Vietnam, among them George Ball, under secretary of state, and Townsend Hoopes, deputy assistant secretary of defense. Several officials in the Central Intelligence Agency who dared to question the efficacy of administration policy were, like Ball and Hoopes, cut out of the inner circle of decision makers.

5. Nixon, *U.S. Foreign Policy for the 1970's*, p. 22.

6. These groups had been established already in the Johnson administration.

7. *U.S. Foreign Policy for the 1970's*, pp. 20, 21.

8. The *Washington Post,* for example, carried an article on March 28, 1977, entitled "Brzezinski, Vance are Watched for Hint of a Policy Struggle."

9. Dom Bonafede, *National Journal,* October 15, 1977, p. 1598.

10. The three-year reign of Henry Kissinger during the last part of the Nixon presidency and the Ford interregnum, from 1973 to 1976, is not considered an exception, because Kissinger has a low opinion of the State Department bureaucracy and operated with only a few close aides while there. In effect, Kissinger moved the top NSC staff to the State Department in 1973. In his view, the Foreign Service did not respond adequately to the opportunities he provided to develop new policies. On the other hand, Kissinger's management style did not instill loyalty toward him in the career Foreign Service either.

11. The roll call vote in the House on July 18 showed 244 in favor and 170 against its bill. The Senate's version was approved on July 18 by a margin of seventy-two in favor and eighteen against.

12. *Congressional Quarterly,* October 13, 1973, p. 2741.

13. See Public Law 93-148, 93rd Cong., H. J. Res, 542, Nov. 7, 1973.

14. "The War Powers Resolution: Striking a Balance between the Executive and Legislative Branches," p. 4. Delivered by Gerald R. Ford on April 11, 1977, at the University of Kentucky in Louisville. The text was reprinted by the American Enterprise Institute, Washington, D.C.

15. Ibid., p. 6.

16. *Washington Post,* October 25, 1977, p. A19.

Chapter 8

1. David McCullough, *The Path between the Seas: The Creation of the Panama Canal, 1870-1914* (New York, 1977), p. 11.

2. Ibid., p. 139.

3. Ibid., pp. 388-395.

4. Juan Antonio Tack, *Letter to the Secretary General of the United Nations, U Thant,* October 4, 1971. Ministry of Foreign Affairs of the Republic of Panama, pp. 24-25.

5. McCullough, *Path between the Seas,* pp. 383-384. Emphasis added.

6. *Congressional Digest,* April 1976, p. 128.

7. Tack, *Letter to the Secretary General,* pp. 26, 27, 28, 31.

8. U.S., Department of State, Address by Sol Linowitz, "Why a New Panama Canal Treaty?" delivered at Denver, Colorado, August 19, 1977, p. 1.

9. U.S., Department of State, News Release, September 27, 1977, "Defense Authorities Discuss Panama Canal Treaties," p. 3.

10. Ibid., p. 2.

11. U.S., Department of State, Statement, "New Panama Canal Treaties," September 8, 1977, p. 1.

12. U.S., Department of State, Statement, "New Panama Canal Treaties," September 26, 1977, pp. 1, 2.

13. Ibid., p. 3.

14. Ibid., p. 2.

15. U.S., Department of State, Speech by Ambassador Bunker before the World Affairs Council of Pittsburgh, "The Panama Canal and the Imperative of Change," October 14, 1977, pp. 2, 3.

16. *Congressional Digest*, April 1976, pp. 107, 128.

17. *Weekly Compilation of Presidential Documents* 12, no. 41 (October 11, 1976): 1456.

18. *Washington Post*, October 15, 1977, p. 1.

19. U.S., Department of State, "Why a New Panama Canal Treaty?" August 19, 1977, pp. 1-2.

20. *Washington Post*, October 11, 1977, p. A2.

21. *Washington Post*, October 23, 1977, p. A30.

22. *Washington Post*, November 21, 1977, p. A5.

23. The Senate ratified the treaties on March 10 and on April 18, 1978. The vote was the same in both cases, 68 for and 32 against.

Chapter 9

1. *New York Times*, December 7, 1976, p. 1.

2. Ibid., December 27, 1976, p. 1.

3. For a perceptive account of the French Canadian role in confederation, see Dale C. Thompson, "Quebec and the Bicultural Dimension," in *Canada-United States Relations*, ed. H. Edward English (New York, 1976).

4. In the 1975 federal elections, the Liberals captured 60 out of 74 Quebec seats in parliament. This represented 40 percent of their 141 seats, a very significant part of their national support.

5. *New York Times*, November 4, 1977, p. 1.

6. It is noteworthy that the methodology used to arrive at these policy statements was similar to the framework outlined in Chapter 1 of this volume.

7. Canada, Department of External Affairs, *Foreign Policy for Canadians* (Ottawa, 1970), p. 9.

8. Ibid., pp. 10-11.

9. Ibid., pp. 20-21.

10. Thompson, "Quebec and the Bicultural Dimension," p. 31.

11. Mitchell Sharp, "Canada-U.S. Relations," *International Perspectives*, Autumn 1972, p. 1.

12. Ibid., p. 13.

13. Ibid., p. 17.

14. After August 1971, Canadian government representatives were much tougher in their negotiations with the United States. It was in that month that Secretary of the Treasury John Connally, alienated Canadian officials by insisting that Canada alter its trading relations with the United States on the same basis as Japan and the West European countries. Connally's apparently brutal handling of the Canadians at that time effectively ended the "special relationship" Ottawa had with Washington in economic matters, and Canadians drew the inevitable conclusions. By 1977 this attitude changed to a more cooperative spirit, but not to the pre-1971 good feeling.

15. *Summary of the Programme of the Statutes of the Parti Québécois*, Montreal, 1975, p. 4.

16. Ibid., p. 5.

17. A poll conducted in Quebec in October 1977 by the respected team of Maurice Pinard and Richard Hamilton found that only 15 percent of respondents favored outright independence from Canada and that an additional 26 percent were in favor of independence "in economic association" with the rest of Canada. Furthermore, 42 percent had a favorable attitude toward the Lévesque government.

18. *Foreign Affairs*, July 1976, pp. 741, 744.

19. Canadian Embassy, Washington, D.C., "Address by Pierre Elliott Trudeau," February 22, 1977.

20. *New York Times*, February 24, 1977, p. 22. Emphasis added.

21. *Washington Post*, February 26, 1977, p. A12.

22. In May 1977 five Canadian provinces, including Ontario, declared that they would not favor an economic association with Quebec if it decided to become independent. *New York Times*, May 4, 1977, p. 5.

23. *New York Times*, January 1, 1978, p. 1.

24. See Wayne G. Reilly, "Canada, Quebec and Theories of Internal War," *The American Review of Canadian Studies*, Autumn 1973, pp. 67-75.

25. Richard Simeon, ed., *Must Canada Fail* (Montreal, 1977), p. 1.

26. In October 1977, a splinter group did split from Lévesque's party and formed the Movement for Quebec Independence (MIQ). It was uncertain whether it would operate as a full political party or

become a radical pressure group for Quebec separation from Canada, with or without economic ties.

27. Bruce Hutchison, "Canada's Time of Troubles," *Foreign Affairs*, October 1977, pp. 188-189.

Chapter 10

1. *New York Times*, December 7, 1977, p. 1.

2. John de St. Jarre, "Inside the Laager: White Power in South Africa," *Foreign Affairs*, October 1976, p. 172.

3. Ibid., p. 149.

4. U.S., Department of State, Statement by Under Secretary Philip Habib, "Southern Africa in the Global Context," March 3, 1977, p. 4.

5. *New York Times Magazine*, November 13, 1977, p. 111.

6. *Time*, "The Defiant White Tribe," November 21, 1977, p. 62.

7. *Department of State Bulletin*, June 20, 1977, p. 666.

8. The translation of Vorster's August 5 speech was made by the U.S. Embassy in Pretoria.

9. *Washington Post*, October 25, 1977, p. A14.

10. Ibid., November 30, 1977, p. A6.

11. *New York Times Magazine*, November 13, 1977, p. 111.

12. U.S., Department of State, "The Challenges of Africa." Speech by Secretary of State Kissinger, August 31, 1976.

13. U.S., Department of State, "The United States and Africa: Strengthened Ties for an Era of Challenge," August 2, 1976.

14. Interview with the vice-president by the *Rand Daily Mail*, October 18, 1977. Text released by the Office of the Vice-President.

15. George Ball, "Asking for Trouble in South Africa," *Atlantic Monthly*, October 1977, pp. 46-47. Emphasis added.

16. Ibid., p. 47.

17. *New York Times Magazine*, November 13, 1977, p. 106.

Chapter 11

1. "The War Powers Resolution: Striking a Balance between the Executive and Legislative Branches," p. 4. Delivered by Gerald R. Ford on April 11, 1977, at the University of Kentucky in Louisville. The text was reprinted by the American Enterprise Institute, Washington, D.C.

Index